H.G. Wells on Film

ALSO BY DON G. SMITH

Lon Chaney, Jr.:
Horror Film Star, 1906–1973
(McFarland, 1996)

The Poe Cinema:
A Critical Filmography of Theatrical Releases
Based on the Works of Edgar Allan Poe
(McFarland, 1999)

H.G. Wells on Film

The Utopian Nightmare

by DON G. SMITH

McFarland & Company, Inc., Publishers
Jefferson, North Carolina, and London

Library of Congress Cataloguing-in-Publication Data

Smith, Don G., 1950–
H.G. Wells on film : the utopian nightmare / by Don G. Smith.
p.   cm.
Includes bibliographical references and index.
ISBN 0-7864-1058-2 (illustrated case binding : 50# alkaline paper) ∞
1. Wells, H.G. (Herbert George), 1866–1946—Film and video adaptations.
2. Science fiction films—History and criticism.
3. Dystopias.
I. Title.
PR5778.F55S64   2002   791.43'6—dc21   2002005063

British Library cataloguing data are available

Cover art ©2002 Wood River Gallery

Manufactured in the United States of America

*McFarland & Company, Inc., Publishers
Box 611, Jefferson, North Carolina 28640
www.mcfarlandpub.com*

For my Fanex friends—
Carol, Christy, and Mike.

Contents

Introduction

Herbert George Wells (1866–1946), one of the most influential men of his generation, is best known today as the author of such pioneer science fiction romances as *The Time Machine, The Island of Dr. Moreau, The Invisible Man, The War of the Worlds, First Men in the Moon,* and *The Food of the Gods.* Those more familiar with Wells, however, would quickly suggest a much broader legacy. As a young Darwinist taught by T. H. Huxley, he wrote many articles in magazines and newspapers arguing for science-education reform. In fact, Wells should be considered a pioneer in the field of progressive educational theory. As a socialist and radical opponent of the status quo, he championed women's rights and racial equality before such positions were fashionable. Convinced that humanity's survival depended on education, he used fiction to disseminate his salvific ideas to the masses. Though a critic of the League of Nations, he tirelessly promoted a unified world order. His vision was magnificent. As he wrote in the early essay "Human Evolution," "In the future, it is at least conceivable, that men with a trained reason and a sounder science, both of matter and psychology, may conduct this operation far more intelligently, unan-imously, and effectively, and work towards, and at last attain and preserve, a social organization so cunningly balanced against exterior necessities on the one hand, and the artificial factor in the individual on the other, that the life of every human being, and, indeed, through man, of every sentient creature on earth, may be generally happy."

The carnage of the two world wars severely tested Wells' optimism. As he wrote in *The World Brain,* "In the race between education and catastrophe, catastrophe is winning." The title of his final book, *Mind at the End of Its Tether,* indicates the extent to which his utopian dream had turned into a nightmare.

Considering Wells' influence in literature, politics, economics, and education, it is not surprising that his writings directly and indirectly inspired many films. In fact, Wells' literary art and the art of cinema came of age almost simultaneously. In 1891, Thomas Edison applied for patents on his camera, the Kinetograph, and its peephole viewer, the Kinetoscope. In 1895, Major Woodville Latham and his two sons made one of the first successful projections. Then, in March of 1895, after pirating Edison's Kinetograph and Kinetoscope, France's Lumière brothers showed

1

their first film to an invited audience of scientists and friends.

Also in 1895, the year that H.G. Wells published his first novel, *The Time Machine*, fellow Englishmen Robert William Paul and Birt Acres conceived of the Theatrograph, a combination of camera and projector that recorded visuals on a celluloid strip. Toward the end of 1895, Paul invited Wells to his office to discuss the possibility of filming *The Time Machine*. The author expressed interest, and the two men patented the Theatroscope on October 24, 1895.

The patent stated:

> My invention consists of a novel form of exhibition whereby the spectators have presented to their view scenes which are supposed to occur in the future or past, while they are given the sensation of voyaging upon a machine through time, and means for presenting these scenes simultaneously and in conjunction with the production of the sensations by the mechanism described below, or its equivalent.

Nothing came of the proposed *Time Machine* film, but Wells later mistakenly claimed that he and Paul had jointly invented the first motion picture projector! Though Wells disliked dealing with "cinema people," his growing understanding of film as a teaching tool led to a collaboration with Charles Laughton and Elsa Lanchester in 1927. They produced three short subjects: *Bluebottles*, *The Tonic*, and *Daydreams*. That same year, Wells began a novel to be adapted to film. Originally called *The Peace of the World*, he later retitled it *The King Who Was a King*. The film was never produced.

Whither Mankind?, his film treatment based on *The Shape of Things to Come* and *The Work, Wealth and Happiness of Mankind*, was filmed successfully in 1936 as *Things to Come*. During production, Wells expressed so much confidence in the future

of the cinema that he vowed to abandon novels and devote himself solely to film treatments. This proposed change upset his friends and readers. However, after his disappointment with the film *Things to Come*, he abandoned his cinematic plans and returned to writing novels.

Generally, Wells did not take an active part in the filming of his works. Aside from the aforementioned instances, his presence at the filming of *Kipps* is the only other example of attention to the films on his part. Most of the time, he sold the rights to his books only to express disappointment at the resulting films. For Wells, film eventually joined literature as another failed tool in the education of the masses, and his interest in the medium flagged after the production of *The Man Who Could Work Miracles* in 1936.

What has never flagged, however, is the interest of filmmakers in Wells' writings. The resulting films range in quality from relatively serious, grand entertainment to poorly produced, egregious betrayals of Wells' vision. This work examines every theatrically released film from 1909 to 1997 (both credited and uncredited) based on the writings of H.G. Wells. I have structured the text by first discussing the fictional work itself and the circumstances behind its creation, then listing in chronological order all the films based on that work, approaching them from the following standpoints:

1. Film Synopsis

2. Adaptation—a comparison of Wells' literary work and the film adaptation.

3. Production and Marketing—a discussion of the film's production, including a look at the careers of those involved, and a description, when known, of how the studio marketed the film.

4. Strengths—an examination of the film's assets.

5. Weaknesses—an examination of the film's liabilities.

6. Rating—a numerical rating of the film using the following scale: 4. excellent, 3. good, 2. average, and 1. poor.

A question that arises in assessing strengths and weaknesses is whether or not a film should be evaluated in part on its faithfulness as an adaptation. My view is that a film should be judged on its aesthetic qualities alone. In other words, an unfaithful adaptation can be a good film and a faithful adaptation can be bad. To cite an example, Edgar Ulmer's *The Black Cat* (1934) claims Poe's short story as its source, yet, except for the presence of a black cat, only the film's mood and atmosphere owe anything to Poe. Nevertheless, though far from a faithful adaptation, the film is aesthetically good to excellent. Similar cases can be made for most of Roger Corman's Poe adaptations and for Stanley Kubrick's adaptation of Stephen King's *The Shining*. Literature and film are different media and must be evaluated accordingly. If you want Poe, read Poe; if you want King, read King. If you want the cinematic visions of Ulmer, Corman, or Kubrick, then watch their films. And so, while I will examine the faithfulness of film adaptations, the films must stand on their own.

Since most of the earliest films no longer exist, I must approach them based on what little information exists today. If I have not seen the film under discussion, I have said so.

1

The Time Machine (1895)

THE NOVEL

H.G. Wells was born in Bromley, Kent, on September 21, 1886. His father, Joseph, was a struggling crockery salesman, and his mother, Sarah, was first a homemaker and later a maid. When Wells broke his leg at the age of seven his convalescence was devoted to reading books such as Wood's *Natural History*, a biography of the Duke of Wellington, and bound volumes of *Punch and Fun*, all of which opened new worlds to his imagination. Wells got his first taste of formal education at a local dame school, where he was instructed by "an incompetent woman and her equally incompetent daughter." His mother then saw fit to send him to Morley's Academy, Bromley, rather than to the National School for working-class children. The rivalry between the two schools led to student conflicts fought with sticks and staves. It is possible that Wells' distrust of the working class, so prominent in *The Time Machine* and other writings, grew partially from these experiences.

When Joseph suffered a broken leg and could no longer provide enough family income, the traditionally religious and staunchly Victorian Sarah took a position as a maid at Up Park, where she had worked as a domestic before her marriage. Wells found at Up Park an "atmosphere of unhurried liberal enquiry" that was attractive to his developing sense of himself as an intellectual.

Sarah nudged a reluctant Wells into the draper's apprenticeship, as she had done his two older brothers. He found the draper's trade stifling and beneath his abilities. In fact, he considered most of his schooling inadequate. After threatening suicide if he were not allowed to continue his schooling he was sent to Midhurst Grammar School, Sussex, after which he won a scholarship to the Normal School (later Royal College), where he trained to be a secondary school science teacher. Throughout his life he disparaged most of his school instructors, considering them intellectually dull and condescending toward his lower middle-class background. He had three teachers, however—one formal and two informal—who strongly shaped his world view. One was his Normal School biology teacher, Darwinist Thomas H. Huxley, from whom he adopted the view of an ever-changing universe in process. Huxley taught that human beings, like all animals, must adapt to change or risk extinction. Second was Plato, whose ancient Greek text, *The Republic,* taught him that social systems can be altered by human planning and intelligence. Third was French socio-economic theorist Saint-Simon, whose books touted the need for a technological elite (the Council of Newton) capable of molding the world's laborers into a unified global workforce and of enforcing social peace by uniting all people in selfless devotion to useful work. All of these foundations exert considerable influence on Wells' 1895 novel *The Time Machine.*

At the Normal School, Wells founded and edited the *Science Schools Journal.* After leaving, he taught science at Holt Academy, North Wales, where he suffered a football injury and contracted tuberculosis. During his recovery he wrote "The Chronic Argonauts," a science fiction short story serialized in 1888 in the *Science Schools Journal.* The story was the first draft of what would later become *The Time Machine.*

After a brief stint as science teacher at Henley House School, Kilburn, he took his Bachelor of Science degree in 1890. Shortly thereafter he tutored for University Correspondence College and met and married his cousin, Isabel Wells, in 1891. In 1892 he met and moved in with Amy Catherine Robbins ("Jane"), one of his students. This, of course, ended his already shaky marriage. As his health deteriorated in 1892 and 1893, Wells turned to journalism, regularly publishing articles on science and science education.

In 1894, Wells serialized "The Time Traveller's Story" in the *National Observer.* This was the fourth version of what would soon become *The Time Machine* (he had reworked the story twice between 1889 and 1892). After marrying Jane in 1895, Wells took her to live in Woking, where he turned his time traveller story into *The Time Machine* and published it that same year to great critical acclaim. At the age of twenty-nine, H.G. Wells was suddenly a deservedly famous novelist.

Novel Scenario and Commentary

A character identified only as the Time Traveller reveals to his dinner guests the theoretical justification for time travel and, when met with skepticism, produces a miniature model of a newly constructed time machine. The machine disappears when activated but fails to convince the assembly that it has vanished into the past or the future. The Traveller invites his friends to dinner three days hence, at which time he promises proof. When all but one of the guests return, the Traveller, appearing in a disheveled state, relates a story of his journey to the year 802,701.

Upon "landing" in the future, the traveller discovers a huge sphinx atop a bronze pedestal. Not knowing what to make of it, he explores what apparently is a paradisal environment populated by a race of people he calls the Eloi. Weak and childlike, they eat, sleep, and laze about in a world of apparent innocence and plenty. The Traveller chooses to return to his own time but discovers the time machine missing, a fact the Eloi apparently cannot explain. When the Eloi ignore the cries of one of their own drowning, the Traveller rescues the young woman identified as Weena, and she becomes the Traveller's companion.

The Traveller soon discovers, however, that all is not bliss. Below the ground lives a race of short ape-like creatures called Morlocks, who keep the Eloi well fed and clothed as a means of harvesting them for food. When the Morlocks attack the Traveller and Weena in the forest, the Traveller escapes, but Weena is killed. The traveller discovers that the Morlocks have moved the time machine into the Sphinx's pedestal in an effort to lure him into a trap. Having few options, the Traveller enters the pedestal and goes forward into the future before the Morlocks can kill or capture him. At the far reaches of time, the Traveller observes a dying world populated only by crab-like creatures and mudfish. He then manages to return to his own time where he relates his story to his guests.

The only proof he has of having travelled into the future are two strange white flowers given to him by Weena—flowers that don't exist in the present time. Later, the Time Traveller disappears for good, leaving one of the guests to muse in the epilogue about the comfort he takes in learning that in the future "even when mind and strength had gone, gratitude and a mutual tenderness still live on in the heart of man [as exemplified in Weena's giving the flowers to the Time Traveller]."

Commentators have described the story as a fable with satiric undertones and as an adventure with the depth of an H. Rider Haggard novel. The first description seems more appropriate. Adventure is certainly abundant, but as Leon Stover documents in his annotated edition of *The Time Machine*, the story is Wells' warning of what will occur if humanity does not solve the riddle of the Sphinx. Readers of Carlyle (a disciple of Saint-Simon's brand of socialism) would have known that the Sphinx's riddle asks how humanity will resolve the conflict between the ruling class (or the captains of industry) and working class labor leaders. In *The Time Machine*, the workers evolve into Morlocks and the members of ruling class evolve into Eloi. Unchecked, the Morlocks will finally evolve into crab-like creatures and the Eloi into mudfish. The solution to the riddle and the salvation of humanity is the control of labor by the intellectual leaders of society. If the intellectuals become complacent and soft, they will evolve into Eloi. If the working classes are not controlled and their energies channeled into productive and docile labor, they will become Morlocks.

Also prominent in the novel is a perceived conflict between men of science and anti-scientific humanists. The Time Traveller represents the man of science, and the author of the epilogue represents the anti-science humanists (as do the Eloi).

THE FILMS

The Time Machine (1960)   MGM, U.S.A. / Running Time: 103 minutes / Release Date: August 4, 1960

CREDITS: Produced and Directed by George Pal; Screenplay by David Duncan, based on the novel by H.G. Wells; Art Direction by George W. Davis and William Ferrari; Set decoration by Henry Grace and Keogh Gleason; Production Illustrated by Mentor Huebner; Special Photographic effects by Project Unlimited (Gene Warren, Wah Chang, and Tim Baar); Stop-Motion Animation by David Pal and Don Sahlin; Matte Paintings by Bill Brace; Edited by George Tomasini; Music by Russell Garcia; Recording supervised by Franklin Milton; Rerecording mixer: William Steinkamp; Makeup by Charles Schram and Ron Berkeley; Make-up supervised by William Tuttle; Morlock design by George Pal; Hairstyles by Mary Keats; Hairstyles supervised by Sydney Guilaroff; Assistant Director: William Shanks; Assistant to the Producer: Gae Griffith; Color consultant: Charles K. Hagedon.

CAST: Rod Taylor (George, the Time Traveller), Yvette Mimieux (Weena), Alan Young (David Filby and James Filby), Sebastion Cabot (Dr. Philip Hillyer), Tom Helmore (Anthony Bridewell), Whit Bissell (Walter Kemp), Doris Lloyd (Mrs. Watchett), Rob Barran (First Eloi), James Skelly (Second Eloi, in white); Paul Frees (voice of the Talking Rings).

Film Synopsis

In the first days of 1900, David Filby, Dr. Hillyer, Anthony Bridewell, and Walter Kemp meet for dinner in the home of their friend George, only to find their host missing. As the guests prepare to dine without him, George enters the dining room from his laboratory. Exhausted and in a disheveled state, he tells of his adventure in flashback.

George invited his friends for dinner and cigars on December 31, 1899, at which time he explained his theory of time travel and produced a miniature time machine. When Dr. Hillyer scoffs loudest, George places one of Hillyer's cigars on the seat of the time machine, advances a level on the machine's controls, and watches as the vertical disc behind the seat begins to turn. The machine emits a hum that shakes the dishes and promptly disappears.

George explains to the astonished skeptics that the time machine is travelling through the fourth dimension into the future where it will "land" in the very spot from which it departed. When everyone except David Filby leaves, George says that he has little liking for his own time and that he plans to travel into the future in a full-size time machine. George offers to show Filby the time machine, but his displeased friend refuses and begs George to destroy the time machine. When Filby leaves, George enters his laboratory and heads into the future. The rapidly rising and setting sun marks the passage of time as trees quickly bloom and bear fruit and the clothes on the mannequin in Filby's shop change with the fleeting years. He stops the machine on September 13, 1917, only to learn from James Filby, David's son, now a soldier, that his friend had died the previous year. Not realizing who he is talking to, James tells George that his father kept up George's house for years in expectation of the vanished man's return.

Upset by both his friend's death and the war, George speeds forward into the future and stops briefly on June 19, 1940,

Rod Taylor at the controls of *The Time Machine* (1960)

when he is rocked by explosions. Depressed that another war has begun, he launches the time machine forward into the future, stopping on August 18, 1966. There, he meets James, now an old man, who warns him that they must seek shelter from an atomic satellite. Just as James recognizes George from their previous meeting, the satellite explodes and George is lucky to return to his time machine before being killed. The ground splits and lava floods the streets. Lava covers the machine, and George must push it into the future until the mountain surrounding it has worn away. At that point in time, the Earth appears green again and George watches as men and machines build a city in the distance. The city stands in splendor for a few centuries and then degenerates into ruin. Wondering why, George stops the time machine on the 12th of October, 802,701.

As rain falls, George hikes to the buildings for shelter. Initially, the lush splendor pleases him. Then he fears that it would be no paradise without other people to share it with. He finds them, boys and girls about the age of twenty, bathing and playing on the bank of a stream. When the swiftly flowing water threatens to drown one of the pretty girls, everyone else sits casually by, making no effort to help. Astonished at what he is seeing, George discards his smoking jacket and pulls the girl to safety. At first she doesn't even thank him, but later she expresses a degree of gratitude. She identifies her kind as Eloi, identifies herself as Weena, and leads him to a dome where the Eloi sit laughing and eating fruits and vegetables. In disinterested response to George's many questions, one of the male Eloi says that they have no government, and no laws. They do, however, have books. When the male takes George to see the books, he is angered to find them crumbling to powder.

The indifference and lack of intellectual curiosity are finally too much for George. In anger he shouts, "What have you done? Thousands of years of building and rebuilding, creating and recreating, so that you can let it crumble to dust. A million yesterdays of sensitive men dying for their dreams. For what? So you can swim and dance and play."

Fed up with the Eloi and ready to return in dismay to his own time, George returns to the spot where he left the time machine only to find it missing, dragged inside the pedestal of the Sphinx. As he pounds on the door of the pedestal, Weena appears and warns him about the Morlocks, who will appear out of the oncoming darkness. Rather than return with her to the dome, he suggests that they build a fire and wait for a chance to enter the pedestal. Though Weena is fearful, she complies. As they build a fire, however, Weena is attacked by a Morlock and saved once again by George. Weena explains that the Morlocks live below the ground, and that when they sound a siren, the Eloi must go below.

The next day, Weena leads George to a museum and demonstrates the talking rings. When spun upon a table, a voice from the rings explains that when the centuries old war between the East and the West finally came to an end, some of the survivors retreated into caverns for a new start while the others remained above ground. George understands now that the cave dwellers evolved (or devolved) into Morlocks and the others into the Eloi.

Weena next takes George to a barren meadow where craters lead below the earth. He is about to descend when a siren calls the Eloi, who walk trance-like toward the doors of the pedestal. Before George can stop her, Weena enters with about a dozen other Eloi. Then the doors close once again. One of the remaining Eloi tells George that it is now "all clear." Apparently

METRO·GOLDWYN·MAYER presents
A GEORGE PAL PRODUCTION

H.G. WELLS' THE TIME MACHINE

in futuristic METROCOLOR

YOU
WILL
ORBIT
INTO
THE
FANTASTIC
FUTURE!

STARRING
ROD TAYLOR
ALAN YOUNG · YVETTE MIMIEUX
SEBASTIAN CABOT · TOM HELMORE

Screen Play by DAVID DUNCAN · Based on the Novel by H. G. WELLS · Directed by GEORGE PAL

The title lobby card for *The Time Machine* (1960)

exhibiting conditioning from a previous age, the Eloi consider the siren some sort of bomb warning.

In an effort to save Weena, George descends one of the craters and discovers that the Morlocks have been breeding the Eloi for food. The Morlocks are cannibals and the Eloi their docile cattle. George engages the Morlocks in hand-to-hand combat and the Morlocks are winning when one of the Eloi aids George enough for them all to escape. Before climbing out of the crater, George tosses a torch and sets the underground world afire. As George and the Eloi escape, the craters explode and the meadow collapses.

George and Weena retire to a stream where Weena asks George how the girls of his time wear their hair. She also asks if George has a girl like her back home, and he assures her that he does not. In fact, he speaks some endearments and expresses the wish to take her with him if and when he recovers the time machine. Suddenly George notices that the doors of the pedestal are open, making the recovery of the time machine possible. He passes through the doors and motions for Weena to follow. Quickly, the doors close and George is trapped with some surviving Morlocks. He manages to fight them off, however, and escape back into his own time.

Needless to say, his dinner guests do not believe his story. After the guests leave, Filby rushes back into the house and hears a whirring sound from George's laboratory. Filby breaks down the door, but George and the time machine are gone.

Filby points out to the maid, Mrs. Watchett, that the marks on the floor are from George's moving of the time machine back into the laboratory from where the Morlocks had moved it. Mrs. Watchett discovers that George has taken three books with him, but she does not know which books. "Do you think he will ever return?" she asks. "One cannot choose but wonder," Filby answers with an enchanted smile. "You see, he has all the time in the world."

Adaptation

The first thing a Wellsian will notice about the film is its abandonment of the author's central concern: what will happen if the intellectuals and captains of industry fail to subdue labor, and how can this necessary subduing be achieved? In a broader sense, how can we save humanity by producing an aristocracy of intellect rather than of privilege? Duncan's screenplay avoids the tough philosophical questions by explaining away the Morlocks as variations of post-war mutation, an explanation relied on by many Fifties horror/science fiction screenwriters, of which Duncan was one. General audiences would pick up on the film's substituted anti-war message through references to the Boar War, World War I, World War II, and future wars of mass destruction, but Wells' central theme is not addressed.

There are other discrepancies between book and film. One is Duncan's insertion of a developing romantic interest between George and Weena that does not exist in the book. In the book, Weena may be infatuated with George, but Wells' Time Traveller clearly views Weena as sub-humanly bovine, just as the Morlocks are sub-humanly simian. He would not think of taking this empty-headed, child-like sloth back to the twentieth century as "his girl." Apparently, Duncan considered the love interest a necessary concession

to audience expectations, another being Weena's survival in the film as opposed to her death in the book.

Another discrepancy is the ironic and satiric ending of the book as contrasted with the upbeat ending of the film. In the book, Wells gives Hillyer (a literary man, not the film's Doctor Hillyer) the last word. Hillyer speculates about the fate of the Time Traveller and then expresses his own opinion about the future: "But to me the future is still black and blank—is a vast ignorance, lit at a few casual places by the memory of his story. And I have by me, for my comfort, two strange white flowers—shriveled now, and brown and flat and brittle—to witness that even when mind and strength had gone, gratitude and a mutual tenderness still lived on in the heart of man." As Stover explains in his annotated *The Time Machine*:

> In these last words, Hillyer expresses his final humanistic judgment on the Time Traveller's tale. All it means for him, in mooning over the comforting flowers, is that love and a "mutual tenderness" is the only thing possible to endure and all that matters in human affairs, come what may. The crunching of irony is that he has blinded himself to the Time Traveller's caustic view of Weena's depraved animality [p.173].

Wells' identification of Hillyer as a literary man is his way of mocking anti-science humanists. The reader closes the book with a bleak vision of the future and with serious questions to ponder. In the film's finale, Filby is awe struck and optimistic, and the audience leaves the theater on an upbeat note. Perhaps George is travelling into the future to lead humanity aright. Except for the pressing need to substitute idealism for war, perhaps there is nothing ultimately to worry about in the here and now, and nothing to fear regarding humanity's future.

This does not mean that the film is simply a comic book rendering of Wells' general plot line. Except for the differences noted above and a few other modifications expected in a book-to-film adaptation, the screenplay is true to Wells. Particularly Wellsian is the periodic anger George feels toward the Eloi. In fact, when faced with the indolent outcome of humanity's intellectual suicide, the Time Traveller on several occasions restrains an impulse to do the Eloi bodily harm.

Production and Marketing

When the The Time Machine went into production in 1959, the horror/science fiction boom of the Fifties was fizzling as studios aimed low-budget productions at indiscriminating adolescents. Some of these films were excellent: *This Island Earth* (1955), *Invasion of the Body Snatchers* (1956), *Forbidden Planet* (1956) and *The Incredible Shrinking Man* (1957). Some were good: *Earth vs. the Flying Saucers* (1956), *Kronos* (1957), *The Fly* (1958), *Colossus of New York* (1958) and *It! The Terror from Beyond Space* (1958). But the vast majority were mediocre to poor: *King Dinosaur* (1955), *Man Beast* (1956), *The Night the World Exploded* (1957), *Terror from the Year 5000* (1958) and *First Man into Space* (1959). In 1959/ 1960, when Alfred Hitchcock's *Psycho* changed the face of the horror film forever, *The Time Machine* was a serious, albeit low budget, return to quality science fiction.

Pleased with the 1953 Academy Award-winning production of Wells' *The War of the Worlds*, the author's estate offered its director, George Pal (1908–1980), the option on other Wells science fiction novels. Having launched the fifties science fiction film cycle with the Academy Award-winning *Destination Moon* (1950), and the Academy Award-winning *When Worlds Collide* (1951), Pal was eager to enhance his vita with Wells' *The Time Machine*.

For the screenplay, Pal turned to science fiction novelist David Duncan (1913–), who penned *The Shade of Time* (1946) and *Dark Dominion* (1954), as well as a screenplay for the non-science fiction film *Sangaree* (1953). Duncan quickly constructed a *Time Machine* screenplay. Later, he would write the science fiction novels *Beyond Eden* (1955) and *Occam's Razor*, as well as such serviceable horror/science fiction screenplays as *The Black Scorpion* (1957), *The Thing That Couldn't Die* (1958), *Monster on the Campus* (1958), and *The Leech Woman* (1960).

With screenplay in hand, Pal approached studio executives, all to no avail. Apparently, the top brass at Paramount believed that space films exhausted marketable science fiction, and other studios proved equally skeptical of the project's feasibility. Only after Pal's successful *Tom Thumb* (1958) did MGM executives ask the director what else he had. Eagerly, he dusted off *The Time Machine*.

Impressed with Pal but still hesitant about *The Time Machine*, executives gave the go-ahead but put the film on an $8000-plus budget and on a tight 29-day shooting schedule. Everyone had to be very resourceful in planning everything down to the smallest detail. Getting almost everything to work on the first take, especially special effects, became imperative.

Special effects were handled by Projects Unlimited (Gene Warren, Wah Chank, and Tim Barr). Working as an apprentice was a young Jim Danforth, who would go on to become one of America's premiere special effects masters. Also crucial was the Morlock makeup, supervised by Bill Tuttle, whose impressive credits included *Mark of the Vampire* (1935). Later, Tuttle would win an Academy Award for *The 7 Faces of Dr. Lao* (1964) and would provide outstanding makeup for Mel Brooks' *Young Frankenstein* (1974).

The male lead went to Rod Taylor

(1930–). In 1956, the Australian-born Taylor acted in *World Without End*, a film foreshadowing *The Time Machine*. There he plays an astronaut accidentally forwarded to 26th century Earth, where he joins nuclear war survivors in a battle against savage mutants. In a 1986 interview, Taylor admitted that across his long career he has gotten more questions about *The Time Machine* than about any other of his films, adding that "Kids today remember me more from TV reruns of that movie than for anything else I've ever done. I expected it would be a tremendously impressive picture, but I *never* thought it would become a classic." Later, Taylor recalled that Pal asked specifically for him to play the Time Traveller:

> George was a genius. He was a lovely, warm-hearted man. I thought of him as a funny little elf. He was surrounded by tiny puppets and toys, which he brought to life in his movies…. We had lunch several times and discussed the project. He had a marvelous talent for illustrations, and I was fascinated with his pre-production drawings. He knew that I was an artist, so we got along beautifully. We worked in close partnership, and I even helped him find the female lead.

Though MGM initially turned her down as Pal's first choice, the role of Weena eventually went to blond Yvette Mimieux (1942–). Pal remembered noticing her innocent look in a screen test he had seen, but when he reviewed the test and asked for her, he learned that she had been let go because she could not act. Still, Pal insisted Mimieux be called back for a screen test. Taylor, too, acknowledged the difficulty in casting Weena:

> I suggested that I test with different girls. *My* first choice was Shirley Knight. Yvette and I have since become dear friends, but at that time, I thought she was kind of a strange little hippie child. I was afraid she would be hard to work

with…. I knew when I did her screen test that Yvette couldn't act at all. But she had a sulky quality which George believed was right.

An interesting piece of trivia is that MGM violated child labor laws in signing Mimieux to play Weena. She lied to Pal about her age, claiming to be 18 when she was only 17. Pal was suspicious but took her word. Luckily, there was no lawsuit.

In retrospect, Mimieux agrees that she was uncomfortably green on the set of *The Time Machine*:

> I suppose the whole crazy production made me more lost than I already was at the time. I'd never acted before, let alone appeared in a film—which is in itself a very technical event. I would come to the set every day and see 100 men and all this equipment; I was never really quite sure where the camera was. And, of course, it didn't occur to the people who hired me that I didn't know, so no one was explaining anything and I was too embarrassed to show my ignorance by asking questions.

Though Mimieux struggled making *The Time Machine*, she improved steadily as production progressed. Among the first scenes shot was the one near the end of the picture in which George and Weena engage in tender conversation. As shooting reached completion, Mimieux had improved so much that Pal ordered the scene reshot to take advantage of her enhanced talent. After *The Time Machine*, the actress continued working at her craft, reuniting with Pal for *The Wonderful World of the Brothers Grimm* (1963), and going on to star in films throughout the sixties and seventies. She married director Stanley Donen in 1972.

Because of the tight budget and time constraints, Pal, Duncan, and everyone else closely associated with production had to have everything designed before the cameras could roll. Even the composer was part of the brainstorming sessions, writing much of the music before the film was even shot. To save money, Pal had the Eloi dome built without a ceiling in order to take advantage of inexpensive natural light. Pal's greatest production difficulty, however, was yet to come—the underground battle between the Time Traveller and the Morlocks.

Pal first filmed entire fight sequences of the Morlocks running, leaping, and then landing, an approach prompting the cost-conscious studio head to call and warn Pal to cut the amount of film being used. At a meeting, Pal pleaded for time to edit the sequence so it would be clear what he was trying to do. Fortunately, the studio head agreed, and Pal worked over a weekend with editor George Tomasini to cut the sequence into shape. In an interview with Ed Naha, Pal recalled the resulting showdown:

> Monday, at noon, we met with the head of the studio and his hangers-on, his "yes men." All those people were just waiting for the blood to flow. That's the nature of a motion picture studio. They were all primed for a good head chopping. We showed the Morlock scene and it looked pretty good. But no one in the room would say a word. Everyone was looking at the boss, waiting for him to say something. He walked over to me and said: "Congratulations, George. You were right." I pointed to George Tomasini sitting next to me and said, "You're congratulating the wrong George. HE put it together." As if by magic, everyone in the room suddenly began nodding their heads and saying, "Yes, it is very wonderful, isn't it."

A special effects accident, which seems humorous only in retrospect, occurred when Gene Warren and Wah Chang prepared for the scene of molten lava rushing through the streets of London. Always cutting costs, the special effects wizards sub-stituted oatmeal for lava. Warren and Chang whipped up the oatmeal on a Friday and left for the weekend, during which time temperatures climbed and the oatmeal fermented. When work resumed on Monday, Warren and Chang set up their cameras at the end of the miniature London street and signaled operators to unleash the oatmeal. When the chute opened, a foul stench filled the air as the sickening liquid spewed toward them. After the clean-up crew earned its money, the special effects crew executed the successful take we see in the film.

According to the film's pressbook, MGM technicians used the entire sprinkler system available on Stage 29 to put out the largest indoor fire ever staged on the lot. Other special effects devices included stop motion photography and matte paintings. The most impressive use of the former is the gruesome decomposition of a Morlock over a period of only seconds. Engineered by George Pal's son, David, the scene remains vividly repulsive to this day.

Apparently pleased with what it had, MGM vigorously promoted *The Time Machine* with a large-format twenty-page pressbook, a Dell comic book tie-in, a Lion label 33 r.p.m. record album tie-in based on *Classics Illustrated* adaptations of four Wells novels, and a Berkley Medallion paperback tie-in of Wells' novel.

As might be expected, film ads hyped the celebrated author of *The Time Machine*: "H.G. Wells the greatest prophet of our time tells his most astounding tale! You will orbit thru Time and face the fantastic human races that dwell above and below the earth in the year 800,000 A.D.!"

In a pressbook news release, Pal praised Wells as a prophet:

> Wells was a remarkable writer but an even more remarkable forecaster. Writing "The Time Machine" in 1895, he

foresaw a future war in which mankind would become capable of destroying our entire civilization. We now know that this is a terrible possibility.

Also, Wells wrote of the fourth dimension, Time, well before Einstein produced his theory of it. Since Wells predicted space travel, in his book, "War of the Worlds," which I also had the pleasure of turning into a movie in 1953, I cannot help but believe that time travel is a possibility although probably not in our lifetime.

Interestingly, one of the film's ads commits a blooper. While most ads show Morlocks carrying whips, some ads show a Morlock carrying a flaming torch. Since Morlocks fear fire, such a rendering is inaccurate and misleading—but also relatively insignificant.

Strengths

One of *The Time Machine*'s greatest strengths is its director, George Pal. Pal knew what he wanted and, even on a low budget, he got it. Though his direction is rarely inventive, he controls the film's mood throughout.

The Time Machine won an Academy Award for special effects. Among the most impressive are the passing of the seasons and years as George journeys into the future, George's burial and subsequent escape from a lava mountain, most of the matte paintings, and the disintegration of the Morlock in the Sphinx near the film's end. In addition, the Victorian sets in the film's opening scenes convey a sense of charming nostalgia.

Though the construction of the Morlocks is not entirely successful, their glowing eyes are effectively eerie.

Rod Taylor is fine as the daring, inventive Time Traveller, conveniently rugged, tender, and intellectually curious. Sebastian Cabot, Whit Bissell, and Allan Young also give impressive performances.

Weaknesses

Though the special effects were award-winning, some of them are below par. For example, the atomic satellite explosion and subsequent lava flood during which toy cars float about in thick red oatmeal doesn't work, and the landscape with openings leading underground looks too much like a set.

The acting by those playing the Eloi is weak in comparison to the rest of the cast. In Mimieux's case, lack of experience luckily translates as innocence and fragility. In the others, it just translates as lack of experience.

Though the screenplay generally produces good entertainment, it is at times contrived. For example, the odds that a person in a time machine would make three stops and encounter three wars are not likely.

The biggest weakness in the film is the Morlock makeup. The short and stout Morlocks appear powerful, yet they are rather easily overcome in physical combat. At one point, even an effeminate Eloi decks one with a punch. Though the camera never dwells on a Morlock face for very long, when it does the effect is comical rather than frightening as the Morlocks' buck teeth and long white hair remind us of Walt Disney's Goofy. We are also left to wonder why evolution produced hair on top of the Morlock's arms and legs but not on the underside.

Finally, the film should have wrestled with more of the social issues raised in the novel, but few, if any, Wells science fiction adaptations have successfully done so. The general theme of the film seems to be that Western culture must remain strong, curious, progressive, and peaceful if we are to survive. We find that theme in Wells' novel, but we also find so much more. Though the film doesn't challenge, it does entertain. Wells' novel does both.

Rating: 3

2

The Wonderful Visit (1895)

THE NOVEL

Made famous overnight by *The Time Machine*, Wells felt that he had more to teach the world. He took as the theme of his next book a remark attributed to John Ruskin to the effect that if an angel visited earth, most Englishmen would mistake it as a new species of bird and shoot it. Applying Swiftian satire to Ruskin's comment, Wells quickly produced *The Wonderful Visit*.

Novel Scenario and Commentary

Mr. Hilyer, the vicar of lovely Sussex village, is an avid ornithologist. Hearing that a strange large bird has been sited in the countryside, Hilyer grabs his gun and goes in search of what must be the member of a new species. After winging the strange creature, he is astonished to discover that he has shot an angel. Rather than being the pale type of angel with whom the English are acquainted in their art, this is an "Angel of Italian Art, polychromatic and gay." The angel's wings are brightly colored, his long hair flows, and his short tunic exposes bare legs, giving the strange being a decidedly effeminate appearance.

When Hilyer returns to the vicarage with the angel, the Curate's wife and daughters assume that the vicar is secreting a female into his house. Hilyer then sends for Dr. Crump, who refuses to believe that the wounded creature is an angel. The wings, he asserts, must be abnormal growths susceptible to surgical removal. He also judges the creature to be a matoid with signs of mental weakness exhibited in its fairness and kindness.

Hilyer insists that the angel wear unattractive, uncomfortable Victorian clothing so as to better adapt to the social environment. Of course, holes are allowed for the wings to stick out. Hilyer also notes that the angel can play the violin with otherworldly skill and beauty.

In a short time, the angel is physically attacked by a drunken tinker, stoned with husks by children, and threatened by dogs. As the angel is forced to patiently suffer the brutish behavior of uncomprehending villagers, one human being, the servant girl Delia, loves him for his tender qualities. Though the angel is grateful for Delia, he becomes increasingly disappointed and frustrated by his interaction with the villagers. As a last straw, the angel strikes Sir John Gotch, who has accused him of trespassing. Mistakenly thinking he has killed Gotch, the angel concludes: "Truly, this is no world for an Angel! It is a World of Pain, a World of Death."

The angel's release comes when he rushes into a burning building to save Delia. Though the two are assumed to have perished in the fire, a little village girl fancies seeing "two figures with wings, that flashed up and vanished among the flames." Thereafter, the vicar never seems happy and dies within a year of the fire.

Wells addresses several key themes in *The Wonderful Visit*: First, human beings are generally close-minded, provincial, resistant to change, and hostile toward anything differing from their narrow expectations. Dr. Crump, for example, refuses to believe what his own eyes tell him.

Secondly, human beings are hypocritical. Though the villagers, as Christians, profess to believe in the traits of goodness, kindness, forgiveness, and understanding, they heap scorn on the angel who exemplifies their faith. Wells notes that for average folk "eccentricity, in fact, is immorality … is madness." Even the vicar himself admits to the angel that his faith is largely a sham. As he explains: "And afterwards, when they are falling to pieces, I try and persuade them of a strange world in which I scarcely believe myself, where life is altogether different than they had—or desire." The vicar also reports that while he preaches, "some are ministering to one appetite and eating sweets, others—the old men—are slumbering, the youths glance at the maidens, the grown men protrude white waistcoats and gold chains, pomp and vanity on a substratum of carnal substance, and their wives flaunt garish bonnets at one another."

A third theme is that science is destructive in the hands of the unimaginative and the ignorant. As Wells satirically editorializes, "If it were not for collectors England would be full, so to speak, of rare birds and wonderful butterflies, strange flowers and a thousand interesting things. But happily the collector prevents all that, either killing with his own hands or, by buying extravagantly, procuring people of the lower classes to kill such eccentricities as appear…. In the name of Science." At one point, the vicar tries to explain to the angel that he kills beautiful birds because they interest him. The angel, of course, does not see the "logic." And Dr. Crump, the village's "man of science," exhibits no more sense than anyone else.

A fourth key theme in *The Wonderful Visit* is that human beings shamelessly exploit their own. The angel is puzzled to see the poor laboring and the wealthy living lives of comparative leisure. When the angel openly questions the situation, Sir John Gotch warns the vicar to send the angel away because the latter has been going about the village preaching socialism: "He has. He has been buttonholing every yokel he came across, and asking them why they had to work, while we—I and you, you know—did nothing."

And a fifth theme is that social institutions, such as schools, exist to instill patriotism and conformity in pliable youth. A tramp who dropped out of school explains to the angel that schools pith children like vivisectionists pith frogs:

> They take 'em young into that school, and they says to them, "come in 'ere and we'll improve your minds," they says, and in the little kiddies go as good as gold. And they begins shovin' it into them. Bit by bit and 'ard and dry, shovin' out the nice juicy brains. Dates and lists and things. Out they comes, no brains in their 'eads, and wound up nice and tight, ready to touch their 'ats to any one who looks at them…. And they runs about spry and does all the dirty work, and feels thankful they're allowed to live.

The angel learns, just as the Time Traveller learns in *The Time Machine*, that the mass of humanity refuses to change in a world that changes around them, that humanity resists improvement and goes about its merry way toward a dark future. At the same time, *The Wonderful Visit* demonstrates Wells' affection for the rural life he knew as a boy. Wells likes his villagers even as he satirizes them.

Though *The Wonderful Visit* remains largely unread today, critics of the time praised its wit and motivation, which, according to Wells, was "to suggest to people the littleness, the narrow horizon of their ordinary lives by bringing into sharp contrast with typical characters a being who is free from ordinary human limitations."

THE FILMS

La Merveilleuse Visite **(1974)** aka *The Wonderful Visit* Capa-Rocher, France / Running Time: 102 minutes

CREDITS: Directed by Marcel Carné; Produced by Jacques Quintard and Roger Delpey; Screenplay by Didier Decois; Cinematography by Marcel Carné, Didier Decois, and Robert Valey; Photography Directed by Edmond Richards; Cameraman—Bernard Sury; Music by Alan Stivel.

CAST: Gilles Kohler, Deborah Berger, Leland Lesaffre, Jean-Pierre Castaldi, Yves Barsacq, Pierre Repeo, Mary Marquet, Lucien Barjo, Jean Gras, Marcel Rouze, Louis Navarre, Jeanne Perez, Louis Pelissier.

Film Synopsis

A figure walks slowly and unsteadily through the water at the edge of the sea, but his reflection in the water glimmers, distorted and indistinct. After leaving the home of a newly-made widow, the vicar and his servant Menard climb into their wagon and head back to the vicarage.

As they ride, they spot a young man lying unconscious on the beach. His beautiful face and wavy blonde hair are striking. After determining that the young man is still alive, the vicar and Menard lift him into the wagon bed and proceed to the vicarage. On the way, they notice that the wagon's rearview mirror has shattered.

At the vicarage, the vicar and Menard place the young man on a couch. When Menard brings a mirror from upstairs, it shatters. The young man soon regains consciousness and explains that he fell from the sky. There was wind, he says, and the sound of silk being torn. Then, to the incredulity of the vicar and the awe of Menard, the young man identifies himself as an angel. When Dr. Jantel arrives, he examines the angel and pronounces him fit. He tells the vicar, however, that while he believes that Jesus was born of a virgin and rose from the dead, he does not believe that the young man is an angel.

Menard dresses the angel in clothes resembling a potato sack. At breakfast, the vicar discovers that the angel is not used to eating food. Simply because the angel needs a name, Menard calls him "John." John soon finds that he cannot cut himself with a razor by pressing it across his arm. He also finds that mirrors break when he walks before them.

Soon, John is ready to venture into the village. On the way he befriends a boy frolicking in a wheat field. The two walk into town hand-in-hand, where they are spotted by François, a milk truck driver engaged to marry the vicar's servant girl Delia. François guesses to his friends that the angel is actually a hippie. When the boy points out the candy store, the innocent John walks in, helps himself to candy, and gives it to the excited boy. As they leave the store, the owner runs after them, demanding that they pay for the candy they have "stolen." As a crowd gathers, Dr. Jantel happens on the scene and tries to explain the concept of money to the angel. The doctor gives the angel the money to pay for the candy, and the angel pays, though he never appears to really understand capitalism.

Back at the vicarage, John plays the vicar's violin beautifully and effortlessly, after which the vicar is amazed to learn that the angel cannot read music. While the angel is playing the violin, Delia arrives. Later, Delia makes François jealous by telling him of having met the most beautiful boy. Delia and François then make love, after which François gives her a pair of pants decorated with a heart. It is time for church, and Delia arrives late. At the church service John again plays the violin beautifully and moves the heart of the Dutchess of the manor and all who hear. After the service, the Dutchess arranges for her photographer to get a picture of John for *Echo of Audierne*, the magazine that she publishes. Later, after the photographer poses John for a picture, he finds that the angel's image is not on the print.

John and the boy retire to the countryside to fly a kite. "How beautiful," John says. "The sky, the country, and you in it." The boy replies that John is beautiful, but John reveals that he knows nothing about his own beauty because he has never seen himself. At the boy's suggestion, John walks to a pool of water, but his reflection dissolves in ripples, just as it did when he staggered in the shallow sea water of the beach immediately after his fall.

Later, thinking them an improvement over what John is wearing, Delia gives him the pants that François had given to her. Unknown to Delia and John, Menard is watching, and he sees her kiss him on the cheek. Menard, who believed John to be an angel, is disappointed. Apparently John is just another human susceptible to the sex drive and all else that is human. When Menard and John speak later, Menard is abrupt. His faith in something beyond this life has been weakened.

Later, John is walking in the countryside when he comes upon a funeral and afterward approaches the gravedigger in order to understand something about death. The gravedigger is disgusted by John's apparel and says he should be ashamed for entering a cemetery dressed as he is. From there, John goes to the village and magically paints the widow's drab home with psychedelic colors and art. The widow, however, is horrified and screams her displeasure. The vicar arrives and hustles John back to the vicarage. On the way, John tells the vicar that no one believes in eternal life. They only believe in it when they are well fed and in good health. Otherwise, they would play music and dance at funerals. When the vicar disagrees, John calls him a hypocrite. "You don't believe I'm an angel!" he charges. "I believe in only what I can see," the vicar blusters.

Meanwhile, Dr. Jantel has concluded that John is a paranoid who might be dangerous if left to loaf about the village. The only answer to the problem, the doctor volunteers, is love. Mental patients only do harm when alone and when people are afraid of them.

By this time, the villagers are quite uneasy about the visitor. That evening, John goes for a walk and encounters Delia. Menard follows. After walking at low tide to an island, John and Delia discuss dreams, and she explains that she is in love with Francois. "Love is not as clear cut ... as solid as a rock," John explains. "Love can be of different kinds. Love can take on thousands of colors." "What color is yours?" Delia asks. "Transparence," John answers.

Then John sees himself for the first time as a reflection in Delia's eyes, and he is relieved when her eyes do not shatter. She insists that he continue looking.

Delia's life has changed as a result of her time with John. They love each other, but their love is spiritual, of the heart.

Menard phones François and tells

him that John and Delia have spent the night together. When François confronts Delia, she says that John didn't steal anything from him, that the words to describe her love for John do not exist. François apologizes for his jealousy.

John restores Menard's faith by magically restoring a boat he had hoped to salvage and sail away on. Menard would never have the money to salvage the boat, but magically, there it sits in the water, restored. John and Menard agree that they will sail to the world's end and beyond.

John becomes convinced that animals will die if cooped up or caged. Therefore, he releases all the farmers' animals, which run through the village streets causing chaos. Menard upbraids the vicar for not intervening when the villagers want to call the police.

François sees the pants that John is wearing and wrecks his milk truck after challenging the angel to a fight. John checks François and fears that he is dead, and that he, John, is responsible. François regains consciousness and returns to the village, claiming that John attacked and injured him. The villagers form a mob and pursue the angel and Menard. When a villager threatens the angel with a pistol, he purposely falls backward over a cliff overlooking the sea, and a dove rises in flight from where the angel disappeared.

Adaptation

The first thing one notices in examining Carné's adaptation based on Decois' screenplay is its difference in tone from Wells' novel. The novel is a satire, generally comic in tone. The film is a parable, generally serious in tone. Of course, there are moments of humor in the film as when Menard questions the vicar's apparent refusal to believe seriously in the supernatural, and when the angel concludes that the villagers' reaction to death points out

their corresponding disbelief in eternal life. In these scenes, Carné adapts Wells' satiric attacks on hypocrisy. Carné indulges in light-hearted humor when the angel paints the widow's house in psychedelic colors, but the number of humorous moments in the film are otherwise few.

With some differences, Carné and Decois follow the general plot of Wells' novel. An angel falls from the sky and is taken in by a vicar. The remainder of both novel and film highlights the inability of a truly perfect being to fit into and be accepted by a hypocritical modern society.

In the book, the vicar shoots the angel, allowing Wells to satirize amateur ornithologists. In the film, the vicar and Menard find the angel unconscious on the beach. In the novel, the angel retains his wings; in the film, he does not. In the film, the angel cannot cast a reflection. The novel makes no such mention. The role of Menard is minute in the novel, but it is central in the film. The film's jealous François stands in for the novel's Sir John Gotch, adding more conflict to the film than Gotch does to the novel. Many of the colorful secondary characters in Wells' novel, such as the tramp, do not find their way into the film. The bittersweet escape of the angel from earthly existence concludes both book and film, though in the film, unlike in the book, Delia does not accompany him.

Carné and Decois approach Wells' novel respectfully as they adapt it to their own thematic purposes. While Wells can look at modern society through Swiftian eyes, Carné directs in a mode of bittersweet sadness, generally keeping satire at arm's length. The foibles of modern life are as present in the film as they are in the novel, but Carné and Decois would rather move us to tears than nudge us to laughter.

Production and Marketing

Many cinema historians nominate Marcel Carné (1909–1996) as history's most brilliant French director. In the thirties, novelist/poet Jacques Prévert (1900–1977) wrote Carné a series of film scripts emphasizing the themes of fatalism and death. Therein, generally admirable men die simply because it is human destiny to die. Reluctantly drawn into dangerous, complicated situations, the men fail to achieve what they want and finally achieve what they had hoped to avoid. Moving through a world of dark, foggy film noir, the men seek love and humanity but find only emptiness, chaos, despair, and death. The ensuing collaboration between Carné and Prévert is existentialism before Sartre—the restriction of human freedom as a result of the human condition.

In *Drôle de Drame* (1937, aka *Port of Shadows*), a young soldier fleeing from something unknown to the viewer falls in love with Nelly, who returns his love. A dog, whose life was saved by the soldier, irrationally follows the soldier everywhere just as the soldier follows Nelly. When danger closes in, the soldier refuses to save himself and is unexpectedly killed while protecting Nelly. He has died to save another human being—but to what end, to what purpose?

In the Carné/Prévert masterpiece *Les Enfants du Paradis* (1944, aka *The Children of Paradise*), four main characters search for meaning in life, only to find that life is meaningless. As was *Drôle de Drame*, *Les Enfants du Paradis* is peopled with unsavory secondary characters and at least one character representing Prévert's nihilism. In both films, humanity engages in great hustle and bustle, all without purpose or meaning.

Carné's later films are generally considered mere shadows compared to his best work of the thirties.

Soundtrack composer and artist Alan Stivell (1944–) learned piano and harp as a child in Paris. He is today a master of the Breton harp, which had not been played for four centuries. The main theme from *La Merveilleuse Visite* is called "YS," the name of the capital of the kingdom of Cornwall in 5th century Amorica. According to legend, YS was swallowed up by the sea as punishment for sin. As in the book of *Genesis*, the flood symbolizes the catastrophe that occurs when human material progress outstrips peoples' respect for each other.

Though a subtitled version in English was produced, the film received little attention in the United States and received no notable reviews.

Strengths

Structurally, *La Merveilleuse Visite* is sound. Carné introduces the two major characters in the first scenes and their discovery of the angel. The conflict is at first an internal one: how will human beings who profess religious belief act in the face of an angel? Of course, most doubt because their faith is a matter of convenience or hypocrisy only. Even Menard, who believes, loses his faith when he misinterprets a secret meeting between the angel and Delia. And what of the angel? How will he act in the face of hypocritical, ignorant, and sometimes cruel human beings? The cast is strong enough to make us care, and as the angel encounters other village folk, his conflict (and their's) intensifies. The perfect and the incurably imperfect just don't mix.

As the angel continues to act as an angel should act, the villagers continue to act as human beings should not act, but usually do. Only Delia seems to understand the angel and the love he represents. The climax comes when François lies to the villagers and leads them as a mob to kill the angel. The resolution is both beautiful and satisfactory. The angel realizes his goal of escape, and Menard regains a degree of hope. Still, the emotion that remains is sadness. While the resolution is positive, human nature remains what it is.

Unlike Carné's early films, *La Merveilleuse Visite* is visually bright. Bernard Sury's camera gives us a feast of glittering water, warm sunlight, and plush green fields. Successfully contrasted with natural beauty is "man's inhumanity to man."

As the film opens, an exchange of dialogue beautifully mirrors what is to come. "What's the matter? Tired?" the vicar asks. "I can hardly breathe," Menard replies. "It is as if the sky were bearing down on me." "Indeed," the vicar agrees, "the sky seems to join the earth this morning ... for once." Indeed, the sky does join the earth in the form of the beautiful blond angel. This is only one example of the effective dialogue sprinkled throughout the film.

Also of considerable merit is Stivell's haunting soundtrack. The music inspired by the destruction of YS perfectly conveys the melancholia produced by humanity's moral incapacity in the face of material progress.

Weaknesses

The film's late 1960s or early 1970s setting accounts for the "angel as hippie" element that periodically arises. Of course, the hippies of that era were viewed by some as innocents searching for a lost Eden. To that extent the element works, but on occasion (such as the painting of the widow's house) it makes the film appear dated.

Some viewers may find the film slow. Though visually striking, it is considerably longer on talk than on action. While the talk is interesting and necessary for character development, it may cause some viewers to squirm. *La Merveilleuse Visite* is not a "popcorn movie." It is a film of ideas and emotions, and therefore not for everyone.

Rating: 3

3

The Island of
Doctor Moreau (1896)

THE NOVEL

As Wells constructed his follow-up to *The Wonderful Visit*, England was reexamining nature and human nature from a Darwinist perspective, two central concerns being the problem of pain and the plasticity of individual organisms. *The Island of Doctor Moreau* was originally subtitled *A Satire* or *A Satirical Grotesque*, indicating Wells' intent to write another Swiftian romance of sorts. As with all great satires, *Island* is deadly serious. Besides Swift's *Gulliver's Travels*, other important influences are Lombroso's theory of criminal types, Poe's *The Narrative of Arthur Gordon Pym*, Defoe's *Robinson Crusoe*, Stevenson's *Dr. Jekyll and Mr. Hyde*, and Kipling's *Second Jungle Book*. Wells had dealt with the prominent themes in *Island* in some of his earlier articles, particularly "The Limits of Individual Plasticity" (1895) and "Human Evolution, An Artificial Process" (1896).

Novel Scenario and Commentary

Prendick survives a sinking ship only to be rescued by a drunken, cruel sea cap- tain transporting animals to a mysterious island outpost. Most instrumental in returning Prendick to health is Montgomery, the assistant of Dr. Moreau, who buys animals for the doctor's secret experiments. After Moreau, Montgomery, and Montgomery's beast-like servant M'ling unload the animals with the help of some other "animalistic" servants, the captain tosses Prendick overboard, leaving him at the mercy of Moreau. Moreau and Montgomery reluctantly offer Prendick a place to stay until another ship arrives.

Prendick recalls that Moreau was the notorious vivisectionist driven from England for experiments deemed cruel by British society and illegal by a British law requiring anesthetic be used during animal vivisection. In conversations with the alcoholic Montgomery, Prendick learns that Moreau took Montgomery with him to the island after the latter was arrested for breaking some unspecified law. Though grateful for the gesture, Montgomery serves Moreau unwillingly. Prendick soon discovers Moreau operating on a creature that appears to be a woman howling in agony as she is surgically turned into a puma. Fearing that he will be the next experimental victim, Prendick runs into the forest and discovers a colony of Beast Folk who, led by a gray figure known as the Sayer of the Law, chant a series of laws affirming their humanity and worshipping Moreau as a god. Those who break the law (e.g. eat flesh, suck up drink, run on all fours, etc.) are subject to the House of Pain. The hand that creates is the hand that wounds and the hand that heals.

Moreau and Montgomery track and capture Prendick, after which Moreau explains that the Beast Folk began as animals, not as humans. Moreau has advanced evolution with the knife, turning them into approximations of human beings. Unfortunately, the animal flesh and beastly tendencies return and Moreau must turn his experiments loose on the island where they form a society of half-human, half-animal. Their chants and pseudo-religion have resulted from the blundering missionary work of a Kanaka native.

Though Prendick no longer feels threatened, he shares with Montgomery a revulsion for Moreau's work. Later, Montgomery and Prendick discover a dead rabbit in the forest. One or more of the Beast Folk has broken the law and tasted blood. Because of behavior previously observed by Prendick, suspicion falls on the Leopard Man. Moreau calls the Beast Folk together and asks, with a thundering voice, who has broken the law. Fear of the House of Pain compels the Leopard Man to attack Moreau. Unhurt, Moreau joins Montgomery, Prendick, M'ling and the Beast Folk in pursuit of the fleeing Leopard Man. When the Leopard Man is cornered, Prendick shoots it out of pity.

About six weeks later, the she-puma observed earlier by Prendick rips loose, attacks Moreau and Prendick, and flees into the forest. Armed with a pistol, Moreau trails the she-puma and is subsequently killed by the escaped beast. Rather than tell the Beast Folk the truth, Prendick explains that Moreau is not really dead, that he has left his body and still watches over them. The "invisible" Moreau will still punish lawbreakers in the House of Pain.

Prendick's ruse works only briefly as the Beast Folk revert to increasingly animalistic behavior. As is his practice, Montgomery gets drunk and curses the situation that he and Prendick are in. Finally, Montgomery leaves the safety of the compound, offers M'ling whiskey and leads the Beast Folk in song. Shortly afterward, shots ring out. Fearing the worst, Prendick rushes outside and sees that the boathouse is burning. Along the beach, he finds Montgomery mortally wounded and M'ling and several other Beast Folk dead. Montgomery's bender has ended in carnage.

Prendick remains on the island as the Beast Folk further revert to their former natures. He builds a raft, escapes from the island and is rescued by a brig heading for San Francisco. Returning to London after about a year on the island, Prendick devotes his time to reading, experiments in chemistry, and astronomy, all the while living in fear of the beast within us all.

In *The Island of Doctor Moreau* Wells returns to a theme of some of his earliest writing: that of nature and nurture. Human beings, Wells wrote, are not the slaves of blind evolution—helpless puppets in the hands of an uncontrolled environment. Instead, human beings can control their evolution through the artificial process of education. Moreau is an educator, a director of evolution. As Wells writes in "Human Evolution, An Artificial Process," (1896), "[*The Island of Doctor Moreau*] provides a novel definition of Education, which obviously should be the careful and systematic manufacture of the artificial factor in man."

Also of concern to Wells is the theme of chance. In *Island*, various characters attribute to chance what happens to themselves and to others. Undirected by human beings, evolution is a process of blind chance—"a vast pitiless mechanism." Like nature itself, Moreau is pitiless in guiding evolution. As in nature, pain is his instrument of progress.

Another of Wells' purposes is to ridicule what Carlyle called "Pig Philosophy"—the Utilitarian position that equates the greatest amount of pleasure as the greatest good. Moreau rejects "Pig Philosophy," preferring the view that pain must be used to end pain. Through a dictatorship of education, human beings must have the beast burned out of them. Only then can humanity be saved. Satire is clear, however, as Wells suggests that bestial cravings and violent activities are more appealing to human beings than law and religion.

Closely related to this theme is that of vivisection morality. In his *Text-Book of Biology*, Wells justified vivisection. In *Island*, he has Moreau say that "the study of Nature makes a man at last as remorseless as Nature." The hero of *The Island of Doctor Moreau* is Moreau himself, not Prendick. Moreau is Wells' scientific man of the future, the almost more-than-human educational dictator who dares to guide the evolution of society.

In his preface to the novel in his collected works, Wells writes that "There was a scandalous trial about that time, the graceless and pitiless downfall of a man of genius, and this story was the response of an imaginative mind to the reminder that humanity is but animal, rough-hewn to a reasonable shape and in perpetual internal conflict between instinct and injunction. The story embodies this ideal, but apart from this embodiment it has no allegorical quality." The trial to which Wells refers is that of Oscar Wilde, who was charged with homosexuality.

THE FILMS

Island of Lost Souls (1933)   Paramount, U.S.A / Running Time: 72 minutes / Release Date: January 11, 1933

CREDITS: Directed by Erle C. Kenton; Screenplay by Waldemar Young and Philip Wylie, from the novel *The Island of Doctor Moreau* by H.G. Wells; Cinematography by Karl Struss; Art Direction by Hans Dreier; Special Effects by Gordon Jennings; Makeup by Wally Westmore.

CAST: Charles Laughton (Dr. Moreau), Richard Arlen (Edward Parker), Leila Hyams (Ruth Thomas), Bela Lugosi (Sayer of the Law), Kathleen Burke (Panther Woman), Arthur Hohl (Montgomery), Stanley Fields (Captain Davies), Paul Hurst (Donohue), Hans Steinke (Ouran), Tetsu Komai (M'ling), George Irving (the Consul).

Film Synopsis

Edward Parker is on his way to Apia where he plans to marry his fiancée, Ruth Thomas. When his ship sinks, he is rescued from the water by the SS *Covena*. On board, Parker is nursed back to health by Montgomery, a physician wanted in England for having committed some unnamed professional indiscretion. Montgomery now serves as an assistant to Dr. Moreau, supervising the transportation of animals to Moreau's island.

The drunken captain of the SS *Covena* assaults Montgomery's servant, M'ling, and is castigated by Parker for his cruelty. Parker notices, however, that M'ling looks a bit like an animal and has pointed, furry ears under his long hair.

Dr. Moreau's boat arrives and his strange looking servants take possession of the animals. As the boat is leaving, the captain tosses Parker overboard, leaving him at the mercy of Moreau. Having no choice, Moreau and Montgomery take Parker to the island, where he catches a glimpse of its strange, misshapen occupants.

Though Moreau protests taking responsibility for Parker, he soon realizes that the unfortunate man can be used as part of his experiments. Moreau, a vivisectionist exiled from England, has created human-like creatures from animals. One of them is Lota, an exotic young woman created from a panther. She is Moreau's most successful experiment to date, and Moreau wants to see what her reaction will be when introduced to the handsome young Parker.

That night, Moreau, Montgomery, and Parker are dining when horrible screams of agony emanate from a nearby house. Known as the House of Pain, it is where Moreau creates his Beast Folk after numerous sessions of torturous vivisection. Parker tries to escape with Lota, but they are stopped in the forest by the Beast Folk. Moreau arrives, cracks his whip and demands that the creatures repeat the Law. Led by the Sayer of the Law, the Beast Folk engage in a pitiful parody of a religious ceremony, vowing to avoid such animal activities as running on all fours, eating meat, and spilling blood. They also express fear of their God-like creator, Moreau, and the House of Pain, a place of punishment for any creature that breaks the law.

When Moreau convinces Parker that the Beast Folk are animals turned into humans, not humans turned into animals, Parker somewhat settles down enough to listen as Moreau explains the nature of "My work, My discoveries, mine alone— with these I have wiped out hundreds of thousands of years of evolution." To ensure that Montgomery remains longer as part of the Lota experiment, Moreau has his own schooner destroyed, leaving no way for anyone to leave the island. Meanwhile, when Ruth discovers that Edward was left on an obscure island by the captain of the SS *Covena*, she approaches the American Consulate and arranges for Captain Donohue to transport her there.

Moreau is, of course, distressed at the arrival of Captain Donohue and Ruth. During the first night of their stay, with Moreau's approval, a beast-man called Ouran tries to break into the compound and take possession of Ruth. By this time, Montgomery would rather risk prison in England than help Moreau any longer with his experiments. In hopes of leaving with the rescuers, Montgomery helps Ruth and Captain Donohue escape and run for Donohue's boat. Moreau, however, orders Ouran to kill Donohue, which the Beast-Man does. When Ouran carries Donohue's body to the beast village, the Beast Folk charge him with breaking the law. Ouran explains that Moreau ordered the killing, and the Sayer of the Law proclaims that the Law is no more. Moreau is no longer a god. Cracking his whip no longer subdues the Beast Folk as they lift torches and move en masse toward him. In the process, they inadvertently start fires that spread over the island. Moreau escapes to his house but is pursued by the Beast Folk, who carry him to the House of Pain, pin him to an operating table, take knives and scalpels in hand, and subject him to the tortures of the damned.

Meanwhile, Ouran pursues Montgomery, Parker, Donohue, and Ruth. Lota, who has become attracted to Parker, leaps on Ouran and gives her life protecting the escapees. As Donohue's boat pulls away from the flame-engulfed island, Montgomery observes that "the fire will destroy all of Moreau's work."

Adaptation

Except for one major digression, and several minor changes, *The Island of Lost Souls* is remarkably faithful to its source. Of course, the major digression is that of Moreau as hero to Moreau as mad scientist and villain. In 1933, Wells panned the film for its "misrepresentation" of Moreau.

Original one-sheet poster for *The Island of Lost Souls* (1932) featuring the Panther Woman, who played no part in Wells' novel *The Island of Dr. Moreau*.

In Wells' book Moreau is clearly no mad scientist. He is a brilliant man who has become as ruthless as nature in an effort to guide and shape nature. He inflicts pain not for his own pleasure but for the sake of progress. He is willing to risk prosecution in England in order to present the results of his work to the scientific community. He is not a paranoid; he desires vindication, not so much because he believes in himself but because he believes in his ideas. He is not suffering from a god complex; he is not hungry for power. In *Island of Lost Souls*, however, Moreau seems more interested in stressing HIS work as HIS. He is a megalomaniac.

The minor changes in *Island* are as follows:

1) In the book there is no Lota, Ruth, Captain Donohue, or Ouran.
2) In the book, Moreau's death does not suggest that justice has been served.

Let us examine these differences. Today, the panther woman is so identified with filmed adaptations of *The Island of Doctor Moreau* that most people probably assume the character was part of the original source. She was not. It can only be assumed that the writers, Young and Wylie, created Lota and Ruth as an additional source of conflict within the film, which is not and cannot be a philosophical treatise. In the thirties, American audiences were not particularly interested in Wells' core ideas. In fact, had they been more familiar with them, they probably would have been appalled. The film had to be sold as a melodrama, as a vehicle of entertainment. The creation of Lota and Ruth satisfies that requirement. We have a love interest of the traditional kind threatened by the spawn of Moreau's cold-hearted experiments. Lota is sympathetic, but she is unnatural. That is why she must lose in the conflict and why she must die at the end.

Since the film presents Moreau as a mad scientist who inflicts pain on defenseless animals, justice requires that he answer in kind. Therefore, he is dragged to the House of Pain and subjected to what the audience must imagine to be an excruciating death. Justice is done. Of course, the message sent by the film is the polar opposite of that sent by Wells' book. No wonder he expressed such dissatisfaction with the adaptation.

Production and Marketing

The Island of Lost Souls was the best film directed by Earl C. Kenton (1896–1980). Other than *Island*, his most notable films are probably *Ghost of Frankenstein* (1942), *House of Frankenstein* (1945) and *House of Dracula* (1945). *Ghost* is an underrated sequel to Universal's first three Frankenstein films starring Boris Karloff. It starred Lon Chaney, Jr. as the Frankenstein monster and Bela Lugosi as Igor. The two *House* films were later sequels that never measured up to the Universal classics. We must understand, however, that Kenton was given a budget and topline co-workers on *Island*. Universal gave him some good players such Lon Chaney, Jr., Boris Karloff, John Carradine, Jane Adams, J. Carroll Naish, and Onslow Stevens, but the workers behind the scenes were not in the same class as those he worked with during the making of *Island*. In fact, most of Kenton's work at Universal required him to turn out minor films made to cash in on previously popular pictures. He was a victim of time and circumstance. Perhaps *Island* is some indication of what he could have done if sufficiently backed by a studio.

Of those who assisted Kenton on *Island*, top honors must go to cinematographer Karl Struss (1891–1981). Struss received an Academy Award for *Sunrise* (1927) and shot such classics as *Ben-Hur*

(1926), *The Sign of the Cross* (1932), *Dr. Jekyll and Mr. Hyde* (1932), *The Great Dictator* (1940), and *Limelight* (1952). He also commanded the camera on such perennial favorites as *The Macomber Affair* (1947, based on Ernest Hemingway's short story), *Rocketship X-M* (1950, a pioneer science fiction film), *Kronos* (1957), and *The Fly* (1958, a classic film that, along with *House of Wax*, launched Vincent Price's career as a horror film star).

Island's cast was headed by British character actor Charles Laughton (1899–1962). Before being cast as Dr. Moreau, Laughton appeared in three British shorts scripted by Wells: *Bluebottles*, *The Tonic*, and *Daydreams* (all 1928). He went on to record successes in *The Old Dark House* (1932), *The Sign of the Cross* (1932, as Nero), and *If I Had a Million* (1932). After *Island*, his career rocketed with an Academy Award-winning performance in *The Private Lives of Henry VIII* (1933). Though he turned into a ham in many of his later performances, he is remembered particularly in *The Barretts of Wimpole Street* (1934), *Ruggles of Red Gap* (1935), *Les Miserables* (1935), *Mutiny on the Bounty* (1935, for which he received an Academy Award nomination), *Rembrandt* (1936), *The Hunchback of Notre Dame* (1939, as Quasimodo), and *Witness for the Prosecution* (1957, for which he received an Academy Award nomination). He also directed the excellent *Night of the Hunter* (1955, based on the fine novel by Davis Grubb).

Before *Island*, Richard Arlen (1898–1976) had appeared in the highly acclaimed *Wings* (1927, which won the first ever Academy Award for Best Picture), *The Four Feathers* (1928), and *The Virginian* (1929). He went on to become a hero in numerous "B" movies. He ended his career as a bit actor in such films as *The Crawling Hand* (1963), *Law of the Lawless* (1964), *The Human Duplicators* (1965), *Apache Uprising* (1966), and *Buckskin* (1968).

Leila Hyams (1905–1977) served as a blonde leading lady in 1920s films and continued in the horror genre with *The Phantom of Paris* (1931) and *Freaks* (1932).

Besides Laughton, the most notable player in *Island* is Bela Lugosi, who starred in *Dracula* (1931), *The Murders in the Rue Morgue* (1932), *White Zombie* (1932), and *Chandu the Magician* (1932). Lugosi accepted fourth billing in *Island*, a foreshadowing of what he would be forced to do for much of the rest of his career. Lugosi would act in many low-budget horror films along with a few very fine horror films throughout his life. His reputation as a drug addict and alcoholic, is well known.

According to publicity releases, Kathleen Burke (1913–1980) was chosen to play Lota, the Panther Woman, after a national search to cast the character. According to the *Los Angeles Examiner* (Sept. 30, 1932), Cecil B. DeMille, Ernst Lubitsch, Rouben Mamoulian, Norman Taurog, Stuart Walker and Erle C. Kenton chose the actress and awarded her a $200 per week contract and a five-week guarantee. Though she went on to appear in a few 1930s films, *Island* remains her only memorable achievement.

American character actor Arthur Hohl (1889–1964) filled serviceable roles in such films as *Cleopatra* (1934), *Show Boat* (1936), *Kidnapped* (1938), *The Scarlet Claw* (1944, one of Universal's best Sherlock Holmes films), and *The Yearling* (1946).

Stanley Fields (1884–1941) was a former prizefighter and vaudevillian. He appeared in the classic *Little Caesar* (1930) but appeared in nothing memorable after *Island*.

Paul Hurst (1889–1953) appeared in roles as gangsters, bartenders, criminals, and cops in many films. He committed suicide in 1953. Certainly of note, he appeared briefly in *Gone with the Wind* (1939).

Hans Steinke (1893–1971) was a professional wrestler who acted in films. A German native, Steinke emigrated to the United States at an early age. The New York State Athletic Commission recognized him as World Heavyweight Wrestling Champion in 1928. Among his other films were *Deception* (1933), *People Will Talk* (1935), *Once in a Blue Moon* (1936), and *The Bucaneer* (1938).

Japanese-American Tetsu Komai (1893–1970) appeared in such films as *Daughter of the Dragon* (1931), *Tokyo Joe* (1949, with Humphrey Bogart), *Japanese War Bride* (1952), and *The Night Walker* (1964, directed by William Castle).

American character actor George Irving (1874–1961) appeared in a number of inconsequential films before *Island*. Later he worked briefly in the Cary Grant/Katharine Hepburn comedy classic *Bringing Up Baby* (1938), in the underrated *Son of Dracula* (1943, starring Lon Chaney, Jr.), and in William Wellman's excellent *Magic Town* (1947).

There were uncredited appearances in *Island* by Alan Ladd and Randolph Scott, who both would later work as leading men in the 1940s.

Posters for the film featured Kathleen Burke as the panther woman, set among forbidding eyes that peer through lush greenery. The absence of other actors or actresses in the posters stressed the horror/sex element over cast. The posters, nonetheless, are quite attractive.

Strengths

Island of Lost Souls is a powerful film registering most of its components as strengths. The film's greatest strength is Karl Struss' cinematography. Struss shoots the opening scenes in fog, giving the setting a dreamlike or nightmarelike aura. From those opening minutes, the film explores terrible themes in the context of this nightmarish environment. Struss' most effective technique is having characters move in for close-ups toward a static camera. In the tense scene before Parker slugs Moreau, the doctor and his assailant move toward one another as described. The effect is unnerving. Toward the film's end, the Beast Folk move toward the camera, oblivious to the pain of Moreau's whip, and the audience experiences Moreau's fear. Struss's technique directly involves the audience as few cinematic techniques can.

The use of off-camera sound is also one the film's strengths. We first hear animal sounds off camera on the SS *Covena*. Why are they there? What kind of ship is this? The technique of off-camera sound is used throughout the film to heighten tension, as in the scenes in which Lota grapples silently with Ouran as the audience hears the cries of Moreau and the creatures in the House of Pain. As Parker cradles the dying Lota in his arms, sounds from the House of Pain permeate the air.

The cast is led by Charles Laughton, basing his Moreau on an occultist he had patronized, even to the extent of adopting the occultist's Satanic beard. Laughton, himself a homosexual or bi-sexual, brings an evil sweetness to the role, his glances indicating that Montgomery is more than just his assistant. Nothing in Montgomery's actions indicates otherwise. In contrast, Leon Stover suggests in his critical text of *Island* that Wells' Montgomery fled England for violating a law against homosexuality and that Moreau is an asexual genius interested only in worthy scientific pursuits. Regardless, the suggestion of homosexuality is a strength of the film as Moreau seems to find sex of all kinds interesting and natural, including bestiality (Lota and Parker).

As Rhona J. Bernstein notes in her *Attack of the Leading Ladies*, "Despite the happy heterosexual reunion between

Parker and Thomas, homosexual desire circulates through most of the film..." (p.148) When the schooner arrives on the island, Montgomery volunteers to stay with Parker on the schooner until morning in order to get an early start to the mainland. Moreau insists on taking Parker up to the house, however, because he has "something in mind." As Moreau leads him to the compound, Parker remarks about the strange looking natives he sees hiding in the foliage. Moreau touches his whip to Parker's chest and says, "You'll be wanting a cold shower, I think, before dinner." Moreau continues a sinister flirtation with Parker throughout most of the film. As Bernstein suggests, Moreau expresses his proclivities through Lota, planning to offer Parker to her as part of an experiment. How else would a 1932 Paramount Picture handle such subject matter? Some writers tend to see homosexual elements in films where none exist, but in this case, the elements are definitely there in both the novel and the film, and they add an interesting dimension to the proceedings.

Newcomer Kathleen Burke gives a splendid account of herself as Lota. Her sensuous beast woman is all anyone could ask. Not a professional actress, she delivers the lines as directed, and she does so innocently and child-like, as one would expect of only relatively humanized Animal Folk. Some critics claim that she is too human and therefore unbelievable, but surely we can believe that Moreau's work at its best could produce a "woman" like Lota. In most cases, an inexperienced actress given such high billing would not work, but in this case it does.

One of the greatest strengths of the film is Bela Lugosi as the Sayer of the Law. His foreign accent heightens the pathos of his lines as he protests against Moreau's turning the Beast Folk not into humans, not into animals, but into *things*. The turning point of the film is the Say-er's enlightened understanding that the man-made law is no more. Struss's close-up of Lugosi as he moves toward the camera in pursuit of Moreau is as scary as cinema gets. Lugosi appeared in many films throughout his long career, but his performance as the Sayer of the Law is one of his best.

Director Earl C. Kenton deserves credit for the overall product. A director is like an author, synthesizing the varied parts of his work into a consistent and effective whole. Kenton shows here what an adequate artist can do when given proper clay with which to work.

Several scenes are testaments to Kenton's creativity. In one, Moreau has sent the ape man Ouran, by night to rape Ruth. After Edward has shown Ruth to her room, Kenton increases suspense by juxtaposing scenes of Ruth preparing for bed and the ape man approaching her window. As Ruth disrobes, Kenton and Struss give us a close-up of the ape man's face as he glares through the bars of Ruth's window. Ruth keeps her candle burning, while in another room, Moreau extinguishes his, symbolizing the encroaching darkness of evil. Ruth lies behind the gauze of mosquito netting, giving those scenes a light, filmy aura. By contrast, scenes of the ape man at the bars are hard and threatening. Kenton's alternating shots of innocent femininity contrast effectively with those of the ape man's crude brutality.

Another strength is the way in which the film utilizes the theme of lost souls. In Wells' novel, Prendick fears that if subjected to vivisection he will become a "lost soul." Presumably, Paramount took the title of the film from Prendick's utterance. The idea that human beings deprived of their nature are lost souls certainly is paramount (no pun intended) in the film. The corollary, that animals deprived of their natures are also lost souls, is vividly brought to life by Lugosi's Sayer of the

Law as he discovers the man-made flaws of his man-made nature. This film is rightfully anti-vivisectionist. Though Wells' novel leaves readers with more food for thought, the film leaves viewers with a more morally defensible message.

The setting certainly enhances the film, as does Wally Westmore's makeup. The unblinking approach allowed by Paramount makes *Island of Lost Souls* one of the 10 best horror films of the 1930s.

Weaknesses

The only criticism one can lodge against this film is the relatively weak performance of Richard Arlen as Parker. Overall, his performance is not bad. In scenes in which he is called upon to exhibit thankfulness, ignorance, affection, or revulsion, he is adequate. However, when called upon to exhibit anger, he is unconvincing.

As a film, *Island of Lost Souls* is an unrelenting horror film. Its weaknesses are negligible, its strengths overpowering. Like few other films, it transcends its own time to address perennially significant issues of nature and nature's sovereignty.

Rating: 3½

Terror Is a Man (1959)   Valiant Films Corporation, U.S.A. and Phillipines / Running Time: 89 minutes / Release Date: December, 1959

CREDITS: Directed by Gerardo (Gerry) de Leon; screenplay by Harry Paul Harber, based on *The Island of Doctor Moreau* by H.G. Wells (uncredited); Cinematography by Emmanuel I. Rojas; Music Composed and Conducted by Ariston Auelino; Makeup by Remedios Amazan; Production Supervised by Joseph Salzburg; Production Coordinated by Artemio B. Tecson; Production Designed by Vincente Bonus; Special Effects by Hilario Santos; Edited by Gervasio Santos.

CAST: Francis Lederer (Dr. Girard), Greta Thyssen (Frances Girard), Richard Derr (Fitzgerald), Oscar Keesee (Walter), Lilia Duran (Selene), Peyton Keesee (Tiago), Flory Carlos (The Man).

Film Synopsis

Fitzgerald, the only survivor of a sunken freighter, drifts ashore on Blood Island, a remote outpost in the Philippines. Dr. Girard and his swarthy assistant Walter find Fitzgerald and bring him to their luxurious home—the only house on the island—where Dr. Girard's lovely wife Frances and servants Tiago and Tiago's sister Selena nurse Fitzgerald back to health. Fitzgerald learns that Dr. Girard has sacrificed a profitable Park Avenue medical practice for the isolation of Blood Island.

A strange, bandaged creature attacks a native village killing two of the inhabitants. The rest of the villagers flee the island in their canoes. Later, when Fitzgerald takes a walk, he finds newly dug graves near the empty village and becomes uneasy upon seeing Dr. Girard and Walter setting traps for a large animal.

Frances, a former nurse, tells Fitzgerald that the escaped animal, and killer, is a panther used by Girard in his experiments. Apparently, the parents of Tiago and Selena were the villagers killed. Because of the torture inflicted on the beast and because her love for Girard has died, Frances asks Fitzgerald to help her escape Blood Island. Since he has fallen in love with her, Fitzgerald promises his assistance.

After recapturing the creature, Girard catches Fitzgerald in the act of searching the study. Girard explains that he is in the process of surgically turning one species into another, of turning a panther into a man. After over fifty operations, all of which the panther found excruciatingly painful, Girard's beast man is nearing perfection. Girard boasts that the creature is able to walk on two legs and will soon be able to speak. When Fitzgerald is incredulous, Girard invites him to observe next day's surgery. When they leave the laboratory, Frances enters to clean up and is lustfully attacked by Walter. Frances has always treated the beast man with kindness. Now, strapped to a lab table and still bandaged head to foot like a mummy, the beast man strains helplessly as Frances fights off her brutal attacker.

Fitzgerald remains unconvinced about the morality of turning a panther into a human being, but he is astonished when Girard makes the creature say the word "man." When Walter enters the lab, the creature breaks loose and attacks the man who earlier accosted Frances. Walter responds by torching the creature's bandages, burning it badly, and, with the help of Girard and Fitzgerald, subduing it.

The fiery battle between man and creature spurs Frances to confess to Girard her love for Fitzgerald. Meanwhile, the creature breaks loose and kills Walter. Knowing that the creature must be stopped, Girard and Fitzgerald leave Frances, Selena, and Tiago at the house and go hunting. The creature, however, doubles back, kills Selena, and abducts Frances. Responding to Frances' screams, Girard and Fitzgerald confront the creature as it carries the woman toward a cliff. When the creature drops Frances and tosses Girard over the cliff, Fitzgerald fires a bullet into it. The mortally wounded creature stumbles along the beach and is helped into a boat by Tiago. Tiago pushes the boat out to sea as a stunned Fitzgerald and Frances walk away in silence.

Adaptation

Though *Terror Is a Man* does not credit H.G. Wells, it is undoubtedly an adaptation of *The Island of Doctor Moreau*.

In both book and film, the lone survivor of a shipwreck (Prendick/Fitzgerald) ends up on an isolated island ruled by a vivisectionist (Moreau/Girard). The survivor objects to the doctor's attempt to humanize an animal/animals. The doctor has an assistant (Montgomery/Walter) who is killed, and the doctor himself is killed by a puma creature or panther creature of his own creation. The shipwrecked survivor finally escapes the island and returns to civilization. In both book and film, the panther creature dies from gunshot wounds, though the killers are inconsequentially different.

There are differences, of course. In the book, Moreau is vivisecting on a much larger scale than is Girard, and in the film, the addition of Frances Girard provides a love interest that is absent from the book but present in the 1932 *Island of Lost Souls*. The film obviously takes the intruder's side, as the book does not, and the film leaves almost all of Wells' themes behind in order to concentrate on the horror and love elements considered to be of more interest to target audiences.

Production and Marketing

Terror Is a Man was the first Philippine horror film released in the United States. Directors Gerry de Leon (1913–1981) and his assistant Eddie Romero (1924–) are almost solely responsible for helping Phillipine films find an overseas market. Romero, the son of a former Phillipine Senator and Ambassador to the Court of St. James, began as a screenwriter at the age of 16 and later directed such films as *The Day of the Trumpet* (1957) before joining forces with Leon on *Terror is a Man*. Leon and Romero teamed as co-directors for *Brides of Blood* (1968, aka *Brides of Blood Island*), a science fiction film in which atomic testing produces frightening mutations, and for its sequel

The Mad Doctor of Blood Island (1968), in which a scientist turns his romantic rival into a chlorophyll monster. Leon then bowed out of the Blood Island series, handed over the reins to Romero, and went on to direct *Curse of the Vampires* (1970). Romero continued the Blood Island series, resurrecting the chlorophyll monster in *Beast of Blood* (1970). Inspired again by H.G. Wells' *The Island of Doctor Moreau*, Romero then directed *The Twilight People* in 1971. The Blood Island series was financially successful enough to inspire a Phillipino rip-off titled *Superbeast* (1972) and Al Adamson's American drive-in vehicle *Brain of Blood* (1971).

Romero's other directorial outings include *Moro Witch Doctor* (1964), *The Beast of the Yellow Night* (1970), *Woman Hunt* (1972), *Beyond Atlantis* (1973), *Sudden Death* (1977), *Desire* (1983), *The White Force* (1988), and *A Case of Honor* (1988). According to press material, Romero is also the prolific author of magazine articles devoted to politics, economics, and sociology.

Czech-born actor Francis Lederer (1906–1999) came to *Terror Is a Man* after years of European stage and film experience. He rose to stardom as Romeo in Max Reinhardt's Czech production of *Romeo and Juliet* and scored big again in the London production of *Meet My Sister*, in which he learned the dialogue phonetically in six weeks—shades of the early Bela Lugosi. After performing in G. W. Pabst's *Pandora's Box* (1928), he travelled to the United States in 1932 and garnered excellent reviews for his starring role in the stage play *Autumn Crocus*. After that, his most notable screen efforts are probably *Confessions of a Nazi Spy* (1939), *Midnight* (1939) *Captain Carey, U.S.A* (1949), *The Bridge of San Luis Rey* (1944), *A Woman of Distinction* (1950), and *Lisbon* (1956). He is probably best remembered today for his effective, underplayed per-

formance in the title role of *Return of Dracula* (1958). Mixing feigned gentleness and menace, Lederer leaves no doubt that he was once a fine romantic leading man/continental seducer. The *Terror Is a Man* pressbook calls Lederer one of the world's few truly international stars. Ironically, he left acting after *Terror Is a Man* and lived well in California on money he made from successful real-estate investments.

Greta Thyssen launched her career by winning the Miss Denmark competition in 1954. The *Terror Is a Man* pressbook lists her measurements as 39-20-35. After studying with Lee Strasberg, Thyssen starred in *The Beast of Budapest* (1958, a political drama about communist Hungary hyped as a horror film), *Bus Stop* (1956, with Marilyn Monroe), *The Double-Barrelled Detective Story* (1965), and *Cottonpickin' Chickenpluckers* (1967). She is probably best known today for *Terror is a Man* and for *Journey to the Seventh Planet* (1961). Her stage performances include *Solid Gold Cadillac*, *Pajama Tops*, *For Love of Money*, and *I Am a Camera*. In addition, she made television appearances on *The Steve Allen Show*, *The Sid Caesar Show*, *Perry Mason*, *Matinee Theatre*, *Schlitz Playhouse*, *Fireside Theatre*, and *Dragnet* (Just the facts, Greta). Now in retirement, she makes occasional appearances at film conventions.

American leading man Richard Derr (1917–1992) was active in films since the 1940s, usually in minor productions. Among his pre–*Terror* vita enhancers are *Joan of Arc* (1948, with Ingrid Bergman), and the science fiction classic *When Worlds Collide* (1951). He later appeared in *The Drowning Pool* (1976, with Paul Newman and Joanne Woodward). Derr was also successful on stage, winning a Theatre World Award for his performance in *The Traitor* (produced by Jed Harris, based on Herman Wouk's novel). Other stage performances included *Dial M for Murder* (with Maurice

The original one-sheet poster for *Terror Is a Man* (1959)

Evans), *Dream Girl* (with Judy Holliday), *Happy Birthday* (with Joan Blondell), *Elmer the Great* (with Joe E. Brown), *Cat on a Hot Tin Roof*, and *Mister Roberts*. He appeared in television's *Studio One*, *The Robert Montgomery Show*, *Silver Theatre*, and *Circle Theatre*.

Though *Terror is a Man* draws heavily on H.G. Wells, it also mines and fails to credit Hammer's *The Curse of Frankenstein* (1957), one of the late fifties' top money-making genre films. In both *Curse* and *Terror* a driven scientist "defies the laws of God." In both films, a woman tries to love the scientist but finds it hard due to his ambitions. In both films, an unwelcome outsider intrudes on the scientist and falls in love with his woman. In both films, the scientist creates a "monster" that he ultimately cannot control. In both films the monster is sympathetic, more sinned against than sinning, and in both films, the monster either directly or indirectly causes the scientist's death.

Terror Is a Man is a horror film, and, thanks to director William Castle, horror films of the late fifties sometimes resorted to outlandish but profitable ticket selling gimmicks. Castle's *Macabre* (1958), for example, offered $1000 to anyone who died of fright, his *The House on Haunted Hill* (1959) featured Emergo, the appearance in the theatre of a skeleton on a wire, and his *The Tingler* (1959), which hyped *Percepto*, provided electrically wired theatre seats. The Valiant Films publicity department hyped *Terror Is a Man* by announcing that a bell would ring before a scene "so shocking" that the audience may want to close its eyes!

Ads for the film promoted the gimmick: "SO DIFFERENT—a Bell System Has Been Installed For the SQUEAMISH and FAINT-HEARTED!!! When the Bell Rings we suggest you CLOSE YOUR EYES! It will ring again when it's safe to open them!"

Posters and ads for the film featured a terrified and reclining Greta Thyssen superimposed before the creature's eyes. Girard (Lederer) is identified as "THE DOCTOR—His obsession was driving everyone mad." As for Frances (Greta Thyssen) the ads read "THE WIFE—She'll do anything to escape." For Fitzgerald (Richard Derr), the ads read "THE INTRUDER—He knew this was against the laws of nature." All of this is fair and responsible advertising.

During its original release, *Terror is a Man* headed a double bill with B feature *The Scavengers* ("Hong Kong, City of Sin and Violence, where Enslaved Beauties are the Bait and a Bullet is the Pay-off"). *Terror Is a Man* was re-released in 1965 as *Blood Creature* in order to capitalize on the popular Blood Island titles issuing from the Phillipines. Relying again on the bell gimmick, ads read "THE BELL TELLS. Close your eyes/You're CHICKEN… /Keep them open/ you're COOL … LISTEN FOR THE BELL!" Greta Thyssen received top billing, and the film was released as the top half of a double bill with *The Walls of Hell* ("AMERICAN COURAGE DEFEATS THE JAPANESE STAND AT THE WALLED CITY OF MANILA"). The more subtle and accurate title *Terror Is a Man*, derived from Girard's philosophical query, "What is a man?" better suits the film.

Strengths

Terror Is a Man remains the best horror/science fiction film made in the Phillipines. Only the wild *Night of the Bloody Apes* (1969, aka *Horror and Sex*) rivals it through sheer brutal audacity. *Terror* exhibits a sensitivity missing from other Phillipine horror films and missing from most other horror films of the late 1950s. This sensitivity is expressed in the title itself. Working titles included *Beast from Blood Island*,

Creature from Blood Island, and (least favorable) *The Gory Creatures*. *Terror Is a Man* is more representative of the film's mood, pace, and sensitivity. Should producers call a beautiful horror film like *The Innocents* (1961) something like *Curse of the Sex-Starved Ghosts?*

Contributing to the film's sensitivity is the panther man, a truly pitiable creature. A repeated victim of heartless vivisection by a "mad scientist," he escapes and kills according to his feral nature. At other times, he desperately tries to please his captors by speaking, which is against his nature. He responds to kindness as any animal or human being would, and he responds to torture as expected. *Terror Is a Man* explores the horror of vivisection as powerfully as does its predecessor *Island of Lost Souls*. Though Wells would not approve of the film's point of view, most audiences do.

Rojas' black and white photography enhances the film's brooding atmosphere, lending it a sense of foreboding and bleak beauty.

Francis Lederer turns in a fine performance as Dr. Girard. He is alternately self-centered, arrogant, ruthless, charming, and sophisticated. Like Charles Laughton in *Island of Lost Souls*, Lederer is an example of the driven scientist masking his bloody intentions behind a smooth exterior.

Though Lederer generally commands our attention, Richard Derr turns in a believable performance as Fitzgerald. Less charismatic than Lederer, he comes across as a principled average guy thrown into a strange situation requiring inner strength and resolve. Derr was a capable actor, and his skills are a strength in *Terror Is a Man*.

Greta Thyssen is a beautiful actress capable of carrying out less demanding roles such as that of Frances Girard. A stronger actress may have helped proceedings, but Greta does not hurt them.

Remedios Amazon handles the makeup well. The panther man expresses himself through his eyes, and when unmasked, he terrifies. Let us give credit here also to the panther man himself, Flory Carlos. His cat-like movements, size, and melancholy eyes combine to produce a minor but memorable performance.

Weaknesses

The film's greatest weakness is that it could have been so much better. Dr. Girard gives no convincing reasons why anyone should turn a panther into a human being. Why climb Mount Everest? Because it is there! Of course there is the view of speeding up evolution, but why? Wells' novel is brimming with philosophically challenging themes, but screenwriter Harber prefers simplicity and traditional horror. Perhaps that is what he thought his audience expected, and he was probably right. But if you are going to go for shock, go for it! It *is* possible to synthesize horror and ideas. The great horror films have done it, but this film does not.

Another weakness is the film's gimmick—the bell system—designed to warn squeamish patrons when a shocking scene is about to unfold. Such gimmicks, popular in the late fifties and early sixties, today appear more silly than scary, especially since the bell rings to signal a singularly non-horrifying scalpel incision.

A third weakness is the film's pace. There are some tedious, talky stretches, none of them *too* long, but long enough to stir mild viewer impatience.

Rating: 2½

The Twilight People (1972) aka ***Beasts*** Four Associates and Dimension Pictures, U.S.A and Phillipines / Time: 84 minutes

CREDITS: Produced by John Ashley and Tito Arevalo; Directed by Eddie Romero; Music composed and conducted by Ariston Avelino, Cinematography by Fredy Conde; Supervising film editor—Ben Barcelon; Production design by Robert A. Formosa; Sets and optical effects by Richard Abelardo; Makeup by Antonio Artieda; Production managed by Mario David; Assistant director—Mario Abelardo; Dialogue supervised by Ethel Fernandez; Associate producer—Bev Miller; Executive producers—Larry Woolner and David Cohen; Screenplay by Jerome Small and Eddie Romero, based on *The Island of Doctor Moreau* by H.G. Wells (uncredited).

CAST: John Ashley (Farrell), Pat Woodell (Neva); Jan Merlin (Steinman), Charles Macaulay (Dr. Gordon); Pam Grier (panther woman); Ken Metcalf (antelope man); Kim Ramos (ape man), Tony Gonsalvey (bat man); Mona Morena (wolf woman); Eddie Garcia (Pereira).

Film Synopsis

Farrell, a vigorous young man, is kidnapped while scuba diving and whisked away by boat to an isolated island. As Farrell is transported to the compound of a scientist, a hideous face watches from the greenery. Upon arriving at the doctor's compound, Farrell is informed of his situation. He was kidnapped by Steinman, a young, blond Aryan who exudes confidence and a certain touch of sadism, and by several henchmen. Dr. Gordon, who fled to the island after a scandal in the United States, chose Farrell as an experimental subject because of his obvious mental and physical strength. Assisting Dr. Gordon is his beautiful daughter, Dr. Neva Gordon. As father Gordon explains, the world is changing rapidly, but mankind isn't. Man will be forced to find other environments, under the sea perhaps, and lower animals are best suited to such environments. Gordon wants to produce a master species—human beings provided with animal characteristics that en-

hance their chance for survival. Convinced that he is on the right track, Gordon shrugs it off when Farrell compares him to Hitler.

Next day, Gordon, Steinman, and assorted henchmen hunt down the creature that watched them from the jungle the day before. Though Gordon wants to capture this "boar man" alive, Steinman's love for killing gets the best of him and he shoots the creature dead.

Soon after, Farrell makes the acquaintance of Pereira, another island captive. Unlike Farrell, Pareira appears in good spirits, believing that Dr. Gordon has great things in store for him.

As Gordon experiments on a "manimal," Farrell explores areas of the compound and discovers the secrets of the doctor's scandals. Later, Steinman confronts Farrell regarding his spying and offers the captive a chance to escape with a three-hour head start, after which Steinman will pursue. Farrell refuses. Neva then enters and shows some perfunctory interest in Farrell as a man.

"Bring the subject in—no sedation," Dr. Gordon orders. Another experiment is about to begin. Neva is disturbed that Farrell will be the subject of her father's ultimate experiment. She reads Farrell's dossier and goes to him at night. The two are obviously attracted to each other, but conflicting emotions force Neva to leave. Farrell follows Neva to the basement where she is attacked by the panther woman. Farrell rescues Neva and forces the panther woman back into her cage.

Neva later charges her father with committing murder. He responds by pointing out that "the human race has always wallowed in self-destruction." Gordon claims that he is offering Farrell immortality by transferring his essence into each of the "super beings."

Farrell observes unnoticed as the affable Pereira is subjected to a torturous

Manimals take aim in this scene from *The Twilight People* (1972), an uncredited adaptation of Wells' *The Island of Dr. Moreau*.

experiment. Disgusted, Neva flees the lab and attempts suicide. Farrell follows her, saves her, and ends up on the floor kissing her, embracing her, and promising to help her escape. Unfortunately, Gordon and Steinman walk in and consign Farrell to a cage in the basement. Steinman taunts the caged Farrell and asks him why he didn't accept his offer to try to escape. Farrell answers that he couldn't escape because he wants to stay long enough to kill Steinman. The Aryan just smiles, retires to his room and treats himself to a large glass of milk.

As Steinman sits on his bed, Neva appears with a gun. Steinman wrestles the gun away from her and pins her to his bed. Neva then accuses Steinman of having homosexual desires for Farrell and of wanting to kill him so nobody else can have him.

This enrages Steinman, but before he can do Neva physical harm, he passes out as a result of the drug she placed in his milk.

With Steinman unconscious, Neva frees Farrell and a passel of manimals. Farrell takes Dr. Gordon by gunpoint toward the beach, and Neva leads the manimals in the same direction. When Steinman regains consciousness, he assembles the henchmen and goes hunting for the escapees. After a trek involving the killing of henchmen by manimals and the killing of manimals by henchmen, Dr. Gordon finally escapes back to the compound where he is killed by his beastly wife, who volunteered for an early botched experiment. Steinman holds Farrell at gunpoint, but Farrell soon unaccountably returns to the scene of Dr. Gordon's death and Neva's grief.

Adaptation

The Twilight People is obviously a loose adaptation of Wells' The Island of Doctor Moreau. The major switch is that Doctor Moreau is turning animals into humans while Dr. Gordon is turning humans into animals. Both are attempting to benefit humanity through their efforts. Still, in The Twilight People, the doctor is portrayed as evil because he resorts to kidnapping. At least Moreau began with animals, absolving him of moral censure in the mind of H.G. Wells. Of course, the audiences for The Twilight People would be predictably outraged at Gordon's atrocities.

In Romero's film, Gordon stands in for Moreau, Steinman for Montgomery, and Farrell for Prendick. We see, of course, that both the novel and the 1933 film adaptation had to have a panther woman, though her role in the novel is quite different from her role in the films, and her role in the films are quite different from one another. For better or for worse, the panther woman has become a staple in films based on Wells' novel.

Interestingly, The Twilight People is the first Moreau adaptation to blatantly portray the Montgomery character as homosexual. The Island of Doctor Moreau does so indirectly, but The Twilight People does so frontally.

Wells' novel raises issues of perennial importance to humanity; Romero's film raises few important issues, if any. Wells provides the intellectual fodder, but Romero is either financially incapable or otherwise unwilling to adapt it in any kind of challenging way.

Production and Marketing

Director Eddie Romero had already worked on one H.G. Wells film before tackling The Twilight People. For information on Romero, see the Production and Marketing section of Terror Is a Man.

American leading man John Ashley began his film career as a teenager and later went on to appear in Hud (1963, with Paul Newman), Beach Party (1963), Muscle Beach Party (1964), Bikini Beach (1964), Beach Blanket Bingo (1965), and Beast of the Yellow Night (1971, directed by Eddie Romero). Ashley also co-starred on the television show Straightaway, as well as in episodes of The Beverly Hillbillies and The Wild, Wild West. Today, he is remembered primarily for his campy beach party movies.

Boston-born Pat Woodell began her career as a child actress and went on to star as the original Bobbie Jo on television's Petticoat Junction. She then appeared as the only other artist in Jack Benny's One Man Show. Her later film credits include The Big Doll House (1971) and Class of '74 (1973).

American leading lady Pam Grier (1949–) appeared in Russ Meyer's Beyond the Valley of the Dolls (1970) before essaying the role of the panther woman in The Twilight People. Her career would soon take off, however, with such successful Black exploitation hits as Blacula (1972), Hit Man (1972), Coffy (1974, Grier's biggest hit), Black Mama, White Mama (1974), Sheba Baby (1975), and Friday Foster (1975). Her role as a homicidal prostitute in Fort Apache, the Bronx (1981) earned her critical acclaim, and she remains a popular star in the new millennium, appearing in films such as Bones (2001) and others.

Ads for The Twilight People featured such catch phrases as "Animal Desires ... Human Lust," and "Test Tube Terrors Half Beast ... All Monster." Posters show a beast man carrying off a woman, a bat man spreading its wings, and other assorted horrors.

Strengths

Let's begin with the title itself, The Twilight People, which suggests a people trapped between daylight and dark. The manimals in the film are caught between the human and the animal; therefore, the title evokes consideration of the film's dilemmas and dichotomies.

Of the actors, Jan Merlin as Steinman is at least serviceable, if not impressive. Regardless, he must be considered a strength. He delivers his lines more naturally than most of the cast, and he physically fulfills the role of homosexual sadist. He is one of the few believable cast members.

Pam Grier as the panther woman is also a strength. Unlike the rest of the manimals, Grier exhibits more genuinely appropriate animal characteristics. She is sensual as well as beastly. In fact, Grier was and is one of the most sensual women in contemporary cinema. The 1933 version depicted a very human panther woman, and the 1959 version depicted a panther man. Grier is more like the panther woman (she-puma) created by Wells, and as such, she works.

The bat man has his moments as well. Tony Gonsalvey is frightening in close-up as he stares through the window at the hated Dr. Gordon, and his soaring for victims stands out among the surrounding boredom. The bat man's final flight into the night is done via effects borrowed from *Son of Dracula* (1943) and *Abbott and Costello Meet Frankenstein* (1948).

Weaknesses

The major weakness of the film is its pace, its inescapable boredom. For perhaps thirty minutes the film intrigues us, then collapses. The escape of the captives should be exciting; instead, it is an eternity of dullness. Even as the manimals kill henchmen and henchmen kill manimals, the whole affair is slow and uninteresting.

Part of the fault is the wooden performances of stars Ashley, Woodell, and Macaulay. The same can be said for much of the cast.

Though cinematographer Conde provides some early interesting underwater photography, except for some shots featuring the bat man, the film is visually uninteresting. The photography isn't bad, but it needs to be much more engrossing to make up for the film's myriad defects. When a pedestrian cinematographer shoots a dull film, the result can be nothing but dull.

Antonio Artieda's makeup is pretty bad, ranging from the serviceable (Pam Grier's panther woman) to the laughable (Ken Metcalf's antelope man). Except for the bat man, the manimal makeup is head work only. This is suspicious to say the least. How are such abortions to survive in the future as Dr. Gordon predicts? Do they really lack only Farrell's intelligence? Generally, the makeup could be equaled by any good Halloween trick-or-treater.

The film's soundtrack is dull and repetitious. The mediocre and repetitive upfront guitar and horns eventually fail to carry forth any tension or terror.

Director Romero fails to convey any of the mood that he and Leon brought to *Terror is a Man*, perhaps suggesting that Leon was the most talented of the two. Romero is undoubtedly working on a low budget; nevertheless, some talented low budget directors have infused their films with interest and style. Romero doesn't.

Of course, some of Romero's problems could have been the screenplay. Unfortunately for him, he co-wrote it. Actually, the dialogue isn't bad, but after thirty minutes, the pace kills.

The biggest fault comes near the end of the film, as we see Steinman pointing a gun at Farrell and we see Farrell drop his weapon and surrender. What happens next? In one print, we never find out. Farrell appears moments later with a gun to aid Neva, and Steinman is seen no more.

According to the film's pressbook synopsis, Farrell kills Steinman. That much seems obvious, but we don't see it happen. Since Steinman v.s. Farrell is one of the film's few engrossing conflicts, why is it not resolved before our eyes? Did the editors cut it? Was the scene cut from video releases only? Whatever the reason, what a mess!

Rating: 1½

The Island of Dr. Moreau (1977)

Cinema 77/American International Pictures, U.S.A. / Running Time: 104 minutes. / Release Date: July 8, 1977

CREDITS: Executive producers—Samuel Z. Arkoff and Sandy Howard; Produced by John Temple-Smith and Skip Steloff; Directed by Don Taylor; Screenplay by John Herman Shaner and Al Ramrus, based on the novel by H.G. Wells; Cinematography by Gerry Fisher; AIP executive—Elliot Schick; Post production supervised by Salvatore Billitteri; Music by Laurence Rosenthal; Production managed by John Wilson; Production designed by Philip Jeffries; Edited by Marion Rothman; Casting by Betty Martin; Production coordinated by Kathleen Sumner; Wardrobe designed by Richart La Motte; Creative make-up by John Chambers; Animals supervised by Ralph Helfer; Head animal trainer—Carl Thompson; Creative consultant—David Winters; Publicist—Jay Remer.

CAST: Burt Lancaster (Dr. Moreau), Michael York (Braddock), Nigel Davenport (Montgomery), Barbara Carrera (Maria), Richard Basehart (Sayer of the Law), M'Ling (Nick Cravat), The Great John "L." (Boarman), Bob Ozman (Bullman), Fumio Demura (Hyenaman), Gary Baxley (Lionman), John Gillespie (Tigerman), David Cass (Bearman).

Film Synopsis

Andrew Braddock and a fellow traveler are shipwrecked and float ashore on a lonely island in the Pacific. Braddock leaves his exhausted friend propped against a tree and sets out through the lush foliage to explore their new environment. While Braddock is gone, his companion screams in terror and is dragged away through the jungle. Pursued by hyenas, Braddock is rescued by a taciturn, powerful man named Montogomery and taken to a spacious, comfortable compound carved in the middle of the jungle. A tall, sturdy gate surrounds the buildings.

Within the compound, Braddock meets the awkward-walking M'ling, a grotesquely ugly servant who gives him a tin of water. Later, Braddock meets Dr. Moreau, a middle-aged scientist, and Maria, a lovely young woman Braddock is attracted to. Moreau explains that because the island is off the scheduled run, Braddock cannot leave until a supply ship arrives. Furthermore, Moreau describes himself as self-exiled. Having left a prestigious university, he has been conducting experiments on the island for eleven years. He stops short, however, of divulging the nature of those experiments.

The next day, Braddock is helping Maria chase her pet cat through the jungle when they come upon M'Ling down on all fours like an animal sucking up water from a pool. M'ling glances up, grins hideously, and bounds off into the jungle. Puzzled, Braddock and Maria find the cat and return to the compound.

When Braddock asks questions about M'ling, a drunken Montgomery refers Braddock to Dr. Moreau. Montgomery does reveal, however, that he was once a bounty hunter and the killer of many men. Does the memory of his bloody past and the knowledge that he himself is a hunted man cause his heavy drinking in exile?

That night, Braddock spies Montgomery and Moreau loading a captive M'ling into a wagon. The servant's face has changed and become more animalistic. Among his coarsened, brutish features are elongated teeth and the emergence of a snout. When Braddock later questions Moreau, the doctor answers vaguely that M'ling is a special kind of man under treatment at the compound.

Suspicious of what he has seen on the island, Braddock secretly begins repairing the dinghy in which he arrived. Returning from such an outing, he finds Maria's cat viciously slaughtered and is stalked by a strange creature that walks first on two legs and then on all fours. After returning safely to the compound, Braddock again tries unsuccessfully to pry an explanation from Moreau.

When Moreau and Montgomery are away from the compound, Braddock explores one of the outbuildings and discovers a collection of wild animals. Seeing a figure lying under a sheet in the laboratory, Braddock unveils a creature in agony—a creature part bear and part man. Outraged, Braddock demands that Moreau explain why he is subjecting creatures to the tortures of vivisection. Moreau explains that he has almost proven the existence of a cell particle that controls the shape of living organisms. Moreau is attempting to turn animals into human beings in order to control heredity and eventually wipe out diseases and biological defects. He tells Braddock that he might as well aid in the experiments since a supply ship will not arrive for another two years! Braddock refuses, preferring to begin a love affair with Maria instead.

Later, Braddock ventures into the jungle and discovers a cave populated by Moreau's humanimals. They are led by The Sayer of the Law, a wolf man who constantly repeats Moreau's credo for their behavior as humans. Moreau arrives and calls for a repetition of the law, after which he informs the humanimals that the law has been broken. Blood has been spilled. The culprit is the bull man, and the humanimals pursue him into the jungle.

When the bull man is injured, Braddock comes upon him first. The bull man pleads with Braddock to kill him rather than return him to the House of Pain. Out of compassion, Braddock shoots the bull man. Unknown to Braddock, however, some of the humanimals observe his act. If it is against the law to spill blood, why has Braddock done so?

Braddock tries to escape the island with Maria but is captured and subjected to Moreau's attempt to turn him into an animal. As changes affect his body and brain, Braddock strains furiously to retain his humanity. Upon discovering what Moreau is up to, Montgomery castigates him for experimenting on a human being and vows to leave the island. Moreau makes the error of shooting Montgomery in view of some humanimals keeping watch from outside the compound. Suddenly, the humanimals understand that human beings are susceptible to death, just as they are. With all they have seen, they proclaim that the law is no more. A revolt ensues, during which the humanimals kill Moreau and pursue Braddock and Maria through the jungle to the sea. The lovers escape and drift away from the island. As days pass, Braddock loses the animal features he had developed. Finally, when Braddock sights an approaching ship, Maria, who was one of Moreau's experiments, reverts to panther characteristics and attacks her savior.

At least one alternate ending was filmed, and possibly two. In a less shocking ending, the escapees are able to rejoice at the sight of an approaching ship. Maria was never one of Moreau's experiments, and the lovers apparently live happily ever after.

In a rumored third ending, a pregnant Maria gives birth to a tiger kitten.

Adaptation

The Island of Dr. Moreau (1977) is in many ways a faithful adaptation.

Burt Lancaster (as Dr. Moreau) surveys the destruction he had caused in this lobby card scene from *The Island of Dr. Moreau* (1977).

Occasionally using dialogue directly from Wells' novel, Lancaster's Moreau emerges as the emotionally detached man of science envisioned by the author. This remains true until late in the film when Moreau assumes the traditional role of mad scientist by experimenting on Braddock (the film's equivalent of Wells' Prendick).

The film's Montgomery differs somewhat from his novel's counterpart, the former being a cynical bounty hunter haunted by the past, the latter being exiled from the world of acceptable science and a possible homosexual. Both Montgomerys are alcoholics, and both come to a bad end, one at the hands of Moreau, the other at the hands of the Beast Folk.

The panther woman, who plays a small but important part in the novel, took on a central role in *The Island of Lost Souls* (1932). In the 1977 version, Maria stands in for the 1933 panther woman. One ending suggests that she was an experimental subject, but the alternate ending suggests she was not. As Moreau explains, he rescued Maria when she was a child in India. Either way, she serves as a love interest for Braddock and is only of peripheral importance to the main themes.

The humanimals are much as Wells depicts them in the novel, the bear man and bull man eliciting our strongest sympathy. The Sayer of the Law repeats the same words written by Wells, Moreau plays the same godlike role in the humanimals' lives, and the House of Pain remains the punishment for those who break the law.

Production and Marketing

Director Don Taylor (1920–1998) began as a leading man, appearing in such films as *Naked City* (1948), *Submarine Command* (1951), *Stalag 17* (1953), and *I'll Cry Tomorrow* (1957). His early directorial outings in the 1960s accounted for several mediocre films, the best being *Ride the Wild Surf* (1964). His fortunes rose in the 1970s, however, when he directed the critically acclaimed and financially successful *Escape from the Planet of the Apes* (1971), the third in a series of five Planet of the Apes films that began in 1968. He then took the helm for the well-received *Tom Sawyer* (1973), *Echoes of a Summer* (1975) and *The Great Scout and Cathouse Thursday* (1976). Following *The Island of Dr. Moreau*, Taylor returned to the terror genre with *Damien: Omen II* (1978), an above average sequel to *The Omen* (1976). In 1980 he turned in what is probably his best directorial effort, *The Final Countdown*, and then made movies for television.

Heading the cast is the venerable and versatile Burt Lancaster (1913–1994). A former circus acrobat, Lancaster began his film career as an actor and dancer in soldier shows during World War II. Among his most memorable film roles are *The Killers* (1946), *The Flame and the Arrow* (1950), *Come Back, Little Sheba* (1953), *From Here to Eternity* (1953, for which he earned an Academy Award nomination), *Vera Cruz* (1954), *Gunfight at the OK Corral* (1957, as Wyatt Earp), *Elmer Gantry* (1960, for which he won an Academy Award), *Judgment at Nuremberg* (1961), *Birdman of Alcatraz* (1962, for which he earned an Academy Award nomination), *The Professionals* (1966), and *The Swimmer* (1967). He gives his best post–1977 performance in *Atlantic City* (1980, for which he won a British Film Award and earned yet another Academy Award nomination). His last film performances were in the wistful *Field of Dreams* (1989), and in the made-for-television movie version of *The Phantom of the Opera* (1990).

In a reputed pressbook interview for *The Island of Dr. Moreau*, Lancaster says that "I took the role because H.G. Wells had a moral point to make. He was an ardent anti-vivisectionist and the film attempts intelligently to explain both sides of the never-ending war between the scientist who must experiment and the moralist repelled by such experiments." Lancaster calls vivisection "another step towards the dehumanization of people. In its fanciful way, it's something like the splitting of the atom or the DNA process so much in today's news. Where, indeed, are we heading?" Apparently concerned with potential audience perception, the actor hastens to add that "the film is not played as a horror piece." While it is questionable whether these words actually issued from the mouth of Burt Lancaster, if they did, it shows a basic unfamiliarity with H.G. Wells, who was not an "ardent anti-vivisectionist." In fact, Wells was a vociferous supporter of animal vivisection. It is certainly true, however, that issues raised by the film were important in 1977 and remain so today.

Lancaster's co-star, English actor Michael York (1942–), began his film career under the direction of Franco Zeffirelli in *The Taming of the Shrew* (1967), under Joseph Losey in *Accident* (1967), and again under Zeffirelli in *Romeo and Juliet* (1968). Before being cast in *Island*, York also appeared in such film hits as *Cabaret* (1972), *The Lost Horizon* (1973), *The Three Musketeers* (1973), *The Four Musketeers* (1974), *Murder on the Orient Express* (1974), and *Logan's Run* (1976). He also appeared in the highly regarded

Michael York and Barbara Carrera enjoy each other's company in this lobby card scene from *The Island of Dr. Moreau* (1977).

made-for-television movie *Jesus of Nazareth* (1977). After *Island*, York turned increasingly to made-for-television movies, one being *The Phantom of the Opera* (1982), which reunited him with Burt Lancaster.

Don Taylor was very pleased with York's work in *Island*, lauding him for his cooperation and his willingness to put in long hours under difficult conditions, particularly the film's early boat and beach scenes.

British actor Nigel Davenport (1928–) came to *Island* based on a distinguished film career, his most memorable being *Peeping Tom* (1959), *A Man for All Seasons* (1967), *The Virgin Soldiers* (1969), and *Living Free* (1972). He also appeared in two

mediocre science fiction films, *No Blade of Grass* (1971) and *Phase IV* (1973), and in the made-for-television version of *Dracula* (1973, as Dr. Van Helsing).

Nicaraguan-born Barbara Carrera (1947–), a former model, had appeared in *Puzzle of a Downfall Child* (1970), *The Master Gunfighter* (1975), and *Embryo* (1976, a science fiction shocker with Rock Hudson) before being cast in *Island*. After *Island*, she would enhance her reputation by appearing in the James Bond thriller *Never Say Never Again* (1983) and by co-starring in Bette Davis' final film *The Wicked Stepmother* (1989). She is probably best known for her role in the popular television series *Dallas* (1985–1986).

Richard Basehart (1914–1984), though

eclipsed by Burt Lancaster, also sported an impressive vita at the time of *Island,* having appeared in such notable films as *He Walked by Night* (1948), *The Black Book* (1949), *Fourteen Hours* (1951), *Titanic* (1953), *La Strada* (1954, directed by Federico Fellini), *Il Bidone* (directed by Federico Fellini), *Moby Dick* (1956, directed by John Huston), *Time Limit* (1957), *The Brothers Karamazov* (1958), and *Hitler* (1963, as Hitler). His science fiction/horror films included *The Satan Bug* (1965), *The City Beneath the Sea* (1971), and *Mansion of the Doomed* (1976). He is probably best remembered today for his starring role in television's *Voyage to the Bottom of the Sea* (1964–1967).

In a pressbook interview, Basehart says, "I love to do strange and different things I never did before.... I had some doubts about doing it [*Island*] when I was still in Hollywood, but I fell in love with it in St. Croix." It was largely his mellifluous voice that landed him the role of the Sayer of the Law, but Basehart didn't mind. "After all," he says, "with my makeup, it didn't really matter what I looked like." According to publicity material, every day for four months Basehart underwent a four hour make-up session commencing at 4 a.m.

Makeup wizards John Chambers and Dan Striepeke, both veterans of *Planet of the Apes* (1968), worked from sketches and models in creating makeup for the humanimals. First they took molds of the actors' faces and augmented the features with clay. The clay then served as models for new molds from which foam rubber appliances were made. Finally, the appliances were affixed to the actors' skin and matched with parts of their still-visible faces. Because the humanimals are seen in varying stages of change, the makeup team created as many as three different makeup designs for each creature.

To ensure the makeup's survival under tropical rainforest conditions, Chambers and Striepeke trimmed, sprayed, and colored an imported fur cloth rather than use real hair. They then added a special adhesive. Fortunately, the makeup resisted every assault, including the hours of retakes of the ocean scenes in which Maria repeatedly belts the hyenaman over the head with balsa wood oars.

To avoid a serious accident, Chambers and Striepeke constructed a fiberglass helmet for the bullman in the scene in which a Bengal tiger snaps off one of his horns during mortal combat. Since the tiger's fangs did at one point strike the bullman's head, the precaution was wise.

American International Pictures went all out in preparing the public for *Island.* Ace published a novelization of the film's screenplay with photos from the film adorning the cover, and Tempo issued a tie-in of the original Wells classic. In addition, Marvel Comics published a special edition of *The Island of Dr. Moreau* to coincide with the film's release. Also coinciding with the film's release were Mego Toys, T-shirt iron-ons, costumes and masks, and key chains—all featuring the humanimals. The studio also released an eight-minute short on *The Making of The Island of Dr. Moreau.*

The film's pressbook encouraged a coloring contest to hype the film, as well as a radio, newspaper, or television sponsored "Famous Doctors of the Movies" contest. It even suggested a travel tie-in hyping the beautiful St. Croix, Virgin Islands. Made on a $6,000,000 budget, boasting an impressive cast, and promoted vigorously, the film certainly held every promise of success.

H.G. Wells receives mention in most ads, but little else. Here is an example:

> The fertile, creative imagination of H.G. Wells depicted Dr. Moreau as a dedicated scientist seeking to isolate and

recombine the chromosomes which determine the shape of all living things ... the moral question posed by Wells, through Moreau, remains the same today as then: how far is science justified in going to prove a thesis? Today's scientists, under the aegis of several large corporations are seriously experimenting with the DNA process. These learned personages of today, no more than did Moreau, are not certain what strange forms of life their experiments will result in.

Strengths

In the film's first half, Burt Lancaster's Moreau approximates Wells' original conception more so than any of his cinematic predecessors. Playing Moreau as a humanitarian, he brings a refreshing, self-controlled dignity to the role.

Though less successful than Lugosi, Richard Basehart admirably brings the Sayer of the Law to life. In fact, thanks largely to Chambers and Striepeke and to a host of actors able to project through heavy makeup, all of the humanimals are impressive. Especially memorable is the tortured bull man who pleads to die rather than return to the House of Pain.

Michael York has several impressive scenes. In one, though earlier discarding moral concerns, he finally expresses the perfect tone of voice and facial expression after being shocked by Moreau's business-like disregard for the suffering of his subjects. Also moving is York's attempt to retain his humanity in the face of Moreau's attempt to turn him into a lower animal. In fact, York gives one of the best performances of his career.

Barbara Carrera is more than adequate as Maria. Though peripheral to most of the film's central concerns, her exotic beauty and smouldering personality make her right for the role.

Gerry Fisher's cinematography is involving at times, particularly early in the film when a moving camera depicts the speed of the brutal abduction of Braddock's partner by an unseen but obviously powerful assailant.

Laurence Rosenthal's music is sinister, but it generally has to battle the bright cinematography for control of the mood.

Weaknesses

A chief weakness of the film is something that in different circumstances would have been a strength. That is, the vivid, lush color photography of the St. Croix tropical paradise. Gone are the shadows and darkness of the brooding 1932 original, and gone is the eeriness that they evoked. One might argue that the paradisal setting effectively contrasts the natural against the unnatural invasion of Moreau's compound, but in this case the approach costs the film more than it adds.

Another weakness is Moreau's change from an overly dedicated humanitarian into a mad scientist, from a man concerned with the future of humanity into a man willing to murder his partner and rob a shipwreck victim of his humanity. The switch lacks the necessary foreshadowing to work.

Neither of the two endings are satisfactory. The ending in which Maria attacks Braddock, proving at the last second that she is the product of a Moreau experiment, is too predictable. By 1977, filmgoers had come to expect the last minute "surprise ending" that worked so well in *Carrie* (1976) and some other genre films. Unfortunately, it doesn't work here. Though somewhat truer to Wells, the ending in which Braddock and Maria are rescued by a ship falls flat. Perhaps the rumored ending in which Maria gives birth to a tiger kitten would have delivered a unique shock.

Rating: 3

The Island of Dr. Moreau (1996)

New Line Cinema (U.S.A.) / Running Time: 96 minutes

CREDITS: Produced by Edward R. Pressman; Directed by John Frankenheimer; Cinematography by William A. Fraker; Screenplay by Richard Stanley and Ron Hutchinson, based on the novel by H.G. Wells; Music by Gary Chang; Casting by Valerie McCaffrey; Production designed by Graham "Grace" Walker; Edited by Paul Rubell; Costumes designed by Norma Moriceau; Special creatures and makeup effects by Stan Winston; Executive producers—Tim Zinneman and Claire Rudnick Polstein.

CAST: Marlon Brando (Dr. Moreau); Val Kilmer (Montgomery); David Thewlis (Edward Douglas); Fairuza Balk (Aissa); Ron Perlman (Sayer of the Law); Marco Hofschneider (M'ling); Temuera Morrison (Azzazillo); William Hootkins (Kiril); Daniel Rigney (Hyena/Swine); Nelson de la Rosa (Majar); Peter Eliot (Assassimon); Mark Dacascos (Lo-Mai); Neil Young (Boar Man); David Hudson (Bison Man); Clare Grant (Fox Lady); Kitty Silver (Sow Lady #1); Fiona Mahl (Sow Lady #2).

Film Synopsis

Three survivors of a plane crash in the Java Sea drift between life and death. After six or seven days, two of the men fight over the last water canteen and end up as shark food. Douglas, the lone survivor, is rescued by a ship. He tells Montgomery, his rescuer, that he was on his way to work on a United Nations peace settlement when his plane crashed. When they dock at an island, Montgomery orders that caged rabbits be brought ashore. He then caresses one of the rabbits before casually breaking its neck. Rabbits aren't allowed on the island, Montgomery explains to the disgusted Douglas, but he has imported some for his own food.

Later, Douglas spots a woman dancing. She explains that her father brought her to the island. When Montgomery approaches, she flees. Douglas remarks that she is beautiful, to which Montgomery replies, "Yeah, she's a pussycat."

Douglas soon learns that he is on the island of Dr. Moreau, a Nobel Prize winning geneticist who has spent seventeen years in isolation obsessed with animal research. Moreau retreated to the island after animal rights activists ran him out of the United States. As a result of a paper he wrote, Montgomery has been Moreau's assistant for ten years. When night falls, Montgomery locks Douglas in his room. Undeterred, however, Douglas breaks out and explores the grounds while strange animal sounds permeate the darkness. He enters a lab filled with caged wild animals and discovers an experiment in progress during which a fetus is delivered. Montgomery cries out and is pursued by an animal-like surgeon. While running, he encounters the girl he met earlier. Her name is Aissa, and she tells him that she wants to leave the island. With the coming of daylight, they see a leopard man drinking in a stream. The creature looks up and guiltily bounds away on all fours. Montgomery and Aissa then find a slaughtered rabbit and suspect the leopard man of having killed it. Soon they arrive at a camp inhabited by animal people. They seek the Sayer of the Law, an animal man who proclaims that they are men because "the father has made us men." The law is not to run on all fours, not to suck drink, and not to kill.

The arrival of Dr. Moreau himself is startling. Sporting a pasty white face, the "Father" benignly gestures as animal men transport him aloft in a chair. As a peace offering, Moreau orders Montgomery to give Douglas his gun. It soon becomes apparent that Moreau controls the animal men by remote control, activating implants that cause them great pain when they misbehave.

At dinner, Moreau introduces his

animal servants to Douglas and proceeds to explain that he has infused animals with human genes. He asks Douglas to judge not so that he be not judged. "There is no peace unto the wicked," Douglas says, to which Moreau replies, "Let he who is without sin cast the first stone." Moreau goes on to explain that he seeks to refine the human species by eradicating destructive elements found in the human psyche. "I have seen the devil in my microscope," he asserts, "and I have chained him ... I have cut him to pieces."

When Moreau learns of the slaughtered rabbit and of Aissa's suspicion of the leopard man, he calls forth all the animal people and announces that the law has been broken. This results in the death of the leopard man. When cremating the body, however, an animal man discovers the implant and learns how to remove his own. Soon the new knowledge is passed around to other animal men.

Meanwhile, Aissa is beginning to change and take on her former animal characteristics. Desperate to remain human, she begs Moreau to give her a treatment. Before anything can be done, four animal men break into the compound and kill Moreau. "No more pain! No more law!" they ferociously declare.

Montgomery fires on the animal men and temporarily restores order. After Moreau's cremation, Montgomery tries to convince the animal people that the Father is still among them as a spirit and that the law still prevails. The charade fails, however, and the animal men kill Montgomery and Aissa. All hell then breaks loose as the animal people arm themselves and set out to establish rule over one another and destroy the compound. The hyena man wants Douglas to tell the others that the hyena man is God. Douglas tells the animal people that they have all eaten the flesh of God (Moreau's burnt remains), so who is the new God? When the

hyena man is killed he pathetically groans, "Father, why?"

After the carnage, Douglas finds his own blood stored in a refrigerator. He had been experimented on without his knowledge. The Sayer of the Law asks Douglas to stay and not leave the island. Douglas refuses but promises to return someday. Sadly, the Sayer realizes that the animal people must be what they are by nature, not what the Father has made them. Later, after Douglas has returned to civilization, he reflects:

> Most times I keep the memory far in the back of my mind, a distant cloud, but there are times when the little cloud spreads until it obscures the sky. And those times, I look about me at my fellow man and I am reminded of some likenesses to the beast people, and I feel as though the animal is surging up in them and they are neither wholly animal nor wholly man, but an unstable combination of both, as unstable as anything Moreau created. And I go in fear.

Adaptation

The screenplay by Richard Stanley and Ron Hutchinson is thematically faithful to the novel, particularly in its mocking of the clergy and religion and in its challenging of illegitimate and unreliable authority. The screenplay dispenses with the captain of the *Lady Vain* as a source of irresponsible authority, but it gives us the grotesque Sayer of the Law as the embodiment of deluded authority. The name Prendick continues to be unacceptable, and the screenwriters change it this time to Douglas. Again we have the panther girl made mandatory by her appearances in *Island of Lost Souls* (1933) and *The Island of Dr. Moreau* (1977), where she was written in as a female presence and potential love interest. As was the case in Wells' first three novels, the screenplay faithfully suggests pessimism regarding the future of humankind.

One significant change is that implants replace the whip as Moreau's controlling device. The pain seems to come from nowhere, enforcing the idea that Moreau is a god with supernatural powers.

Unlike Wells' Moreau, Brando's Moreau suffers from an allergy to sunlight and wears sunblock that renders his skin ghostly white. He is also more whimsical than Wells' creation. Otherwise, Brando's Moreau is the driven, though otherwise bored, gene splitter of Wells' novel.

Production and Marketing

The Island of Dr. Moreau (1996) was the third credited version of H.G. Wells' novel. So why another version? According to the foreword in Tor's paperback tie-in promoting the film, science is closer now than ever to actually realizing Moreau's goal, and of course, closer to suffering Moreau's catastrophy. But thematic timelessness justifies a remake as well because "Wells reaches farther into the human psyche [than organ transplants and transspecies implantations], far beyond physical attributes of 'man.' He dares to define humanity, to question the existence of the beast within each of us, and poses to the reader the idea that perhaps given the proper circumstances and a lack of the laws that keep us civilized, we too could revert to the wild." This may be true, which is why William Golding's *Lord of the Flies* and other novels concerned with human nature continue to intrigue.

At the helm was veteran director John Frankenheimer (1930–). Among Frankenheimer's most notable films were *The Young Stranger* (1957), *The Manchurian Candidate* (1962), *Birdman of Alcatraz* (1962), *Seven Days in May* (1964) and *Seconds* (1966). Both *The Manchurian Candidate* and *Seconds* were excellent science

fiction films. The former concerns the brainwashing of a Korean War veteran for the purpose of political assassination, and the latter explores the life of a bored business executive who falls into the clutches of a powerful and evil organization which physically and psychologically turns him literally into another human being. Unlike most directors of nineties science fiction films, Frankenheimer focuses on the timeless human element first and on the science fiction second.

The off-beat casting of Marlon Brando (1924–) as Dr. Moreau was as much a surprise as the 1977 casting of Burt Lancaster had been. Brando brought to the film a sterling reputation, having starred in such blockbuster critical successes as *A Streetcar Named Desire* (1951), *Viva Zapata* (1953), *Julius Caesar* (1953, as Mark Anthony), *Sayanora* (1957), and *Last Tango in Paris* (1972), all of which earned him Academy Award nominations. He won Academy Awards for *On the Waterfront* (1954) and *The Godfather* (1972).

Val Kilmer (1959–) was best-known for taking over the role of Batman from Michael Keaton in *Batman Forever* (1995), but more significantly, he gave a stunningly realistic performance as hard-living rock icon Jim Morrison in *The Doors* (1991).

English leading man David Thewlis had earned critical acclaim in his role as an alienated drifter in *Naked* (1993). He followed that film with a fine performance in Caroline Thompson's lovely version of *Black Beauty* (1994).

Ron Perlman came to the role of the Sayer of the Law having starred as a sympathetic, heroic "animal man" in the popular television show *Beauty and the Beast*. His other performances consisted of character roles in such films as *The Name of the Rose* (1986).

New Line Cinema promoted the film vigorously. Tor and Modern Library both cooperated by releasing tie-in books, and picture cards were distributed plugging the film. Advertising relied largely on the presence of Marlon Brando. Unfortunately, ads and posters for the film were generally unimaginative. The Tor paperback cover, on the other hand, is a colorful, artistic, and exciting scene of a very un-Brando-like Moreau brandishing a whip as animal men surround him against the backdrop of the burning compound.

Strengths

The film begins by depicting two shipwreck survivors who die in an attempt to prolong their lives at each other's expense. Instead, they end up allowing a shark to preserve its life at their expense— all in keeping with the law of the jungle. Are human beings really any different or more important in the cosmic scheme of things than the rest of the animal kingdom? The opening scene and subsequent events suggest that we are not. The film suggests that all animals are at the mercy of the law of the jungle because God does not exist. Some people, such as priests and the sayers of the law, try to maintain civilized behavior in the masses, but the animal tendencies eventually prevail. Moreau assumes the role of God to his creations, transmitting the law to the Sayer just as God transmitted the Ten Commandments to Moses in the Bible. The film suggests, however, that while all laws have their practical purposes, they are nonetheless man-made, a fact that must be hidden from the masses. To emphasize Moreau's godlike role, Brando first appears as a grotesque caricature of the Pope, waving and gesturing to his creations while being transported aloft on a platform chair. Relating to his creations as a strict, though loving, father would relate to his children, Brando is a benevolent dictator. When one of his children breaks the law,

however, the Father painfully zaps it from afar until it writhes in unbearable pain. Well, maybe he isn't so benevolent; after all, most dictators are not. In many instances, though, he exhibits tenderness, as when he forgives the leopard man moments before one of his "children" defends the law by shooting the miscreant in the head. Moreau is a cultured man who introduces his more successful creations to music and the arts. When the four animal men break into the compound, they confront the Father with questions: "Father... what am I. We are not like you. What are we?" Moreau answers, "You are my children," but hyena man gruffly responds, "No more pain! No more law!" And with that they kill Moreau. As Nietzsche and a cover of *Time Magazine* proclaimed, "God is Dead." And as Tolstoy observed, if God does not exist, everything is possible.

So God is dead. But in the film, the "disciples" still eat the flesh, an obvious allusion to Christian eucharist that Wells does not include in the novel. Montgomery attempts to prolong the faith of the humanimals by suggesting that the Father is still with them in spirit, an obvious allusion to the biblical book of Acts. So who is really God? The answer is anyone's guess. This is one of the most important themes addressed successfully by the film. People seem to need the laws of god in order to behave themselves. When the gods are proven false, natural drives take over, the id overrules the superego, and chaos results.

So how are we to take Moreau in this film? Wells intended him to be a well-intentioned scientist who fails to overcome the fatal flaws in mankind, and Brando's Moreau is such a man. He is not Laughton's sinister mad scientist. He is more in league with Lancaster's Moreau. Lancaster's Moreau, however, becomes the typical mad scientist by film's end, and Brando's Moreau never succumbs. He is killed while trying to interest tortured animal people in atonal classical music. This change of emphasis makes the 1996 *Island of Dr. Moreau* more a parable of the human condition than a horror film. Unfortunately, as seen in the examination of weaknesses, after Brando's death, the film collapses into a special effects popcorn production.

On the positive side, the performances in general should be praised. Particularly impressive are Thewlis and Balk, who try to tread water as Brando and Kilmer go over the top. Still, Brando and Kilmer *are* the stars, and they seem intent that everyone know it. This is not to say that Brando or Kilmer gives a bad performance. On the contrary, Brando is quite good, especially when delivering lines such as "I have seen the devil in my microscope, and I have chained him." Indeed, Moreau's devil resides in the nature of living things. Kilmer's Montgomery is a self-centered hedonist, possibly as a result of his association with Moreau. He lacks any real understanding of Moreau's grand design, but he does live comfortably—and he is, in effect, a demigod, all of which Kilmer brings across effectively.

Most impressive is the cinematography. Opening scene lensing suggests great geographical expanses through long shot photography, which lets us understand that we are far from society's prejudices and climate of opinion. The shark attack scene is also well handled.

Stan Winston's manimal makeup is excellent—state of the art for 1996. The Father's creatures are exactly what one would expect as survivors of such experiments. In addition, the actors can act through the makeup, which all manimals manage to do—evoking both pity and revulsion as Moreau's creations.

Ultimately, the best thing about this film is that it presents an occasion for people to think. But in America, most people don't go to movies to think. They go to buy popcorn and be entertained. This film delivers the entertainment, but it probably left theaters early because it demanded too much from the audience, especially in the first two thirds of the film.

Weaknesses

This seemed to be one of the best genre films of the nineties. With additional viewings, that estimation diminished. Why? The answer is two-fold. The first problem is Brando himself. His whimsical approach to things undercuts his believability as both a benevolent dictator and as a driven, self-centered scientist. Whether this is Brando's fault or Frankenheimer's, it is had to tell. However, Brando's Moreau is ultimately unconvincing despite Brando's technically impressive performance. Perhaps the problem lies in Brando's persona as the "primitive man" as depicted so well in such films as *The Wild One*, *A Streetcar Named Desire*, and *Last Tango in Paris*. In *Island of Dr. Moreau*, Brando is a cultivated man. Still, he exhibits characteristics of the primitive man as he zaps his creations with unbearable pain. We must finally ask, was Brando miscast? He is too fine an actor to be miscast. Some critics have complained that he is obese. Obesity was not part of Wells' description of Moreau, but might not an obese scientist work in the context of the novel and film? So this problem is a mystery. Brando's Moreau is problematic, and elements of his performance leave some audiences unconvinced while others are satisfied.

The major problem with the picture is its devolution into a special effects popcorn movie during its last one third, during which explosions and special effects might satisfy adolescents who squirmed during the first two thirds of the film. The questions raised by the first two thirds are answered in the last segments of the film, but the results are ultimately and curiously unsatisfactory. The problem seems to be the screenplay. Richard Stanley was relieved from the project and Ron Hutchinson and John Frankenheimer (uncredited) took over. Does this account for the problem? That is a possibility.

Rating: 3

4

The Wheels of Chance (1896)

THE NOVEL

Written in 1895 and published in 1896, *The Wheels of Chance* followed hard on the heels of *The Island of Doctor Moreau*. Subtitled *A Holiday Adventure*, it is the light-hearted story of an assistant draper's two week cycling holiday. Against his will, Wells had trained as a draper's assistant, and in this novel he communicates the vocation's drudgery and boredom.

The bicycle is a new invention, and Mr. Hoopdriver is eager for some heroic break in the monotony of his life. In his autobiography, Wells notes that he bought himself a bicycle and rode the same terrain as Hoopdriver's course, all the while laying out geographic settings for his later *The War of the Worlds*. In an 1897 interview, Wells called *Wheels of Chance* his favorite novel, though he considered *The Island of Dr. Moreau* his best.

In 1904, Wells' endeavor to turn his novel into a successful play titled *Hoopdriver's Holiday* ended in failure.

Novel Scenario and Commentary

Mr. Hoopdriver, an assistant draper at the Drapery Emporium, has taken up the daring new hobby of bicycling. Though his body is covered with bruises (as were Wells' legs after his first forays on the bicycle), he takes a week's holiday from work and embarks on a cycling tour of the Southern Coast of England.

On his first day out, he crashes his cycle, does minor repairs, and proceeds on holiday. A short time later, when encountering a young lady cyclist in gray, he crashes again while attempting to appear an experienced operator. After some pleasant conversation, the girl is gone, and Hoopdriver, unable to find her, hopes that their paths will cross again.

Later, Hoopdriver sees the lady in gray weeping at the side of the road with a young man in brown. Wells tells us that the two are masquerading as the Beaumonts—as brother and sister. Fearing for the lady's happiness, Hoopdriver follows the pair from place to place. In fact, Hoopdriver is a playwright of sorts, composing plays in his imagination as he serves as both actor and audience—a precursor to Thurber's Walter Mitty. In this case, Hoopdriver sees himself as a noble knight-errant out to save the lady in gray. Such romance surely beats the life of a draper's assistant!

Hoopdriver soon discovers the real name of the pair: Jessie Milton and Mr. Bechamel. Since the two are obviously trying to remain in disguise, and since Hoopdriver keeps showing up everywhere they go, Bechamel assumes that Hoopdriver is a detective and attempts to find out who hired him. Hoopdriver quickly understands that Bechamel considers him a detective and plays along, discovering in the process that Bechamel is a married art critic who has promised to help Miss Milton flee from her novelist step-mother. On the way, however, he has tried to seduce her, which is why Miss Milton was crying at roadside.

Miss Milton and Bechamel continue their trek, and, consciously playing Sherlock Holmes, Hoopdriver follows. At the next stop, Bechamel leaves Jessie in their room, at which point Hoopdriver enters and offers his services as a gentleman. Miss Milton quickly accepts Hoopdriver's offer and suggests that they escape by bicycle. Hoopdriver and Jessie then escape on the stolen bicycles.

Meantime, Mrs. Milton has dispatched her friends Widgery, Phipps, and Dangle (who all distrust each other) to rescue Jessie from Mr. Bechamel, and all four commence in search of the fugitives.

As they flee, Miss Milton tells Hoopdriver that she wants to live her own life, be a journalist, and write books. She wants to make a difference in the world, and she wants to be unconventional. In fact, her dreams are the same as Hoopdriver's. Hoopdriver knows not where all this is leading, but his daydreams and sense of knight-errantry carry him on. So absorbed is the girl in her own difficulties that she cannot remember the assumed name Hoopdriver has given her so that they might avoid detection. Since he cannot remember either, they change their names constantly from place to place. Hoopdriver, however, is beginning to worry about his money supply. The amount he took with

him for his holiday is quickly dwindling with the addition of Miss Milton.

During a respite, Miss Milton inquires about Hoopdriver's past, and he portrays himself as originally from South Africa where he shot a lion at the age of nine. Of course, Miss Milton is impressed.

Finally, Hoopdriver invites a fist fight at a pub in defense of Miss Milton's honor and luckily emerges unscathed. Mrs. Milton's friends show up and take Jessie into their custody. Hoopdriver agrees not to see Miss Milton again, but she agrees to loan him books so that he might rise above his current social status. Does he deserve to rise above his social status? Will he? Wells leaves the questions unanswered, but the reader concludes that he probably won't.

In his autobiography, Wells notes that *The Wheels of Chance* is a light piece written in haste, and that Mr. Hoopdriver is a "caricature-individuality" rather than a character as might be constructed by Henry James. Wells suggests that though he is proud of his caricature-individualities (which include Mr. Polly in *The History of Mr. Polly*, and his aunt and uncle in *Tono Bungay*), he predicts that most such characters will not endure "into new social phases." As society evolves, they will become incomprehensible to most readers.

Along the same lines, Wells describes Hoopdriver as a character embodying his idea of the "floating *persona*, a dramatized self [which] recurs at various levels of complexity and self-deception." Indeed, Hoopdriver is a Don Quixote, a Walter Mitty—a silly, comic character who earns a degree of respect from the reader through his very struggle to be heroic in the face of his own limitations.

THE FILMS

The Wheels of Chance (1922) Stoll: Great Britain

This scene from the lost film *The Wheels of Chance* (1922) features George K. Arthur as Mr. Hoopdriver (second from right) surrounded by his pursuers.

CREDITS: Directed by Harold Shaw.

CAST: George K. Arthur (Hoopdriver); Gordon Parker, Bertie Wright, Mabel Archdale, Judd Green, Wally Bosco.

Film Synopsis and Adaptation

This silent film is lost. One existing still photo appears to be a scene in which Mrs. Milton and her friends confront Hoopdriver and Jessie. This suggests at least some adherence to the Wells novel. I suspect that the film largely followed the novel, though it may have supplied a happier ending.

Strengths, Weaknesses, and Rating

This silent film is lost; therefore I cannot comment.

5

The Invisible Man (1897)

THE NOVEL

Having received favorable reviews for *The Wheels of Chance*, Wells published *The Invisible Man* in 1897 and told an inverviewer that the early draft contained about 100,000 words before being edited down to only 55,000. He was already at work on, or possibly even had finished *The War of the Worlds*, which would be his next publication, but he chose to take *The Invisible Man* to print first. Of course, Wells did not invent the theme of invisibility. It appeared as early as Plato and continued to appear in philosophy, fantasy, and folklore until Wells provided it a scientific basis.

Novel Scenario and Commentary

A stranger comes to Iping Village in England in early February. Slogging through biting rain and driving snow, he carries a small black portmanteau in his thickly gloved hand. He is wrapped from head to foot, and the brim of his felt hat hides his face. Seeking shelter at the Coach and Horses Inn, he startles the assembled villagers with his appearance. He rents a room in the inn and soon begins a series of mysterious scientific experiments. In an effort to discover what her guest is up to, Mrs. Hall, the proprietress of the inn, becomes a nuisance to the reclusive stranger. As others begin to inquire about the stranger's activities, he becomes increasingly agitated and impatient. Finally, after the vicarage is robbed, Mrs. Hall and others confront him about his mysterious comings and goings.

Fed up with their curiosity and meddling, the stranger removes his clothing and wrappings to reveal himself invisible. No one, including the constable, is capable of preventing the invisible man's escape.

That same day, a mile and a half out of Iping, the invisible man enlists the aid of a frightend tramp, Mr. Marvel, who agrees to bring him food, drink, clothing and the scientific notebooks abandoned in Iping. If Marvel betrays him, the invisible man promises swift punishment. The tramp is for awhile cooperative but, neverthelss, soon betrays the invisible man and flees to the village of Port Burdock for help. With the invisible man in pursuit, Marvel rushes into an inn but is soon accosted by invisible hands. A skermish erupts as those in the inn try to help

Marvel. One man fires a pistol and apparently wounds the invisible attacker, who flees the inn.

In a house near the inn, Dr. Kemp hears the shots and soon discovers his door handle stained with blood. In an effort to enlist Kemp's aid, the invisible man identifies himself as Griffin, a young scientist who was hounded out of medical school for his unusual experiments involving animals. He later took up physics and the study of light and optical density. After intense research, Griffin discovered the secret of invisibility. Unfortunately, he now finds himself a hunted man, susceptible to the cold, and unable to continue experiments designed to restore his visibility. Griffin then requests that Kemp be his confederate, his partner. He needs a place where he can eat and sleep unmolested, a place from which he can launch a Reign of Terror. He will give orders, and those who resist will die. By killing, he will be able to terrify and dominate the ignorant masses. He will be Invisible Man #1, and others will follow.

Kemp soon betrays Griffin to the police, and again the invisible man escapes. Soon Kemp receives a note threatening his life, and the police lay a trap for the invisible man. Using an axe, the invisible man breaks into Kemp's home and battles the police in an attempt to get at Kemp. Kemp flees on foot and Griffin follows. A crowd of villagers gather as Kemp thrashes about on the ground as though being strangled by unseen hands. The crowd soon attacks and kills the invisible assailant. Slowly the bruised and battered outline of a body appears on the ground. Someone brings a sheet and covers Griffin. Then the villagers carry him into a house.

Critics disagree in their interpretations of *The Invisible Man*. Some see Griffin as another mad scientist, just as they saw Dr. Moreau. Both are victims of hubris, destroyed by their own tragic flaw.

In the epilogue (which did not appear in the first edition), Wells writes, "So ends the story of the strange and evil experiment of the Invisible Man." This seems conclusive, but it isn't. Wells is ambivalent about Griffin. Like Moreau, Griffin is a god-man, and Wells is sympathetic to both. Like Prendick, Kemp represents the timid herd mentality. A lowly tramp is understandably willing to betray Griffin, but Griffin is genuinely surprised, disappointed, and outraged when betrayed by a fellow scientist. But Wells is suggesting that he should not have been. The Moreaus and Griffins of the future must not overestimate the herd's understanding, even that of herd scientists. The status quo represents a powerful force resistant to progress and change, which is why Wells represents the villagers in *The Invisible Man* much as he did those in *The Wonderful Visit*: he is fond of their humorous simplicity on one level, but he loathes their stubborn ignorance and lack of vision on another.

In *The Invisible Man*, Wells creates a brilliant, daring protagonist who is as vulnerable in many ways as the common man he despises. In this, Griffin earns our sympathy. Like Moreau, however, Griffin realizes that progress can occur only at the price of suffering—hence, Moreau's experiments and Griffin's proposed Reign of Terror.

Finally, *The Invisible Man* is another Wellsian critique of society in the tradition of Saint-Simon, a "scientific romance" designed to welcome an age of world socialism. A reign of terror might be necessary to ensure human progress and save mankind from democracy. Though Wells professed a disbelief in the possibility of invisibility, the point is that science must be the foundation on which the future is constructed by Carlyle's great men and captains of industry.

The book was well-received critically,

and in his autobiography, Wells comments positively on the 1933 film. Referring to a drawing he reproduces in the autobiography, he writes that "The date of this particular picshua, as the small figure in the corner indicates, was the day of the publication of the *Invisible Man*, a tale, that thanks largely to the excellent film recently produced by James Whale, is still read as much as ever it was."

THE FILMS

The Invisible Fluid (1908)   American Mutoscope and Biograph Company, U.S.A. / Running Time: 12 minutes

CREDITS: Directed by Wallace McCutcheon; inspired by *The Invisible Man* by H.G. Wells; cinematography by G.W. ("Billy") Bitzer.

Film Synopsis

A scientist creates a mysterious fluid which will render objects invisible for ten minutes. He loads the fluid into an atomizer and mails it to his businessman brother whom he hopes will be able to market it. The skeptical brother turns the atomizer upon himself and promptly disappears. The startled delivery boy who delivered the package reads the accompanying letter and envisions the fun he can have with such an invention. First he squirts a girl walking her dog, leaving only the dog chain trailing through the air. Next, the boy causes a fruitcart to vanish along with its angry Italian owner. Two delivery men are then astounded when the heavy trunk they are lifting suddenly disappears. Soon after, a groom disappears while leaving the church with his bride.

By this time, those made invisible have reappeared and chase the boy. When they catch him, he squirts them again and they become invisible. A policeman sneaks up from behind and captures the boy. When in court, the boy squirts himself with the atomizer while demonstrating to the judge how he did what he did. Invisible, he escapes from the courtroom.

Adaptation

Though inspired by Wells' *The Invisible Man*, the film plot shares little with its source. Of course, the film adapts the idea of scientifically induced invisibility and shows the mischevous boy creating humorous havoc somewhat as Griffin does with the villagers. The film is played for humor, however, and addresses none of the philosophical considerations suggested by the novel.

Production and Marketing

The Invisible Fluid, the first American film to credit H.G. Wells, was directed by American Mutoscope and Biograph's prolific helmsman, Wallace McCutcheon. Among McCutcheon's science fiction film credits are *The X-Ray Mirror* (1899), *Dr. Skinum* (1907), *Love Microbe* (1907), and *Energizer* (1908).

Behind the camera was Billy Bitzer (1874–1944), who would later work on the films of D.W. Griffith. Credited with several major developments in cinematography, his work includes *The Avenging Conscience* (1914), *Birth of a Nation* (1915), *Intolerance* (1916), *Hearts of the World* (1918), *Broken Blossoms* (1919), *Way Down East* (1921), and *America* (1924). One of the magic attractions of cinema has always been special effects, and the concept of invisibility gave Billy Bitzer a chance to dazzle early audiences. In this case, he used simple stop-motion to achieve the illusion of disappearance.

Strengths, Weaknesses, and Rating

As one would expect, *The Invisible Fluid* is obviously a primitive special effects film. The stop-motion process would amuse audiences of its day and might even provide a chuckle or two now. Still, even in 1908, the novelty of camera tricks was beginning to wear off, and audiences were looking for better stories and characters. Our primary interest today in such films is to watch pioneers at work. As this film has not been seen, neither its strengths and weaknesses nor rating can be determined.

L'Homme Invisible (1909) aka *An Invisible Thief* Pathé, France / Running Time: 5 minutes

CREDITS: Directed by Ferdinand Zecca [some sources suggest Albert Capellani or Louis Gasnier].

Film Scenario

A young man pores over H.G. Wells' *The Invisible Man*, hoping to reproduce Griffin's experiment. After obtaining the drug monocaine, he mixes up a potion and drinks. His body then fades, leaving his clothes visible. He takes off his clothes and robs a nearby house. He returns home with his ill-gotten gain, puts his clothes on, and dons a mask. Going again into the street, he robs a man and a woman, takes off his clothes and mask, and alludes the police, who flee in terror when attacked by an invisible presence.

Adaptation

Obviously, a five minute film cannot do justice to a novel. The main elements adapted from the book are the concept of invisibility itself and the invisible man's criminal and playful pranks, especially his rousing tussels with the police.

Production and Marketing

Though Pathé in 1909 was one of the world's leading film studios, no one knows much about the production of *L'Homme Invisible*. Probable director Ferdinand Zecca (1864–1947) came to the H.G. Wells novel having made such films as *The Prodigy* (1901), *Catastrophe in Martinique* (1904), *Vendetta* (1905), *Whence Does He Come?* (1906), *Mutiny in Odessa* (1907), and *The Dreyfus Affair* (1908). On the other hand, some sources suggest that either Albert Capellani (1870–1931) or Louis Gasnier (1882–1963) may have directed. Capellani specialized in silent fantasy films and travelled to America in 1915 to direct such films as *Camille* (1915), *Daybreak* (1917), and *The Young Diana* (1922). Gasnier also migrated to America and directed such films as *Darkened Rooms* (1929), *The Last Outpost* (1935), and *Murder on the Yukon* (1942).

It is not known if Pathé paid Wells for use of his book, but since the book itself appears in the film, it probably did. Wells may otherwise have launched a winning lawsuit.

Translations of Wells' books were popular in France, probably helping account for Pathé's profit on the film of eight and a half million francs. In 1914, Wells would sign a contract with Pathé for the filming of his books, only to have the project thwarted by World War I.

All that remains from the film today is a handfull of fuzzy stills.

Strengths, Weaknesses, and Rating

Neither a critique nor a verdict can be provided. According to Phil Hardy's *Overlook Film Encyclopedia: Science Fiction*, however, the special effects are essentially those used by John P. Fulton in the 1933 *Invisible Man*. If so, this 1909 version was a pioneer effort indeed.

The Invisible Thief (1910)   Gaumont, France / Running Time: 5 minutes
CREDITS NOT AVAILABLE

Film Synopsis

A man steals a bicycle and pedals away from two policemen who observe the crime. When they catch him, the man unaccountably vanishes, after which the bicycle pedals away seemingly on its own. As the police watch, the thief reappears in control of the cycle. The police commandeer a passing car and pursue the thief. When they catch the thief for the second time, he again makes himself invisible. After the policemen leave their car and search for the invisible man, he sneaks into the car and drives away, leaving the frustrated police to figure out what happened.

Adaptation

As was the case with Pathé's L'Homme Invisible of the previous year, invisibility and the invisible man's pranks with the police are the main concepts in common with Wells' novel. Unlike in Pathé's film, Wells' novel does not appear here as an explanation for invisibility.

Production and Marketing

Since continental film companies did not have the protection of a copyright office, outright plagiarism was common in the cinema's early years. Though critics sometimes complained, years would pass before film companies were safe from those who would "cover" their productions. This is exactly what Pathé's strongest competitor Gaumont appears to have done. And that is about all that anyone knows about the production of The Invisible Thief.

Since credits do not exist, labeling this an H.G. Wells film is somewhat problematic. It is included here because it is a pirated version of a film based on Wells' novel. Whether it credited Wells or not, no one knows.

Strengths, Weaknesses, and Rating

Unable to provide these details.

The Invisible Cyclist (1912)   Pathé, France / Running Time: 5 minutes
CREDITS NOT AVAILABLE

Film Synopsis

A professional thief discovers the secret of invisibility. When caught in the act by police, he vanishes. He steals a bicycle, the police give chase, and he becomes invisible as the bicycle races down the road seemingly on its own. When the police continue their pursuit, the invisible thief abandons the bicycle for an automobile. As he drives away, he becomes visible and drives wildly through houses and over rooftops before landing in the sea. Still fully visible, he is captured by the police.

Adaptation

As one might expect, this Pathé film, which pirates Gaumont's pirated version of Pathé's L'Homme Invisible, adapts the invisible man's avoidance of the police from Wells' novel.

Production and Marketing

After Gaumont adapted Pathé's adaptation of Wells' novel, Pathé apparently decided to pirate Gaumont's film and emphasize the bicycle and car chases. Confusing though this is, it was apparently common for the times since the continent lacked copyright laws. Nothing else is known about the production of *The Invisible Cyclist*, though surely Mr. Hoopdriver of Wells' *The Wheels of Chance* would have appreciated being invisible as he fled on bicycle from his pursuers.

Films involving invisibility were fairly common in the silent cinema, undoubtedly because it allowed for thrilling "trick photography." Other films adapting the invisibility theme were *Invisibility* (1909) and *Her Invisible Husband* (1916).

Strengths, Weaknesses, and Rating

Since I have not seen this film, I can offer neither a critique nor a rating.

The Invisible Man (1933)   Universal, U.S.A. / Release Date: November 13, 1933 / Running time: 70 minutes

CREDITS: Produced by Carl Laemmle, Jr.; Directed by James Whale; Screenplay by R. C. Sheriff, based on *The Invisible Man* by H.G. Wells; Cinematography by Arthur Edeson; Art Direction by Charles D. Hall; Edited by Ted Kent; Special effects photography by John P. Fulton; Retake photography and miniatures by John J. Mescall; Music by W. Franke Harling; Makeup by Jack Pierce.

CAST: Claude Rains (Dr. Jack Griffin), Gloria Stuart (Flora Cranley), William Harrigan (Dr. Kemp), Henry Travers (Dr. Cranley), Una O'Connor (Jenny Hall), Holmes Herbert (Chief of Police), E.E. Clive (Police Constable Jaffers), Dudley Diggs (Chief of Detectives), Harry Stubbs (Police Inspector Bird), Donald Stuart (Inspector Lane), Merle Tottenham (Milly), Walter Brennan (Bicycle Owner), Dwight Frey (Reporter), Jameson Thomas, Craufurd Kent (Doctors), John Peter Richmond [John Carradine] (Informer), John Merivale (Newsboy), Violet Kemble Cooper (Woman), Robert Brower (Farmer), Bob Reeves, Jack Richardson, Robert Adair (Officials), Monte Montague (Policeman), Ted Billings and D'Arcy Corrigan (Villagers).

Film Synopsis

A stranger whose face is swathed with bandages enters the English country village of Iping during a snow storm and puts up at the village inn. Mr. and Mrs. Hall, the innkeepers, cannot respect the stranger's request for peace and, in a fit of rage, the stranger throws Mr. Hall down the stairs of the inn. When the police arrive and a group from the inn confront the stranger, he takes off his bandages and clothes, revealing emptiness. He is an invisible man. While escaping, the invisible man seriously injures several villagers and creates general chaos.

The events in Iping tip off elderly chemist Dr. Crowley that the Invisible Man may be his former associate, Jack Griffin, who is in love with his daughter Flora. Also contending for Flora's affections is Dr. Kemp, another of Crowley's medical associates. Griffin had been conducting experiments with a drug called Monocane which has been known to bleach animals and finally drive them insane.

Dr. Kemp is in his sitting room listening to radio reports of the invisible man when he feels a thump on his shoulder. Turning, Kemp sees nothing. The voice of Griffin tells Kemp about discovering the secret of invisibility and retiring to Iping in order to reverse the process. When he was interrupted, he decided to teach the people a lesson. He now wants Kemp to aid him in carrying out a Reign of Terror, an invisible campaign of sabotage and murder. He also warns Kemp that death awaits if he double crosses him. Griffin forces Kemp to drive him back to Iping on a mission to recover his abandoned records at the inn. When he meets resistance, Griffin kills the police inspector.

After returning to Kemp's house, Griffin retires to bed, and Kemp phones Dr. Crowley and Flora to tell them of Griffin's return. Then Kemp calls the

"HOW BEAUTIFUL YOU ARE!
I HAD FORGOTTEN UNTIL NOW!"

CARL LAEMMLE
presents
H. G. WELLS'
FANTASTIC SENSATION

"THE INVISIBLE MAN"
A UNIVERSAL PICTURE

Gloria Stuart cowers from Claude Rains in this original lobby card scene from *The Invisible Man* (1933).

police. Dr. Crowley and Flora arrive at Kemp's house, and Flora tries to convince Griffin to give himself up. Griffin refuses, boasting of the fear he can cause and the power he can command. At that point, the police arrive and Griffin realizes that Kemp has betrayed him. Before fleeing the house, Griffin promises to kill Kemp at ten o'clock the following night.

Griffin then embarks on a campaign of terror, wrecking a train, robbing a bank, and scattering the money in the streets. He also commits murder. The police try to use Kemp as bait to capture Griffin, but the plan fails when Griffin invisibly follows when Kemp drives alone into the mountains. Griffin ties the terrified Kemp in the car and sends him over a cliff to his death—at precisely the hour of ten.

Exhausted from his activities, Griffin is forced by the police and townspeople out of a barn where he sought refuge from falling snow. Able to see his footprints in the snow, someone in the crowd fires a pistol twice and an invisible body crumbles to to the ground, forming an outline in the snow.

In the hospital, the dying Griffin calls for Flora. His last words to her are: "I meddled in things that man must leave alone." As he expires, Griffin gradually becomes visible. The invisible man's Reign of Terror is over.

Adaptation

R.C. Sheriff's screenplay faithfully adapts most of the important elements of

H.G. Wells' novel. The introduction of Monocane's insanity-inducing qualities is the screenplay's most striking deviation from Wells. In the novel, Griffin is decidedly not a madman. Like Moreau, he is a superior man opposed by dull-witted commoners. Even though the dull-witted commoners in the novel and film are British, that theme would not have played well to American audiences in the thirties. Another important deviation is that Sheriff's Dr. Kemp commands greater respect from movie audiences than his counterpart does in Wells' novel. Wells' Dr. Kemp, though a physician, is a Judas, a defender of the *status quo* who cannot appreciate Griffin's inspired vision. Sheriff's Kemp is a typical thirties leading man type.

Dr. Crowley and Flora are Sheriff's inventions. After all, there must be a love interest, but the other characters in the film are all Wellsian. Missing from the screenplay is the tramp whom Griffin engages as his first accomplice, but the film does not suffer from the omission. To note a final deviation, Dr. Kemp survives in Wells' novel while he does not in the film.

Despite these deviations, Wells' themes of comical, stupid villagers reminiscent of those in *The Wonderful Visit,* invisibility, laboratory ethics, and urban terrorism translate well from the page to the screen.

Production and Marketing

Fearing that the novel would be impossible to photograph, several studios passed on the chance to produce H.G. Wells' *The Invisible Man.* Universal, who had profited from filming such horror/science fiction films as *Dracula, Frankenstein,* and *The Old Dark House,* and *The Murders in the Rue Morgue* was more optimistic.

At first, Universal had difficulty settling on an acceptable adaptation of Wells' *The Invisible Man.* First announced for

production in 1931, the film was to be directed by Robert Florey and to star Boris Karloff (*Frankenstein,* 1931). It never happened. Universal paid Wells $25,000 for the film rights and acquired rights to Philip Wylie's *The Murderer Invisible,* planning to combine the two novels into one scenario. Between 1931 and 1933, Garrett Fort, John Balderston, Gouverneur Morris, and John Weld took stabs at writing screenplays, but it was R.C. Sheriff (1896–1975), author of James Whale's *Journey's End* (1930), who wrote the final version and received screen credit. In his autobiography *No Leading Lady,* Sheriff wrote that he faced an uncomfortable challenge as screenwriter because if he stuck too closely to Wells' novel, the studio would criticize him for lack of imagination. Universal had certainly filmed loose adaptations of Bram Stoker's *Dracula,* Mary Shelley's *Frankenstein,* and Edgar Allan Poe's "Murders in the Rue Morgue" and they would later film unrecognizable adaptations of Poe's "The Black Cat" and "The Raven." Interestingly, an unrecognizable adaptation of *The Invisible Man* almost occurred as one writer set the scene in Tsarist Russia and another made the invisible man a Martian intent on conquering the earth. In 1932, director James Whale (1896–1957) became interested in the project and even contributed his own story treatment which depicted the invisible man as having been facially mutilated and obsessed with hiding his horrible face from the sight of the world. Like most "mad doctors," he goes insane and longs to kill people who have caused him no harm. Though Whale went on to another project and discarded ideas of filming his own screenplay, he returned in time to direct *The Invisible Man.*

Sheriff ultimately decided to buy a copy of Wells' novel and stay as close as possible to the text. Perhaps this was because, as John Weld has claimed, H.G.

Wells recommended Sheriff as screen-writer after first approving Weld's adaption. So should John Weld be credited along with Sheriff for the screenplay? It depends on whom one believes. Regardless, the result is one of the most faithful genre adaptations Universal ever produced.

When it came time to film, Boris Karloff had already left Universal over a contract dispute. Without an invisible man, Whale vetoed Colin Clive for the role and chose British stage actor Claude Rains (1889–1967). Though unimpressed with Rains' physical features, Whale wanted the actor's voice. After all, Rains would be invisible throughout most of the film. Little seen in his first screen role, Rains would go on to win four Academy Award nominations during a long, successful career.

Though Chester Morris was offered the part of Dr. Kemp, he turned it down upon discovering that Claude Rains would be given top billing. Gloria Stuart (1909–) landed the role of Flora Cranley on the strength of her performance in James Whale's *The Old Dark House* (1932). Sixty-six years after *The Invisible Man* she would win an Academy Award for Best Supporting Actress in *Titanic* (1998). Other notables appearing in bit parts are future three-time Academy Award winner Walter Brennan (1894–1974), John Peter Richmond [John Carradine] (1906–1988), and Dwight Frye (1899–1943).

John P. Fulton solved the problem feared by other studios who passed on *The Invisible Man*. To depict Rains' progressive stages of undress, Fulton began with a hollow dummy head. Rains' hands then appeared from below and removed the false nose and the top of the bandages. Fulton accomplished the rest of the disrobing with a travelling matte. Relying on an old novelty act known as the "the black art," he dressed Rains completely in black from head to foot, dressed him in the clothes of the invisible man, and placed him in front of an equally black background. When photographing Rains, Fulton recorded only the clothes on film, leaving the rest of the frame unexposed. When Rains unwrapped the bandages, his black-hooded head remained unexposed as well. Fulton then produced a traveling matte by striking a series of high-contrast prints from the special effects footage. He then merged the special Rains footage into the scene of the invisible man's room.

Crediting director Whale, photographer Charles Edeson, and makeup man Jack Pierce, the film's lavish pressbook explained that after initially considering and discarding such outmoded effects as wires, the creative team experimented and discovered the possibility of using small mirrors such as magicians employed in creating optical illusions. Actually, this approach appears to have been used very little in the film, if at all. Supposedly James Whale, with a twinkle in his eye, assured everyone that "The Invisible Man is NOT wrapped in cellophane."

A pressbook publicity release pointed out that Rains was made up in the same room where Jack Pierce created the Frankenstein Monster, the Mummy, etc.. Then we get an alleged interview with Claude Rains, who explains how "marvellous" he finds the idea of invisibility:

> For instance, just imagine how consoling it would be to realize that no matter how crooked your nose, how bowed your legs or how cowlicked your hair, no one could see it. Inferiority complexes, inhibitions, Freudian complexes of all sorts would immediately vanish, and the world be just about like it was before Pandora tipped over the fatal box. Creditors, could they find you? No. Salesmen, peddlers, unwelcome admirers, nuisanes of all sorts—completely baffled. Think of the peace.

Continuing to muse on the advantages of invisibility, Rains surmises that President Truman and a number of Hollywood actors would occassionally enjoy the gift of invisibility. As Rains rises to shoot a key scene, the interviewer says, "Well, I'll be seeing you," to which Rains replies, "Oh, no you won't." Though probably not a *bona fide* interview, it is nevertheless good showmanship.

The Invisible Man is the best H.G. Wells film adaptation. It received enthusiastic reviews in 1933 and is rightfully regarded as a classic today. In fact, in Bryan Senn's *Golden Horrors*, a group of thirty well-known writers, editors, and filmmakers in the horror genre ranked *The Invisible Man* the fifth greatest horror film of the thirties, a decade blooming with horror classics. It was Gene Shalit's Critic's Choice Video. On the video box Shalit writes: "Rains is unforgettable as he grasps his character, which is more than the local constables can do when they try to catch him. This spectral spectacle, based on H.G. Wells' famous novel, is a motion picture classic—gripping and haunting."

Strengths

Even as a new millenium begins, John Fulton's 1933 special effects still impress. The initial unmasking scene must have left audiences gasping as Griffin disrobes, revealing that he is "all eaten away." Also unforgettable is the scene in which a stolen pair of pants goes skipping down the road in pursuit of a screaming woman as a disembodied voice sings "Here We Go Gathering Nuts in May."

James Whale's direction is nearly flawless as he sets the camera for maximum variation and effect, even suggesting the community's growing panic with tracking and dissolves, and skewed angles.

R.C. Sheriff's screenplay deftly unfolds Griffin's persona from harassed stranger, to practical joker, to callous murderer. Though Wells suggests that Griffin's excesses are those of a politically calculating great mind, Sheriff's insertion of Monocane as an insanity producing drug allows for greater audience identification with the invisible man. Who wouldn't cheer him on as he loses patience with the insufferably irritating Jenny Hall and her milktoast husband? Who wouldn't smile approvingly when he smashes a bottle of chemicals against the picture of Mrs. Hall that "graces" his rented room while the pompous constable and confused inndwellers press for his arrest?

The audience probably identifies with Griffin until it becomes clear that he is going mad. In a conversation with Kemp, Griffin announces his plans: "We'll start with a Reign of Terror. A few murders here and there. Murders of big men, murders of little men. Just to make sure we make no distinction. We might even wreck a train or two...." In the film's best scenes, Griffin's words again convey the onset of madness. At first he is very human, tender and solicitous toward his worried Flora. Then he begins to rant like a man drunk for power: "Don't you see what it means? Power, power to rule, to make the world grovel at my feet!... Power I said! Power to walk into the gold vaults of the nation, into the secrets of kings, into the holy of holies, power to make multitudes run squealing in terror at the touch of my invisible finger!" Then, with some of the most chilling lines ever uttered in a horror film, he ends by staring out the window and defiantly declaring that "Even the Moon's frightened of me—frightened to death!"

The invisible man is initially a figure of pity and humor, but soon we fear him and what he is becoming. Later, when he knocks over a baby carriage, brutally murders a policeman, and precipitates a train wreck, we know that the great scientist

Claude Rains searches for a cure for invisibiliy in this re-release lobby card scene from *The Invisible Man* (1933).

must be stopped in any way possible. Thus Griffin meets death, as do most of the screen's "mad scientists."

As good as the screenplay is, it benefited immensely from a fine cast. Claude Rains is a screen presence exploiting both voice and physical movement, especially in the egomaniacal scenes with Gloria Stuart and William Harrigan. Stuart and Harrigan are adequate, and the supporting cast of villagers is excellent, especially Una O'Connor, who irritates the audience in *The Bride of Frankenstein* (1935) but irritates only Rains in *The Invisible Man*.

Weaknesses

As Bryan Senn notes in his book *Golden Horrors*, Whale slips up when Kemp follows Flora from the adjoining lab into the house and the camera allows us to see both rooms at the same time. The only other weakness in the film is one of history's most well-known bloopers. As the Invisible Man flees from the barn near the film's conclusion, the camera tracks his prints in the snow. But they aren't footprints; they are *shoe prints*—and the invisible man was not wearing shoes.

Wells, while generally pleased with the film, criticized the insertion of Monocane and its transformation of the invisible man into the invisible lunatic. Indeed, the film would have been more philosophically provocative had Sheriff stuck more closely to Wells' conception of Griffin as a great mind hounded by little people such as Kemp and the country bumpkins.

How would a great man deal with Nietzsche's herd? How should he? Under the circumstances we are invited to chalk up Griffin's actions to madness beyond his control. Sheriff's concept is certainly not bad; it just could have been better had he challenged his audience rather than pandered to it. Griffin's final words, "I meddled in things that man must leave alone," is most un-Wellsian and equates goodness with lack of imagination and mediocrity.

Rating: 4

The Invisible Man Returns (1940)

Universal, U.S.A. / Running Time: 81 minutes. / Release Date: January 12, 1940

CREDITS: Directed by Joe May; Associate Producer—Ken Goldsmith; Screenplay by Lester K. Cole and Kurt [Curt] Siodmak. Original story by Joe May, Kurt [Curt] Siodmak, and Cedric Belfrage (uncredited); Suggested by the novel *The Invisible Man* by H.G. Wells; Cinematography by Milton Krasner; Art direction by Jack Otterson; Associate Art Director—Martin Obzina; Special effects by John P. Fulton; Music by Hans Salter and Frank Skinner; Music directed by Charles Previn; Sound supervised by Bernard B. Brown; Set decoration by Russell A. Gausman; Gowns by Vera West; Technician—William Hedgcock.

CAST: Sir Cedric Hardwicke (Richard Cobb), Vincent Price (Sir Geoffrey Radcliffe), Nan Grey (Helen Manson), John Sutton (Dr. Frank Griffin), Cecil Kellaway (Inspector Sampson), Alan Napier (Willie Spears), Forester Harvey (Ben Jenkins), Harry Stubbs (Constable Tukesberry), Frances Robinson (Nurse), Ivan Simpson (Cotton); Edward Fielding (Prison Governor), Leland [Leyland] Hodgson (Chauffeur), Mary Gordon (Cook), Billy Bevan (a Warden), Dave Thursby (Bob); Matthew Boulton (Policeman), Bruce Lester (Chaplain), Ernie Adams (Man), Paul England (Detective), Ellis Irving, Dennis Tankard, George Lloyd, George Kirby, Harry Cording, George Hyde, Edmund MacDonald (Miners), Louise Brien (Griffin's secretary), Frank Hagney (Bill), Frank O'Connor (Policeman at Colliery), Frank Hill (Policeman attending Cobb), Rex Evans (Officer Briggs), Cyril Thornton, Ed Brady (Policemen), Clara Blore (Woman), Hugh Huntley (Secretary), Colin Kenny (Plainclothesman), Mary Field (Neighbor).

Film Synopsis

Sir Geoffrey Radcliffe is wrongly accused of killing his brother, Sir Michael, and is sentenced to hang. Shortly before the hour of his execution, Radcliffe receives a visit from Dr. Frank Griffin and vanishes into thin air while under guard in his prison cell. Scotland Yard Inspector Sampson, realizing that Radcliffe's friend Griffin is the brother of the late Jack Griffin (The Invisible Man), speculates that the escaped prisoner was administered an invisibility serum.

Radcliffe flees to the home of his fiancée, Helen Manson, and launches a search for the real murderer in order to clear his name. Unfortunately, Radcliffe knows that time is short because the invisibility serum threatens to alter his mind as it did that of Jack Griffin. In fact, Radcliffe starts speaking of ruling the world while he, Dr. Griffin, and Helen have dinner.

When Richard Cobb appoints disreputable night watchman Willie Spears to a ranking position in the family mining operation, Radcliffe becomes suspicious. Radcliffe forces Spears' car off the road and makes the frightened man name Richard Cobb, Radcliffe's cousin, as the murderer. Cobb has been buying the watchman's silence since. Radcliffe gags and binds Spears, places a noose around his neck, and stands him on a chair. He then sets out to find Cobb.

Though Cobb is under heavy police guard, the invisible Radcliffe abducts Cobb at gunpoint and takes him to the

A New Fantastic Sensation
Suggested by "The Invisible Man" by
H. G. WELLS
The **INVISIBLE MAN RETURNS**
A NEW UNIVERSAL PICTURE

Vincent Price pursues the villainous Cedric Hardwicke in this original lobby card scene from *The Invisible Man Returns* **(1940).**

house where Spears is being held captive. When Radcliffe and Cobb arrive, Spears frantically incriminates Cobb, who kicks the chair out from under his betrayer and turns off the lights. With the invisible man in hot pursuit, Cobb flees through the busy streets to the colliery. A battle ensues when the invisible Radcliffe pins Cobb in a moving coal wagon high above the agitated crowd. Someone fires a lucky shot, hitting Radcliffe seconds before the coal wagon dumps Cobb to his death. Seeing Helen, the mortally injured Cobb confesses that he killed Sir Michael.

Suffering from exposure and blood loss, Radcliffe dons the clothes of a scarecrow and makes his way into the village to Dr. Griffin's clinic. Griffin gives Radcliffe an emergency blood transfusion but be-

moans the fact that he cannot operate on an invisible man. Suddenly, Radcliffe materializes on the bed before a startled Griffin. Apparently, the transfusion accomplished what Griffin had hoped the serum would, and now he can begin the operation to save Radcliffe's life.

Adaptation

When James Whale directed *The Bride of Frankenstein* (1935) as a sequel to his *Frankenstein* (1931), screenwriter William Hurlbut returned to Mary Shelley's novel for inspiration. Screenwriters Cole and Siodmak appear to have consulted only Whale's *The Invisible Man* in preparation for its sequel. Again present is the madness-inducing invisibility drug

Duocane (called Monocane in *The Invisible Man*), the race to find an antidote, and the anxious girlfriend and scientist. Returning elements from the film and from Well's novel are the abduction of the invisible man's nemesis from under heavy police guard, the ineffectual constabulary, and the startled villagers. Adapting little from the original novel, this is clearly a film sequel owing little if anything to its literary inspiration.

Production and Marketing

Though *The Invisible Man* (1933) was a financial and critical success, and though the studio had a multipicture contract with H.G. Wells, the studio waited until October 1939 to begin work on a sequel. Rarely, if ever, has a studio waited so long to cash in on a good thing.

Rowland V. Lee, who had directed such fare as *The Mysterious Dr. Fu Manchu* (1929), *The Count of Monte Cristo* (1934), *The Son of Frankenstein* (1939), and *Tower of London* (1939), was scheduled to direct *The Invisible Man Returns*, but the job eventually went to German emigre Joe May (1880–1954). Adept at serials and thrillers, May also worked on the original story for the sequel with fellow German emigre Kurt Siodmak (1902–). Siodmak would go on to pen such memorable screenplays as *The Wolf Man* (1941), *Frankenstein Meets the Wolf Man* (1942), *Son of Dracula* (1943), *I Walked with a Zombie* (1943, with co-writer Ardel Wray) and *The Beast with Five Fingers* (1947). He directed *The Magnetic Monster* in 1951, and later wrote and directed such unfortunate potboilers as *Love Slaves of the Amazon* (1957) and *Ski Fever* (1966).

John P. Fulton again created the special effects, and German emigre Hans J. Salter (1896–1994), composed the music. Salter had a long, successful career as a Hollywood composer, among his best

known scores were *The Mummy's Tomb* (1942), *Frankenstein Meets the Wolf Man* (1942), *House of Frankenstein* (1944), and *The Mole People* (1956).

Universal pegged Vincent Price (1911– 1993) for the role of the Invisible Man. Though Price had appeared with Boris Karloff and Basil Rathbone in Universal's eerie costume drama *Tower of London* (1939), many consider *The Invisible Man Returns* his first real horror film. He would certainly star in many, many more, among his finest being *House of Wax* (1953), *The House on Haunted Hill* (1959), seven Edgar Allan Poe adaptations directed by Roger Corman (1960 to 1965), *Witchfinder General* (1968), *The Abominable Dr. Phibes* (1971), and *Theatre of Blood* (1973).

Commanding top billing was former British stage actor Sir Cedric Hardwicke (1893–1964). Hardwicke's Hollywood films ran the gamut from great to mediocre, his best being *King Solomon's Mines* (1937), *On Borrowed Time* (1939), *Stanley and Livingstone* (1939), *The Hunchback of Notre Dame* (1939), *Tom Brown's Schooldays* (1940, a personal favorite of mine), *Victory* (1940), *The Moon Is Down* (1943), *The Lodger* (1944), *I Remember Mana* (1948), *The Winslow Boy* (1948), and *Richard III* (1955).

Nan Grey (1918–1993) supplied the mandatory love interest. She had gained attention in the popular *Three Smart Girls* (1936) and *Three Smart Girls Grow Up* (1938). She appeared briefly but impressively as a victim of *Dracula's Daughter* (1939) and had co-starred with Karloff and Rathbone in *Tower of London* (1939).

Former British stage actor John Sutton (1908–1963) was cast as the second lead bent on helping the Invisible Man. Along with playing the occassional smooth villain, his career continued in that vein. Near the end of his life, he would reunite with Vincent Price in *The Bat* (1959).

British born Cecil Kellaway (1891–

John Sutton and Nan Grey listen as Vincent Price discusses his dream of world dominance in this re-release lobby card scene from *The Invisible Man Returns* (1940).

1973) based a career on playing the "charming rogue." Among his most memorable films are *Wuthering Heights* (1939), *I Married a Witch* (1942), *Frenchman's Creek* (1944), *Kitty* (1945), *The Luck of the Irish* (1948, for which he received an Academy Award nomination), *Harvey* (1950, my personal favorite), and *Hush, Hush, Sweet Charlotte* (1963).

British character actor Alan Napier (1903–1988) appeared as the self-serving sneak Willie Spears. He later appeared in the ghost classic *The Uninvited* (1944), *Julius Caesar* (1953), *Journey to the Center of the Earth* (1959), *Marnie* (1964, directed by Alfred Hitchcock), *Batman* (1966), and many others.

Universal Studios took *The Invisible*

Man Returns seriously. Budgeted at $253,730 and scheduled for a 27-day shoot, things went awry as director Joe May worked slowly and shot well after hours in an effort to keep pace. Perhaps part of the problem was that May barely spoke English. Vincent Price, who spoke German, asked May to direct him in German as opposed to English. Price believed that the rest of the cast probably didn't understand May a good part of the time. When *The Invisible Man Returns* wrapped on November 11, 1939, the production was $15,000 over budget. Yet, due to an impressive press campaign and a public that fondly remembered *The Invisible Man*, Universal made money on the film and planned yet another sequel. And there would be more Universal sequels suggested by H.G. Wells' novel, but only *The Invisible Man Returns* boasts any connection to the original story at all.

Strengths

Regardless of the problems encountered or caused by director Joe May, we must judge the film as May's product. From that perspective, he doesn't make any notable slips. Particularly impressive are the exciting final colliery scenes in which he shows why he was a successful serial director. John P. Fulton's special effects equal and sometimes exceed those of his first effort, such as Vincent Price's detailed materialization. Hans Salter's romantic musical score heightens emotion in the right places. In addition, the screenplay provides an interesting premise and plot for the showcase of invisibility. While an escaped prisoner's attempt to find the real killer is not a novel idea (it was still being exploited in 1993's highly acclaimed *The Fugitive*), when coupled with the concept of invisibility it takes on some novel twists.

Milton Krasner's cinematography is impressive. Especially nice is a scene designed to create an eerie mood in which Vincent Price walks ghost-like (with bandaged face and hat) through the foggy English countryside.

Price is good as Sir Geoffrey Radcliffe. Effectively using his velvety voice to convey emotions from madness to tenderness, he is a strong (though not superior) successor to Claude Rains. Nan Grey is appropriately vulnerable and noble as the female lead, and John Sutton performs doctorly as Frank Griffin. Particularly appealing is Cecil Kellaway as Inspector Sampson. Both effective as an inspector and comforting as a human being, he adds dimensions to the law enforcement element missing from *The Invisible Man*.

Alan Napier is surprisingly successful as the village representative of Wells' herd. Perhaps he doesn't deserve his final fate in the film, but he does represent the weakness of mediocre humanity trying to get by any way it can.

Weaknesses

The film's most serious weakness is its pace. Halfway through, proceedings drag as Cobb and Sampson pay successive visits to Dr. Griffin that fail to advance the plot.

The plot itself contains some minor weaknesses as well. For example, is Ratcliffe going mad or isn't he? In a dinnertable scene reminiscent of *The Invisible Man*, Radcliffe rants about achieving a clearer view of ant-like humanity and about taking over the world. In *The Invisible Man*, these scenes provide foundation for Jack Griffin's Reign of Terror. But in the sequel, Radcliffe seems to recover and show no more signs of encroaching madness. Obviously, as the protagonist of the film, he could not easily be portrayed as a mass murderer. That would have called for his scripted death. Instead, we are left to wonder if Radcliffe simply got tipsy at the dinner table, a conclusion not supported by either films' premise of Monocane (or Duocane) as a madness-inducing drug. After the dinner table scene, Radcliffe is quite lucid, justice-directed, and uninterested in world conquest—and this hurts the film. Why not be creative and test the implicit tensions rather than tease and then ignore them? Is it that the audience must be allowed to leave the theater unchallenged?

Now, loss of blood did not cause Radcliffe's invisibility, so why does a blood transfusion restore his visibility? There is no answer to this quandry, just careless scripting. Why not allow Griffin to successfully administer his antidote? Could it be that the presence of an available antidote would create problems in the event of a sequel? Maybe no one was thinking that far ahead. Nevertheless the blood transfusion miracle is entirely unbelievable.

Finally, though Nan Grey is a good heroine, she doesn't fit in with the rest of the British cast. Price isn't British either, but the texture of his voice allows him to pass. This may be a minor fault, but it is noticeable.

Whale's wild humor is missing from the sequel. There are some humorous lines, but in general, the sequel is comedically tame. Fulton's special effects were fresh and startling in 1933. By 1940, though still impressive, they were no longer novel. Faced with this problem, instead of increasing the excitement of the disrobing scenes, May's disrobing scenes are disappointingly matter-of-fact.

While Price does an admirable job as the Invisible Man, he fails to present the presence Claude Rains did in *The Invisible Man*. Though part of the problem can be attributed to script limitations, the fact remains that Rains is both sympathetic and frightening, while Price is merely sympathetic.

Finally, *The Invisible Man Returns* is a strong enough sequel to a great film. If we take *The Invisible Man Returns* on its own merits, it ranks with many of Universal's best films of the forties. When judged against *The Invisible Man*, however, it suffers by comparison.

Rating: 3

***The Invisible Woman* (1940)** Universal Pictures, U.S.A. / Running Time: 70 minutes / Release Date: December 27, 1940

CREDITS: Directed by A. Edward Sutherland; Associate producer—Burt Kelly; Screenplay by Robert Lees, Frederic I. Rinaldo, and Gertrude Purcell; Original story by Curt Siodmak, suggested by the character created by H.G. Wells; Cinematography by Elwood Bredell; Special photographic effects by Robert P. Fulton; Art direction by Jack Otterson; Associate art director—Richard H. Riedel; Edited by Frank Gross; Musical direction by Charles Previn; Sound supervised by Bernard B. Brown; Technician—Joe Lapis; Set decoration by Russell A. Gausman; Assistant director—Joseph McDonough; Gowns by Vera West.

CAST: Virginia Bruce (Kitty Carroll), John Barrymore (Professor Gibbs), John Howard (Dick Russell), Charlie Ruggles (George), Oscar Holmolka (Blackie Cole), Edward Brophy (Bill), Donald MacBride (Foghorn), Charles Lane (Growley), Thurston Hall (John Hudson), Margaret Hamilton (Mrs. Jackson), Mary Gordon (Mrs. Bates), Anne Nagel (Jean), Maria Montez (Marie), Shemp Howard (Hammerhead/Frankie), Kathryn Adams (Peggy), Kitty O'Neill (Mrs. Patton), Eddie Conrad (Hernandez), Kay Leslie (Model), Kay Linaker, Sarah Edwards (Fashion Show Buyers), Harry C. Bradley (Want Ad Man), Kernan Cripps (Postman).

Film Synopsis

Irresponsible playboy Dick Russell goes broke and must stop financing the experiments of Professor Gibbs, an absent-minded, eccentric scientist who has created a hypodermic solution and machine, which when combined, makes animals invisible. The Professor advertises for an experimental human subject and catches the eye of Kitty Carroll, a lovely young fashion model who wants to be invisible so as to torment her cruel boss, the aptly named Mr. Growley.

When the experiment proves successful, the Professor calls Dick with the news. Before the time Dick arrives, the invisible Kitty leaves the laboratory and frightens Mr. Growley into becoming as kind and gentle as a pussy cat. "Seeing" no invisible woman, Dick assumes that the

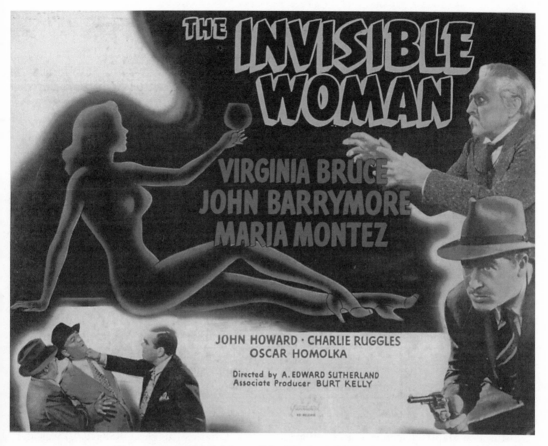

The re-release title lobby card for *The Invisible Woman* (1940)

Professor is just nutty and leaves for his mountain lodge.

Kitty returns, and the Professor takes her to the lodge, where Dick becomes convinced of the Professor's success. Playing tricks with her invisibility, Kitty meanwhile keeps Dick's butler, George, in a humorous uproar. In the midst of the hubub, Kitty and Dick break into continual arguments.

Later, Kitty takes off all her clothes in order to be completely invisible and drinks brandy to warm herself. The alcohol, however, prolongs her invisibility, and she fails to materialize at the proper time. Dick and the Professor immediately rush her back to Dick's estate, where they discover that the invisibility machine has been stolen. The culprit is gangster Blackie

Cole, who is hiding out in Mexico with his three incompetent henchmen. Cole wants to be invisible so as to return unseen to the United States.

Since the gangsters do not have the hypodermic solution, the machine has unforseen effects on the guinea pig henchman known as Foghorn, causing him to speak in a high female voice. Blackie sends the other two henchmen to kidnap the Professor, who meanwhile has discovered a drug to make Kitty visible. Meanwhile, Foghorn turns good guy and goes for help.

Dick arrives at Blackie's Mexican hideout to find the Professor tied up in a chair and Kitty held at gunpoint. Kitty drinks grain alcohol, turns invisible, and disposes of the gangsters. By this time, Kitty and Dick are in love. Later when they are married, their baby turns invisible upon contact with rubbing alcohol. "Hereditary," the Professor observes.

Adaptation

The credits explain that the film is suggested by the character created by H.G. Wells; it is not really an adaptation. Accordingly, except for the theme of invisibility, the film has no connection with Wells' novel.

Production and Marketing

Following the success of *The Invisible Man Returns*, Universal launched *The Invisible Woman*. Since the special effects were by then familiar to audiences, *The Invisible Woman* relies on the new romantic angles invited by an invisible female. Chosen to write the screenplay was always dependable Curt Siodmak. Since the studio was then turning out more light cinematic fare, it soon decided to make the film as a slapstick comedy and replaced Siodmak with veteran comedy writers Fred Rinaldo and Robert Lees. The studio also chose to avoid the costly budget of *The Invisible Man Returns* and proposed the more realistic budget of $300,000.

Considering *The Invisible Woman* an A production, Universal went all out in assembling a fine cast. Because she still owed the studio a film, Universal at first considered Margaret Sullavan for the lead role. Sullavan balked, squabbles began, and Universal hit Sullavan with a restraining order preventing her from working for another studio until she had fulfilled her obligations. All parties finally made peace and Universal cast Sullivan in *Back Street* (1941) instead.

The lead role then went to Virginia Bruce (1910–1982), a popular leading lady throughout the thirties whose contract had just run out at MGM. In the drunken twilight of a once glorious career, John Barrymore (1882–1942) accepted the role of batty Professor Gibbs. The matinee stage idol who had once brilliantly brought Shakespeare's characters to life and starred in such films as *Dr. Jekyll and Mr. Hyde* (1920), *Beau Brummel* (1924), *The Beloved Rogue* (1927), *Dinner at Eight* (1933), and many other classics, found himself starring in a film he must have considered drivel. Apparently making matters worse was Barrymore's reported inability to remember his lines. According to John Howard, the actor solved the problem by cutting up the script and placing the parts around the set—on vases, behind phones, on the backs of other actors, etc. Barrymore made only two more films and died in 1942.

John Howard (1913–1995), the male lead, counted among his credits starring roles in *Lost Horizon* (1937), the Bulldog Drummond series (1937–1939), and *Philadelphia Story* (1940). He later went on to appear mainly in routine films, an exception being *The High and the Mighty* (1954).

Charles Ruggles (1888–1970) was an experienced film actor since 1915. Usually playing comic characters of dignity and diffidence, Ruggles starred in classics such as *Charley's Aunt* (1930), *Love Me Tonight* (1932), *Trouble in Paradise* (1933), *Ruggles of Red Gap* (1935), and *Bringing Up Baby* (1938).

Other notables appearing in the film are Shemp Howard (1891–1955) of Three Stooges fame, Margaret Hamilton (1902–1985), the Wicked Witch of the West in *The Wizard of Oz* (1939), and Maria Montez (1919–1951), the exotic leading lady in many costume adventures.

In a pressbook interview, Virginia Bruce is recorded as saying "This is by far the most interesting assignment I have ever had. It is similar to a radio performance except that I will have a chance to establish a visible character before I disappear. Although I am unseen, audiences should be able to visualize the character and her actions, to conform with dialogue and situations."

The film's pressbook suggests such display lines as the following gems of overblown alliteration:

> At last—a woman you can see through! ... a misty miss who causes the merriest mix-up ... the most riotous romance ... the funniest fun ... you've ever seen!
>
> A gorgeous ghost becomes the toast of the town! She's delightful ... she's kissable ... she's caressable ... but, she's invisible.

One lobby gag suggests that theater owners place a goldfish bowl, empty save for water, in the lobby with an attached card reading: "The 'INVISIBLE WOMAN' offers $500.00 cash reward for anyone guessing the exact amount of fish in this bowl." All the pressbook ballyhoo was designed to sell the film with laughs.

Strengths

Though the pressbook calls Barrymore's performance "one of his most notable acting triumphs," it isn't. He outrageously overacts, but in this case we don't mind. In such a screwball film, he is fun to watch and seems quite at home in the general madness. His banter with Margaret Hamilton is particularly good. The rest of the cast delivers as well, particularly

An invisible Virginia Bruce boots Charlie Ruggles in this re-release lobby card scene for *The Invisible Woman* (1940).

Charlie Ruggles, who displays about every reaction that a befuddled butler can possibly display. Especially enjoyable is Kitty's revenge against Mr. Growley. Charles Lane is perfect as the overbearing, heartless boss, and when Kitty gives him what he deserves, we smile with satisfaction. The jokes generally work, though jokes involving "seeing" become a bit thin early on. The physical stunts are impressive, and the musical soundtrack works. As usual, John Fulton's special effects are interesting.

It is difficult to fairly compare and contrast *The Invisible Woman* with its predecessors. It is a comedy, not a horror film, and the science fiction elements are hardly serious. Apparently considered mildly risqué in its time, the film cannot be considered so today. Still, the level of entertainment is such that audiences, even today, get their money's worth. This third in Universal's "Invisible Series" is a better than average offering, and certainly no disgrace.

Weaknesses

This film starts out with a bang (Ruggles literally slipping and falling down the stairs) and keeps up a hilarious pace until the gangster shennanigans begin. Though Holmolka and the other gangsters are quite up to the task, the action slows and things simply are not as funny. John Fulton's special effects are interesting but no longer startling or novel. Though landing another Academy Award nomination, he attempts nothing new in *The Invisible Woman*.

We might nitpick a few other weaknesses. Though minor, the close-ups are not always seemlessly edited into the film, and John Howard appears uncomfortable when embracing and kissing an invisible (and actually non-existent) Virginia Bruce in the fish pond scene.

Rating: 2½

Invisible Agent (1942)   Universal Pictures, U.S.A. / Release Date: July 31, 1942 / Running Time: 79 minutes

CREDITS: Directed by Edwin L. Marin; Associate producer—George Waggner; Screenplay by Curt Siodmak, suggested by the novel *The Invisible Man* by H.G. Wells; Cinematography by Lew White; Special photographic effects by John P. Fulton; Edited by Edward Curtiss; Art Direction by Jack Otterson, Associate Art Director—Robert Boyle; Assistant director—Vernon Keays; Music directed by Hans J. Salter; Set decoration by Russell A. Gausman; Associate Set decorator—Edward R. Robinson; Sound directed by Bernard B. Brown; Technician—William Hedgcock; Gowns by Vera West.

CAST: Ilona Massey (Maria Sorenson/Maria Goodrich), Jon Hall (Frank Raymond/Frank Griffin), Peter Lorre (Baron Ikito), Sir Cedric Hardwicke (Conrad Stauffer), J. Edward Bromberg (Karl Heiser), Albert Basserman (Arnold Schmidt), John Litel (John Gardiner), Holmes Herbert (Sir Alfred Spencer), Keye Luke (Surgeon), Philip Van Zant (Nazi S.S. Man), Matt Willis (Nazi Assassin), Mabel Colcord (Maid), John Holland (Spencer's Secretary), Marty Faust (Killer), Alberto Morin (Free Frenchman), Wolfgang Zilzer (von Porten), Ferdinand Munier (Bartender), Eddie Dunn, Hans Schumm (S.S. Men), John Burton (RAF Flier), Lee Tung-Foo (General Chin Lee), Milburn Stone (German Sergeant).

Film Synopsis

The time is shortly before World War II. Axis partners Conrad Stauffer and Baron Ikito visit the print shop of Frank Griffin, alias Frank Raymond. Raymond has his grandfather's invisibility formula, and the Axis powers want it. Griffin manages to escape and report to the U.S. government. Raymond admits that he has the formula, but he refuses to turn it over to the American government just as he had refused Stauffer and Ikito. When the Japanese bomb Pearl Harbor, however, Raymond reconsiders and offers the formula to the

U.S. government, who wants to drop an invisible spy behind enemy lines. The catch is that Raymond insists on being that spy. Over a barrell, the United States agrees, and flies Raymond over Berlin where he injects himself with the invisibility formula and parachutes to safety. His mission is to learn about German espionage plans and discover the names of Japanese spies in the U.S.

Raymond makes his way to the home of Maria Sorenson, a lovely Allied spy with connections high up in the Nazi party. The invisible Raymond whistles at Maria as she is about to remove her clothes in the bedroom. When he gives her the password, she relaxes. It so happens that Maria, posing as Stauffer's girl, is expecting a dinner guest: Karl Heiser, Stauffer's subordinate. Heiser has plans of stealing Maria from Stauffer and eventually taking Stauffer's place in the party hierarchy. During dinner, Raymond takes advantage of his invisibility to play pranks on Heiser and to keep Maria on edge. When Maria laughs at Heiser's misfortunes, he loses his temper and puts her under house arrest. Alone with Maria, Raymond rubs cold cream on his face so that she can see his good looks and, exhausted from the day's activities, promptly falls asleep. At that point Stauffer shows up unexpectedly and has Heiser arrested.

When Stauffer returns to his office, Raymond is waiting for him. Stauffer gains the upper hand, however, by having the doors locked and pointing out that any leap from the window will lead to death four stories down. Raymond starts a fire in the room and escapes with a book of names of Japanese spies in the U.S.

Stauffer and Ikito are soon in disagreement about how to handle the situation, both sides making clear that Axis loyalty extends only so far as it benefits their respective countries. At one point, even Ikito appears sickened by the German's attitude.

Raymond visits Heiser in prison and agrees to help him escape if the soon-to-be-executed prisoner will reveal details about a planned German air attack on the United States. Heiser complies and Raymond spirits him out of the prison. When Stauffer gets a phone call from Heiser about the invisible man, he pretends to be pleased at Heiser's escape. Once off the phone, however, he orders Heiser shot on sight.

Meanwhile, Ikito traps Raymond and takes him and Maria to the Japanese Embassy. By this time, Raymond suspects that Maria aided in his capture and distrusts her loyalty.

Raymond, still invisible, soon manages to free himself and escapes with Maria to an airfield where they take off in a plane waiting to attack New York. Ikito kills Stauffer for letting the two escape and then commits hara-kiri himself. After dropping bombs on the German airfield, Raymond becomes ill and is saved by Maria as their plane flies over English soil. Heiser is killed by Stauffer's assassins, and the film ends with Raymond and Maria kissing in close embrace.

Adaptation

Though H.G. Wells received another check from Universal Studios, *Invisible Agent*, like *Invisible Woman* before it, borrows nothing from Wells' *The Invisible Man* except the name of Frank Griffin and the concept of invisibility itself. It is, in fact, not an adaptation of the novel in any way.

Production and Marketing

With World War II raging, Hollywood became a propaganda machine for the Allied war effort. Screenwriter Curt Siodmak, an escapee from Nazi Germany, apparently enjoyed the task of poking fun at Nazis in *Invisible Agent*.

The invisible Jon Hall threatens Cedric Hardwicke as Ilona Massey and J. Edward Bromberg look on in this lobby card scene from *Invisible Agent* (1942).

Originally announced as *Invisible Spy*, the film was to be produced by Frank Lloyd and Jack Skirball. When Skirball withdrew, Universal assigned George Waggner, the director of *The Wolf Man*, as associate producer.

Director Edwin L. Marin (1901–1951) had directed some good films such as *A Christmas Carol* (1938) but generally turned in merely competent jobs. Cedric Hardwick returned to the Invisible Man series, having played the villain in Universal's earlier *The Invisible Man Returns*.

The role of the Invisible Agent went to Jon Hall (1913–1979) who began his career in such films as *Charlie Chan in Shanghai* (1936), *The Girl from Scotland Yard* (1937), and *The Hurricane* (1937). His

career hit its stride with *Invisible Agent* (1942), *Arabian Nights* (1942), *White Savage* (1943), *Ali Baba and the Forty Thieves* (1944), *Cobra Woman* (1944), and *The Invisible Man's Revenge* (1944). The quality of his roles declined in the fifties, hitting bottom in 1965 when he directed and starred in *The Beachgirls and the Monster*. He soon left acting, went into the photography business, and committed suicide in 1979.

Hungarian-born leading lady Ilona Massey (1912–1974) brought a touch of dignity and style to *Invisible Agent*. She had gained critical attention for her fine work in otherwise routine films such as *Rosalie* (1937) and *International Lady* (1941) and is probably best remembered today for her performance as Baroness Frankenstein in *Frankenstein Meets the Wolf Man* (1943).

Hungarian-born character actor Peter Lorre (1904–1964) was cast as the sinister Japanese agent. Before *Invisible Agent*, he had give chilling performances in *M* (1930), *Mad Love* (1935), *Crime and Punishment* (1935), *Island of Doomed Men* (1940), *Stranger on the Third Floor* (1940), and *The Face Behind the Mask* (1941). He also gave critically acclaimed performances in such classics as *The Maltese Falcon* (1941).

Hungarian-born J. Edward Bromberg (1903–1951) had been in films since the mid–1930s, usually in gentle roles. Some of his more memborable films include *Suez* (1938), *Hollywood Cavalcade* (1939), *The Phantom of the Opera* (1943), *Son of Dracula* (1943), and *A Star Is Born* (1948).

Other familiar faces in *Invisible Agent* include Keye Luke (of Charlie Chan fame), Matt Willis (the very effective werewolf of *Return of the Vampire*), and Milburn Stone (Doc on the long-running television hit *Gunsmoke*).

The studio hyped *Invisible Agent* for all it was worth. Posters and ads called the film "TODAY'S MOST AMAZING SENSATION," noting that it was suggested by the H.G. Wells novel. Reviews were generally kind, often noticing Peter Lorre's fine performance.

Strengths

The film's most obvious strength is its fine cast. Ilona Massey is charming and graceful, just the type of lady who would attract the interest of important men (or any

The original title card for *Invisible Agent* (1942)

other men for that matter). Cedric Hardwick is excellent as the intelligent, cold-hearted Stauffel, quite a change from the typical bumbling Nazis that otherwise populate the picture. Peter Lorre is effective as the soft-spoken but obviously dangerous Baron Ikito. Most memorable are the scenes in which he "plays" with a paper cropper while musing about its potential as a torture instrument. J. Edward Bromberg is both piggish and pathetic as the hapless Heiser.

The film is well-paced throughout, and Hans Salter's familiar soundtrack themes are a plus.

Weaknesses

Though the cast is solid, the film could have used a stronger leading man. Hall doesn't detract from the film, but he doesn't give a notable performance either.

The film's main problem is the screenplay. Curt Siodmak repeatedly demonstrated throughout his career the skills of top-notch scenarist, but in *Invisible Agent* he misses the mark. First of all, Siodmak ignores an issue established earlier in the series: the fact that the invisibility drug can drive a person insane. What if Raymond held the fate of the free world in his hands but had to fight insanity and a possible conversion to Naziism inspired by their "Superman" philosophy? Relieved of this troublesome concern, Siodmak is able to shed some of the seriousness and go in a different direction than the two earlier serious Invisible Man pictures were able to go. He is also too eager to denigrate the Nazis at every turn, treating them either as comic buffoons or as sub-human monsters. The following dialogue excerpts are typical:

> Stauffer: There is no place on Earth for the weak.
> Heiser (proudly): The Fuhrer doesn't like people who think for themselves.
> Maria: They [the Nazis] treat women like dogs. I hate them.

> Stauffer: There is no place in our order for sentimentalists.
> Raymond (to Heiser in prison): I pity the devil when you boys start arriving in bunches.

Particularly embarassing is a diatribe that Raymond delivers to the imprisoned Heiser, a most unappreciative captive audience. After a while, we get the point! Also annoying is the slapstick comedy at the expense of the Nazis. Today the approach seems out of place. The Nazis were a real menace; they were not circus clowns. All of this contributes to another problem: is the film a drama or a comedy? It seems it can't make up its mind, and the confusion detracts from any over-all effect.

Though John P. Fulton's special effects aren't bad, they aren't as good as in the previous Invisible Man films. One memorable scene has the invisible Man lathering up his feet and legs in a bathtub, but generally we don't see the usual care taken to produce striking effects. No doubt, such care would have lifted the film a half notch in quality.

The Invisible Agent is the fourth in Universal's Invisible Man series based on or inspired by H.G. Wells' novel. Unfortunately, each new entry in the series represents a slight but clear decline in quality. Uneven and often annoying, *The Invisible Agent* is lightweight, forgettable film fare. It raises no controversial issues and addresses no challenging ideas. Instead, it seeks merely to entertain an indiscriminate audience, which it can do rather successfully.

At least the Invisible Man had not yet met Abbott and Costello, a final indignity still to come.

Rating: 2

The Invisible Man's Revenge (1944)

Universal Pictures, U.S.A. / Release Date: June 9, 1944 / Running Time: 77 minutes

CREDITS: Produced and directed by Ford Beebe; Executive producer—Howard Benedict; Screenplay by Bertram Millhauser, suggested by the novel *The Invisible Man* by H.G. Wells; Cinematography by Milton Krasner; Special photographic effects by John P. Fulton; Edited by Saul A. Goodkind; Camera operated by Maury Gertsman; Assistant director—Fred Frank; Musical score and direction by Hans J. Salter; Art direction by John B. Goodman and Harold H. MacArthur; Set decoration by Russell A. Gausman and Andrew J. Gilmore; Technician—William Hedgock; Property master—Eddie Keyes; Gowns by Vera West.

CAST: Jon Hall (Robert Griffin), Leon Errol (Herbert Higgins), John Carradine (Dr. Peter Drury), Alan Curtis (Mark Foster); Evelyn Ankers (Julie Herrick), Gale Sondergaard (Lady Irene Herrick), Lester Matthews (Sir Jasper Herrick), Halliwell Hobbes (Cleghorn), Leland [Leyland] Hodgson (Sir Frederick Travers), Ian Wolfe (Jim Feeney), Billy Bevan (Police Sergeant), Doris Lloyd (Maud), Cyril Delevanti (Malty Bill), Skelton Knaggs (Alf Parry), Olaf Hytten (Grey), Leonard Carey (Constable), Yorke Sherwood (Yarrow), Tom P. Dillon (Towle), Guy Kingsford (Bill), Jim Aubrey (Wedderburn), Arthur Gould-Porter (Meadows), Lillian Bronson (Norma), Janna DeLoos (Nellie).

Film Synopsis

Paranoiac Robert Griffin escapes from a mental hospital leaving corpses and destruction in his wake. He returns to the home of his former business associates, Sir Jasper Herrick and his wife Irene, and accuses them of trying to kill him while the three were on an African safari in search of a Tanganyika diamond field five years ago. Though innocent of the charge, the Herricks' responses to Griffin make them appear guilty. While demanding half of the Herricks' fortune, Griffin sees a painting of the Herricks' daughter, Julie, and falls in love with her.

When the Herricks dismiss Griffin, he comes upon Herbert Higgins, a shoe-mender-turned-blackmailer who recommends that Griffin consult a lawyer. Having become partners, Griffin and Higgins go to an attorney. When the police enter, Higgins backs off the idea and he and Griffin quickly exit.

Griffin then finds his way to the home of Dr. Peter Drury, a reclusive scientist performing experiments in invisibility. Among the doctor's successes are Methuselah, a parrot, and Brutus, a German Shepherd. Griffin identifies with Brutus because he has been attacked on occasion by the dogs of the gentry. Drury explains that after years of research, he has created a drug that can make any organism invisible. Quite pleased with himself, Drury announces that his name will soon take its place along with those of Copernicus, Faraday, and Darwin.

Griffin talks Drury into turning him invisible and sets off seeking vengeance against the Herricks. When Griffin startles the Herricks with his invisibility, Sir Jasper tries to kill him. Griffin avoids the attack, however, and forces Jasper to sign over all his property to him.

Later, at the Running Nag Inn, the invisible Griffin aids Higgins in a darts game by guiding Higgins' darts to the bullseye. Afterward, Griffin saves Higgins from the game's loser and from the enraged crowd.

In order to appease Jasper Herrick and to begin courting Julie, Griffin returns to Dr. Drury in hopes of regaining his visibility. The doctor has meanwhile discovered that a complete blood transfusion can temporarily restore visibility. Griffin asks Drury to phone Mark Foster, Julie's current love, and invite him over so Griffin can drain his blood. When Drury calls the police instead, the invisible man knocks the doctor out and drains all of the doctor's blood into his own body. This upsets Drury's now-visible dog Brutus, who pursues the visible Griffin back to the Herrick residence.

Under an assumed name, Griffin woos Julie over dinner but slips into a deranged speech about how glorious it must be to possess the power of invisibility. About that time, Griffin begins to fade away and quickly removes himself from the room. Griffin later lures Mark Foster into the wine cellar with the intent of draining his blood. Brutus comes to the rescue, however, and before anyone can save him, Griffin dies under the fang and claw of the late Dr. Drury's lonesome companion.

Adaptation

Though Universal paid Wells for use of his novel's title in the film credits, little if anything seems to have been derived from the novel that could not have been derived from viewing *The Invisible Man* (1933). Once again we have a Griffin as the Invisible Man, though no connection is made in the film between Jon Hall's character and that of Claude Rains. In fact, Dr. Drury seems never to have heard of Jack Griffin's earlier pioneer work in invisibility. It is possible that Leon Errol's Herbert Higgins was modelled on the novel's tramp, Marvel, and it is possible that Dr. Kemp's call to the police betraying the Invisible Man in the novel suggested Dr. Drury's similar call in the 1944 film. It doesn't make much difference since the film, suggested by the book, does not claim to be an adaptation

Production and Marketing

Shortly before shooting began, Universal gave H.G. Wells $7,500 for the right to make two additional Invisible Man sequels. Production began on January 10, 1944, and wrapped in mid-February, at which point John P. Fulton went to work on the special effects.

Director Ford Beebe (1888–1978) directed over 200 films during his long career, most of them low-budget westerns, B features, and serials. He is best remembered today for the serials *Flash Gordon's*

Trip to Mars (1938) and *Riders of Death Valley* (1941), and for the atmospheric horror film *Night Monster* (1942), reputedly admired by Alfred Hitchcock.

Universal hoped to land Claude Rains for the lead role, but when Rains declined, the studio turned to Jon Hall, who had played the transparent one in *Invisible Agent*. Hall had proven adequate in that role and at least knew the ropes.

Australian comedian Leon Errol (1881–1951) was signed to provide comic relief. He left medicine for Broadway and vaudeville in 1910 and played henpecked husbands in many thirties two-reelers and feature films. He is best known today for his portrayal of the drunken Lord Epping in *Mexican Spitfire* (1939, the first of the series starring Errol and Lupe Velez).

John Carradine appears in his second Invisible Man film, this time as a co-star. Because of his many horror film appearances, interviewers frequently pressed him to reveal his "favorite" horror appearance. The only one Carradine ever mentioned warmly was *The Invisible Man's Revenge*. Why? Because he had fun making it. British-born Evelyn Ankers (1918–1985) assayed her familiar role as heroine in a Universal Picture. She came to the film having co-starred in such silver age thrillers as *The Wolf Man* (1941), *The Ghost of Frankenstein* (1942), *The Mad Ghoul* (1943), and *Weird Woman* (1944). Gale Sondergaard (1899–1985) took a break from her usually sinister roles to play an innocent in *The Invisible Man's Revenge*. She had already won an Academy Award for her performance in *Anthony Adverse* (1936) and had established a reputation in such films as *Maid of Salem* (1937), *The Life of Emile Zola* (1937), *The Cat and the Canary* (1939), *The Bluebird* (1940), and *The Spider Woman* (1944).

Advertising for the film featured the heads of the major cast and the outline of an invisible man. At that point, there wasn't much more to do.

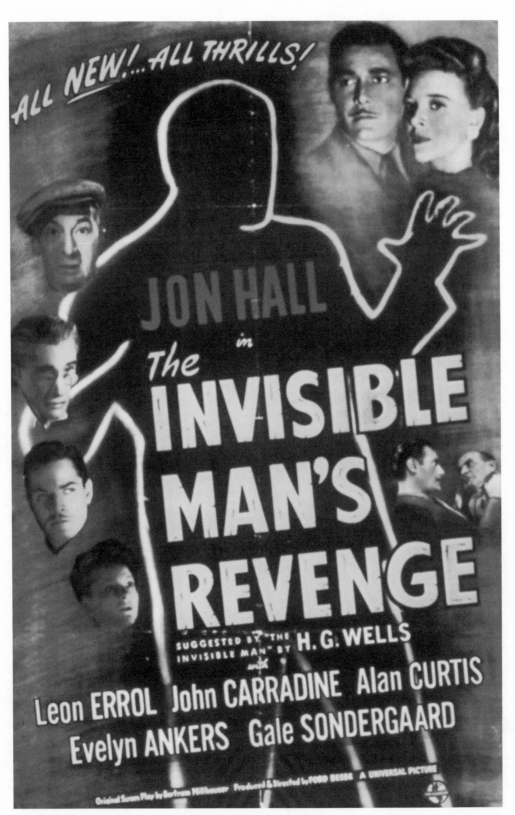

The original one-sheet poster for *The Invisible Man's Revenge* (1944)

Strengths

Two scenes particularly stand out in *The Invisible Man's Revenge*. In one, Griffin runs down a corridor as his flesh slowly becomes invisible. In the other, Griffin splashes aquarium water on his face, creating a ghostly outline that frightens Lady Irene Herrick. We are also treated to Griffin removing his dark glasses, revealing the bandages that circle the back of his head. Also interesting are the invisible animals.

Special effects alone cannot carry a film, however, and the screenwriter throws in the blood transfusion twist to help distinguish the film from its predecesors. The biggest strength of *The Invisible Man's Revenge*, however, is the cast. Hall is sur-

prisingly strong in the role of Griffin, Sondergaard and Matthews are nearly perfect as the Herricks, though Sondergaard sometimes acts guilty and sinister when she is not intended to be. Errol is a mixed bag. He does what he does well, but perhaps he does too much of it. At least he does not deliver the type of annoying comic relief as that delivered with crippling effects by Una O'Connor in *The Bride of Frankenstein* (1935) and Hugh Herbert in *The Black Cat* (1941). Finally, Carradine's over-the-top performance as Dr. Drury is delightful. Though Ankers has little to do, she acquits herself well.

The Invisible Man's Revenge can hold its own against such 1943–1946 Universal contemporaries as the ape girl series, the Inner Sanctum series, the final Mummy

John Carradine looks up to the invisible man in this scene from *The Invisible Man's revenge* (1944).

films, and *House of Frankenstein* and *House of Dracula*. The only clearly superior Universal horror films of the period are *Frankenstein Meets the Wolf Man*, *Son of Dracula*, *The Phantom of the Opera*, and the best of the Sherlock Holmes films

Weaknesses

The film's greatest liability is its tired screenplay. The previous two films suggested by Wells' novel were mediocre because there just wasn't much new to do with the invisibility theme. The same is true here. Perhaps this explains the film's over-reliance on Leon Errol's comic relief. Unfortunately, the terror is not so intense as to require much comic relief. If anything, an eerier atmosphere and increased suspense would have resulted in a better product. As the weak screenplay indicates, Universal had gone as far as it could.

All in all, *The Invisible Man's Revenge* is the forties equivalent of today's popcorn movie on a low budget. It passes the time pleasantly enough, but it isn't very memorable. Still, it is slightly better than its immediate predecessor, *Invisible Agent*.

Rating: 2½

Abbott and Costello Meet the Invisible Man (1951)
Universal-International, U.S.A. / Release Date: March, 1951 / Running Time: 82 minutes

CREDITS: Directed by Charles Lamont; Produced by Howard Christie; Screenplay by Robert Lees, Frederic Renaldo, and John Grant. Original story by Hugh Wedlock, Jr. and Howard Snyder, suggested by *The Invisible Man* by H.G. Wells; Cinematography by George Robinson; Art Direction by Bernard Herzbrun and Richard Riedel; Music directed by Joseph Gershenson; Edited by Virgil Vogel; Set Decoration by Russell A. Gausman and John Austin; Sound by Leslie I. Carey and Robert Pritchard; Hair styles by Joan St. Oeger; Makeup by Bud Westmore; Special Effects by David S. Horsley.

CAST: Bud Abbott (Bud Alexander), Lou Costello (Lou Francis), Nancy Guild (Helen Gray), Arthur Franz (Tommy Nelson), Adele Jergens (Boots Marsden), Sheldon Leonard (Morgan), William Frawley (Detective Roberts), Gavin Muir (Dr. Philip Gray), Sam Balter (Radio Announcer), John Day (Rocky Hanlon), Sid Saylor (Waiter), Billy Wayne (Rooney), George J. Lewis (Torpedo), Frankie Van (Referee), Bobby Barber (Sneaky), Carl Sklover (Lou's Handler), Charles Petter (Rocky's Handler), Paul Maxey (Dr. Turner), Ed Gargan (Milt), Herb Vigran (Stillwell), Russ Conway, Billy Snyder (Newspapermen), Franklin Parker, Ralph Montgomery (Photographers), Ralph Dunn (Motorcycle Cop), Harold Goodwin (Bartender), Richard Bartell (Bald Man).

Film Synopsis

Bud Alexander and Lou Francis graduate from detective school and take the case of Tommy Nelson, a middleweight fighter charged with murdering his manager. Bud and Lou drive Tommy to the home of his fiancée, Helen Gray, where her uncle, Dr. Philip Gray, is trying to perfect the invisibility serum Monocaine and a reagent. Unfortunately, Monocaine still has the potential to drive its user insane. Since Bud has alerted the police, the betrayed Tommy injects himself with Monocaine against Dr. Gray's orders.

Tommy becomes invisible before the startled eyes of Lou, who tries in vain to convince Detective Roberts of what he saw. This lands Lou at police headquarters where he is examined by psychiatrist Dr. Turner. When Turner tries to hypnotize Lou, Lou ends up innocently hypnotizing Turner, two cops, and a cleaning woman.

Later, Lou delivers clothing to Tommy in a fog-shrouded, secluded area. Again Bud has warned the police, and Tommy must escape when they arrive. Tommy

explains to Bud and Lou that he was sup-
posed to take a dive in his fight with
Rocky Hanlon, but instead knocked Hanlon out. He says his manager was then
beaten to death by thugs in Promoter
Morgan's gang, and the blame was placed
on Tommy.

Tommy talks Lou into posing as a
fighter with Bud as his manager. The invisible Tommy then accompanies Bud and
Lou to the gym where Lou stuns onlook-
ers with his boxing speed (all thanks to
Tommy). A match is quickly arranged between Lou, now known as Louie the
Looper, and Rocky Hanlon. Falling into
Tommy's trap, Morgan sends the beautiful Boots Marsden to suggest a fix. If
Lou will throw the fight in the fifth

round, his bank account will grow considerably.

Tommy agrees to accompany Lou to
the ring and work his invisible wonders so
that Lou wins. Then when Morgan and
his men attempt to kill Bud and Lou,
Tommy will expose them as the real
killers. The night of the fight, Dr. Gray
keeps Tommy restrained on a cot at the
time Lou enters the ring to fight Hanlon.
Tommy escapes just in time to save Lou
from a terrible beating and send Hanlon to
the canvas for the ten count.

Morgan and a henchman try to kill
Bud and Lou, but they are stopped by the
invisible Tommy, who is seriously hurt in
the altercation. With Morgan in police
custody, Dr. Gray transfuses Tommy with

Bud Abbott emphasizes a point to Sherlockian Lou Costello in this lobby card scene from *Abbott
and Costello Meet the Invisible Man* (1951).

Lou's blood and saves Tommy's life. Tommy's blood, full of the secret serum leaks a bit into Lou's veins and makes him invisible. When the invisibility wears off, Lou finds his legs are on backwards. Nothing ever goes right for the little guy!

Adaptation

H.G. Wells certainly never conceived of his Invisible Man encountering the comic team of Abbott and Costello. This film, like most other sequels in the Invisible Man series, is suggested by the Wells novel. It is not an adaptation. It does, however, play straight with the first film, *The Invisible Man,* and its immediate sequel, *The Invisible Man Returns.* Monocaine is back with its threat of insanity, and Dr. Gray even has a photograph of Claude Rains on the wall of his laboratory. While the element was probably coincidental, Dr. Gray is somewhat like Wells' Dr. Griffin in that he attempts to betray the Invisible Man rather than risk his reputation in the scientific community. In the film, this is rather clumsily inserted to account for the Invisible Man showing up late at the boxing match.

Production and Marketing

When the comedy team of Bud Abbott (1895–1974) and Lou Costello (1906–1959) began to fade in popularity in the late forties, Universal-International tried teaming them with the Universal monsters, who were also in decline. The result was *Abbott and Costello Meet Frankenstein* (1948), a very successful film that resurrected the career of Abbott and Costello and allowed the Frankenstein Monster, the Wolf Man, and Dracula to be scarier than they had been in years. Universal-International followed up with the tepid *Abbott and Costello Meet the Killer, Boris Karloff* (1949) and then launced *Abbott and*

Costello Meet the Invisible Man in 1951. We last "saw" the Invisible Man at the end of *Abbott and Costello Meet Frankenstein* when Vincent Price arrives too late to share in the fun. In 1951, as portrayed by Arthur Franz, the Invisible Man would at last have his chance with Abbott and Costello.

Arthur Franz (1920–) was an adequate character actor with radio, television, and stage experience. Though he appeared in some fine films such as *Sands of Iwo Jima* (1949), *The Sniper* (1952), *The Caine Mutiny* (1954) and *That Championship Season* (1982), he is probably best remembered today for playing the title role in *Monster on the Campus* (1958).

Hollywood-born actress Nancy Guild returned to the screen after a two-year absense, having co-starred in *Give My Regards to Broadway* in 1948. Playing the ganster's moll was Adele Jergens (1922–), who was a leading lady mainly in B features. Also on board was William Frawley (1887–1966), the balding, cigar-chewing character actor best known today for playing Fred Mertz on the *I Love Lucy* television show (1951–1960). Playing the heavy was Sheldon Leonard (1907–), who made a career out of playing gangsters before quitting acting to produce television series.

Director Charles Lamont (1898–1993) was an established comedy director, guiding several Ma and Pa Kettle and Abbott and Costello films, and even one Francis the Talking Mule picture.

Ads for the film promised "CHILLS! CHUCKLES! That Invisible Man is back on the prowl and oh! what howls ... when he meets Detectives Bud and Lou!" The ad doesn't explain which Invisible Man is back. It certainly wasn't any Invisible Man from a previous film. Along with the chills and chuckles, the film also promised "HAIR RAISING ... HOWL RAISING ... HILARITY!" The comedy-horror connection was stressed, just as it had been in

The original title lobby card for *Abbott and Costello Meet the Invisible Man* (1951)

the case of *Abbott and Costello Meet Frankenstein.*

According to the pressbook, *Abbott and Costello Meet the Invisible Man* was the comedy team's 26th movie together during their eleven years in Hollywood. What was the team's burning ambition? "To make a movie called *Abbott and Costello Meet Abbott and Costello.*"

Strengths

When Abbott and Costello had a good script, they could be very funny, which is the case in *Abbott and Costello Meet the Invisible Man.* In essence, the jokes work, and the slapstick is hilarious. Franz is fine as the Invisible Man, playing it all straight. Frawley is funny as Detective Roberts, and Leonard is cold and menacing as Morgan. Adele Jergens has a good scene in which she tries to convince Lou to throw the fight. Turning on the charm, she tries to get him to agree on which round to dive based on the number of kisses she gives him. Of course, Lou holds out for a later round.

Several scenes particularly stand out. In the one in which Lou delivers a grip full of clothes to the Invisible Man, the foggy forest is more eerie and atmospheric than anything in *The Invisible Man's Revenge*, though otherwise, the mood is comic throughout. In another scene, Abbott and Costello sit helplessly in the back seat of a car as the Invisible Man drives wildly down the road. As the comedy team shudders in fear, the Invisible Man matter-offactly explains that he hopes Dr. Gray will soon discover the reagent because "without it, I might turn into a raving maniac with an uncontrollable urge to kill." Very funny as well are the dinner scenes in which antics by the Invisible Man cause Bud and Lou to cover for him with the baffled waiter. Of course, the boxing match finale is the film's high point, and it doesn't disappoint. What would the reaction be if such a fight were actually captured on tape today and reviewed by boxing officials? The chaos would be completely unexplainable.

The film's action is generally fast-paced throughout, and David Horsley's special effects are superior to John P. Fulton's in *Invisible Agent.*

Weaknesses

For the person who simply hates Abbott and Costello's brand of comedy, this film will lose much of its appeal. Though such people may be few, they will certainly not have enthusiasm for *Abbott and Costello Meet the Invisible Man.* There are a few flaws, however. The scene in which Lou innocently hypnotizes Dr. Turner is predictable and goes on a bit too long, and Nancy Guild, though competent, doesn't bring anything special to the film. Bud and Lou deliver a few warmed over jokes from earlier films, but they are brief and don't really detract from the procedings.

I suppose my biggest complaint is that the film does almost nothing with Monocaine's potential to drive the Invisible Man insane. What if Tommy Nelson, a power-hungry monomaniac due to Monocaine, had somehow thrown in with Morgan at a most inopportune moment. We can only wonder, but such a turn would have improved the film and we still could have had a happy ending. Of course, we do get the old megalomanic speech that we have come to expect in most of

the serious Invisible Man pictures, but it goes nowhere, and, as in *Invisible Man Returns, The Invisible Woman,* and *Invisible Agent,* the Invisible Man's most outrageous behavior can be explained away as the effect of a few too many drinks.

The Invisible Man series went steadily downhill from the excellent *The Invisible Man* (1933) to the mediocre *Invisible Agent* (1942). The series improved by half a point with *The Invisible Man's Revenge* (1944) and delivered everything it promised with *Abbott and Costello Meet the Invisible Man.* Of course, this is the Invisible Man's swan song. The character as envisioned by Wells was by now as far in the distant past as was the Frankenstein Monster as envisioned by Mary Shelley. At least, the Invisible Man joined the Frankenstein Monster, the Wolf Man, and Dracula in getting an entertaining send off. The same cannot be said in the case of *Abbott and Costello Meet Dr. Jekyll and Mr. Hyde* (1953), which even Boris Karloff cannot save, and *Abbott and Costello Meet the Mummy* (1955), both of which disappoint.

Rating: 3

El Hombre Que Logró Ser Invisible (1957) aka *El Hombre Invisible, The Invisible Man, The Invisible Man in Mexico, H. G. Wells' New Invisible Man* Cinematográfica Calderón, Mexico / Release Date: ? / Running Time: 95 minutes

CREDITS: Directed by Alfredo Crevenna; Produced by Guillermo Calderón (Paul Castain); Story by Alfredo Salazar; Screenplay by Julio Alejandro; Cinematography by Raul M. Solares; Edited by Jorge Gustos; Sound edited by Abraham Cruz; Music by A.D. Conde; Special photographic effects by J.A. de Castro.

CAST: Arturo de Córdova (Carlos), Ana Luísa Peluffo (Beatriz), Augusto Benedico (Luis), Raul Meraz, Nestor Barbosa, Jorge Mondragón, Roberto G. Rivera, Roy Fletcher.

Film Synopsis

Carlos and Beatriz are to be married. Carlos' brother Luis, still single, is conducting experiments in invisibility. When Carlos' business partner is murdered, John, another partner, accuses Carlos. Carlos is convicted of murder and sentenced to prison for 99 years. Beatriz turns to Luis for help because Carlos is despondent in prison. Feeling that Carlos is innocent, Luis keeps working on the invisibility serum, even though he knows that the drug could drive a person mad.

After Luis accidently turns an insect invisible and successfully experiments on a rabbit, he goes to the prison and injects Carlos with the drug. Carlos quickly turns invisible, sheds his clothing, and escapes. The invisible Carlos then catches a bus, stops a pickpocket in the act, startles strollers and beats up a thief in the park on his way to meet his fiancée. Beatriz picks up Carlos at a pre-arranged place as the police watch her every move.

Beatriz and Carlos shake the police and hole up in Beatriz's house. In hiding, Carlos muses about using his invisibility to execute lucrative criminal acts. On second thought, however, he decides that he could at this point make just as much money honestly by showing himself as an invisible man—except that he is an escaped convict! Meanwhile, Luis searches for a reagent.

When Carlos goes to inspect the business office for clues in the murder, he overhears a conversation between John and a watchman. The watchman knows more than he should, and John kills him. An ensuing phone call convinces Carlos that John committed the murder in collaboration with Beatriz's father, the company owner. Apparently the other partner would not go along with the conspirators' use of the company as a front for narcotics smuggling.

Carlos returns to Beatriz and announces that he no longer seeks justice; he simply wants to flee the country with Beatriz and wait for Luis to perfect the reagent. He would rather live as a fugitive than break Beatriz's heart by having her father convicted of conspiracy to murder and drug smuggling.

Back in hiding at Luis' laboratory, Carlos applies makeup so as to be partially visible and "feel more human." He also dons goggles, a hat, and an overcoat. The police arrive, and Carlos removes the makeup, ditches the clothes, and escapes. By now, police suspect that Carlos is the invisible man being reported by citizens. The Inspector goes to Beatriz's home and tells everyone there that he knows that an invisible Carlos is in the house. Soon the police and Carlos are embroiled in combat, and Carlos once again escapes. The police take Beatriz to her "worried" father.

Carlos makes John go to Beatriz's father with instructions to make the old man write a letter of confession. The old man beats John nearly to death, however, and wildly fires a pistol in an effort to kill the invisible man. As the old man runs from the room, John shoots him in the back and expires.

Carlos returns to Luis and tells him that he doesn't want his body back. He believes that the Supreme Judge has chosen him from all other mortals to set things right. He calls women inferior beings and claims that mankind has corrupted its soul. All souls must now return to the Creator. "I'm going to destroy all life!" he vows.

Realizing now that Carlos is innocent, Police Chief Forbes pleads for the fugitive to return. Carlos responds by carrying out a threat to shut off all the electrical power in the city and then implies that he will poison the air and water.

Carlos reveals to Beatriz his plan to contaminate the city water supply with an encephalitis virus. She pretends to be a willing accomplice but tries to knock Carlos unconscious. Failing in her attempt, she finds herself being strangled by Carlos, who continues to apply the pressure until she gasps that she adores him. His ego sufficiently soothed, Carlos heads for the water treatment plant. The police are waiting, however, and several shots are fired, one of which hits and kills Luis, who had hoped to persuade Carlos to give himself up. The police form a large circle and discover that Carlos lies wounded by one of the bullets. At the hospital, a doctor administers Luis' perfected reagent, and Carlos becomes visible again. The doctor explains that Carlos needs an immediate operation to remove the bullet, and Beatriz promises she will stay by his side through it all.

Adaptation

El Hombre Que Logró Ser Invisible is not so much an updating or adaptation of H.G. Wells' *The Invisible Man* as it is a remake of Universal's *The Invisible Man Returns*. In both films, a wrongly convicted man employs an invisibility serum to effect a prison break. The fugitive returns to his girlfriend and seeks to uncover the identity of the real killer. In both cases, the real killer is the girlfriend's father, and the invisible fugitive eventually gets revenge. In both films, the invisible man is wounded, returned to visibility, and saved by an operation as their girlfriends stand by. The difference is that the madness element present in Universal's *The Invisible Man* and hinted at in *The Invisible Man Returns* is fully exploited in the last quarter of this Mexican entry. Writers Salazar and Alejandro appear to adapt nothing from Wells' novel except the idea of an invisible man who plays tricks on local citizens. The rest comes from the two Universal films discussed above.

Production and Marketing

In the late fifties and early sixties, Mexican directors such as Alfredo B. Crevenna, Alfonso Cardona Blake, Julien Soler, Federico Curiel, and Rene Cardona began producing low budget black/white horror exploitation films suitable for Saturday matinees. Crevenna would go on to direct such lightweight horror/science fiction films as *La Hella Macabra* (1962), *Aventura al Centro de la Tierra* (1965), *Gigantes Planetarios* (1966), *El Planeta de los Mujeres* (1966), and *La Mujer del Diablo* 1972). He is probably best known for directing *Santo Contra la Invasión de los Marcianos* (1966, aka *Santo Versus the Martian Invasion*), one of the popular Santo series in which a heroic masked wrestler, played by Rodolfo Guzman Huerta, battles werewolves, zombies, vampires, mad scientists, and space aliens.

The lovely Ana Luisa Peluffo originally gained fame as one of the sexy starlets of Urueta's *La Illigitima* (1955).

Strengths

El Hombre Que Logró Ser Invisible can boast two major strengths. The first is its quick pace. From the time we are introduced to the leading characters, events unfold quickly. The second is the decision to allow the invisible man to go mad and pursue a career of terrorism. *The Invisible Man Returns* teased a turn to madness but never delivered. This version allows us the jolt of watching the character we have been pulling for become a narcissistic madman and potential murderer. It is almost like watching our favorite dog come down with rabies.

After watching a dubbed version of the film, comments on the acting performances are not possible though the cast does not appear a liability.

Weaknesses

The film's main weakness is that it could have been so much better. First of all, the special effects are unimpressive. We get the headless coat, footprints in the snow, depressed chair cushion, floating cigarette, and moving typewriter keyes— all of which were very familiar to genre fans. For example, when Carlos is given the reagent, we see a skull appear, and then the actor's face. Nothing special at all. In fact, the special effects in all the Universal Invisible Man films were superior to Castro's.

The screenplay is adequate, but it would have been better had the writer built a foundation for Carlos' madness-inspired religious fanaticism. Though we at one point see Beatriz meditating before a crucifix, Carlos never exhibits any particular religiosity before the onset of madness. Then, his motivations are suddenly "God-inspired." Carlos' variety of madness would have been more believable, and possibly even terrifying, had he earlier demonstrated a belief or deep faith in God.

The story line, though adequate, cannot overcome the obvious low budget. Sets are chintsy and everything has the look of a children's serial.

Also a problem is Crevenna's pedestrian direction. For example, in the key scene in which Cordova strangles Peluffo, she pleads with her attacker as though her breath were not being cut off at all. Still, this may have been a result of shoddy dubbing, not bad direction. Regardless, Crevenna does nothing creative with the camera and simply lets the pace of the screenplay carry the film.

When a company produces an invisible man film in the late fifties, that film's production values should not pale in comparison to those of the thirties. But in this case, they do, and the film suffers correspondingly. As a new *Invisible Man*, the film falls far short of 1933's version. In the final twenty-five minutes, it briefly challenges *The Invisible Man Returns* as a horror film, but the strong finale is insufficient to make it a peer. *El Hombre Que Logró Ser Invisible* is not as entertaining as the more comedic *Invisible Woman*, *Invisible Agent*, and *Abbott and Costello Meet the Invisible Man*, and it doesn't have the style and presence of *The Invisible Man's Revenge*. Perfunctory direction and ho-hum special effects contribute to the film's mediocre look.

Rating: 2

6

"The Man Who Could Work Miracles" (1898)

THE SHORT STORY

In 1896, H.G. Wells retreated to several Channel sites in an effort to recover from kidney trouble. Despite illness, Wells generally managed to write for six or seven hours at a time with only a short break for tea.

Among his friends at the time were such luminaries as George Gissing, Joseph Conrad, Henry James, Ford Madox Ford (previously Hueffer) and J.M. Barrie. Highlights of the year included a trip to Italy with Gissing and serial publication of his next novel *The War of the Worlds*. Since the success of his novels, he was now able to command higher prices for his short stories. One of those stories was "The Man Who Could Work Miracles," published in *The Illustrated London News* in July, 1898.

When H.G. Wells wrote and published "The Man Who Could Work Miracles" he was gaining an international reputation as a writer of science fiction romances, but when he adapted his short story for the screen in 1935–36, he was much more than that. In the interim he addressed the Royal Institution (1902), joined the socialistic Fabians (1903–04), worked with the Ministry of Information on War Propaganda (1918), served on the League of Nations Committee (1918), published the monumental *Outline of History* (1920), visited Russia (1914 and 1920), covered the World Disarmament Conference (1921), stood for Parliament (1922), renewed his connection with Britain's Labor Party (1922), spoke on behalf of the world-wide campaign for peace (1928), was elected international president of PEN (1933), and interviewed both Stalin and FDR—all the while publishing challenging books on education, sociology, and science fantasy. In other words, he was a figure of international significance on a variety of fronts. No wonder the cinema was eager for his collaboration, and no wonder he was eager to use the cinema as a forum for his ideas.

Short Story Scenario and Commentary

George McWhirter Fotheringay, a skeptical draper's assistant, suddenly finds

95

himself endowed with the power to work miracles. He first becomes aware of his "gift" in a pub when his mere word makes a candle invert in the air with its flame pointing down. After being ushered unceremoniously out of the pub, Fotheringay returns to his bedroom and discovers that he can, by word alone, raise candles, make a match appear in his hand, and light a lamp with no personal exertion. He also lifts a piece of paper, turns a glass of water pink and then green, creates a snail, and conjures forth a new toothbrush.

The next day, he reports for work at Gomshott's Drapery and spends most of the day musing about his new-found powers. That evening, he commands and causes roses to blossom on dry wood. When he unwittingly causes his walking stick to hit Constable Winch, he unsuccessfully tries to explain to the enraged lawman that he was merely working miracles. When Winch refuses the explanation, the frustrated Fotheringay cries "Go to Hades! Go, now!" To his surprise, Winch disappears. Feeling remorse that he has sent a man to Hell, Fotheringay reconsiders and sends Winch to San Francisco instead.

On Sunday after chapel, Fotheringay shares his story with Mr. Maydig, a preacher interested in occult matters. When Maydig is skeptical, Fotheringay causes a blue pigeon to appear and flutter about the room. He then conjures up a wonderful dinner for two and later successfully orders the religious conversion of Maydig's housekeeper. Maydig is then convinced that Fotheringay's powers are limitless, and he convinces Fotheringay to perform great miracles for society. At Maydig's suggestion, the two men take a walk during which Fotheringay reforms all the drunkards in the Parliamentary division, greatly improves railroad communications, drains a swamp, improves the soil, and cures the Vicar's wart.

When the clock strikes three, Fotheringay says that he must return home as time is running out for him to sleep before work on Monday. Maydig suggests that Fotheringay simply buy time by stopping the sun as Joshua did in the Bible. Fotheringay thoughtlessly complies, at which point the Earth stops revolving and everything on the planet, including Fotheringay, is cast into space. Having learned his lesson, Fotheringay, in flight, wishes everything back as it was before he discovered his great powers and asks that they leave him. Presto! He is back in the pub shortly before the time he commanded the candle to invert.

"The Man Who Could Work Miracles" is a delightful fantasy as Mr. Wells brings Mr. Fotheringay and other comic commoners to vivid life.

The Films

The Man Who Could Work Miracles (1936)   London Films, Great Britain / Running Time: 82 minutes

CREDITS: Produced by Alexander Korda; Directed by Lothar Mendes; Scenario and dialogue by H.G. Wells, based on his short story "The Man Who Could Work Miracles"; Set design by Vincent Korda; Cinematography by Harold Rosson; Music by Michael Splianski; Music directed by Muir Mathieson; Special effects by Ned Mann; Production managed by David B. Cunynchame; Edited by William Hornbeck; Recorded by A.W. Watkins; Assistant director—Imaly Watts.

CAST: Roland Young (George Fotheringay), Ralph Richardson (Colonel Winstanley), Edward Chapman (Major Grigsby), Ernest Thesinger (Maydig), Joan Gardner (Ada Price), Maggie Hooper (Sophie Stewart), Robert Cochran (Bill Stoker), Lady Tree (Grigsby's Housekeeper), George Zucco (The Colonel's Butler), Joan Hickson (Effie), Ivan Brandt (The Giver of Power), George Sanders.

Film Synopsis

A dispute breaks out among the demigods when the Giver of Power believes that his gift will help improve humanity. When challenged by two other demigods, the Giver grants unlimited power to a randomly chosen commoner, one George Fotheringay. When Fotheringay learns that he can make things happen by simply wishing them, he sets about experimenting with his startling new power. At first he practices in his room by making his lamp and bed move, and by conjuring up a kitten and then turning it into a pin cushion.

At work, Fotheringay makes a bouquet of flowers appear in the hand of Maggie Hooper, cures her sprained arm, and clears up a co-worker's complexion. Later, when accosted by a policeman, he commands that the officer "Go to blazes," but reconsiders and promptly rescues the cop from hell and sends him to San Francisco.

Fotheringay soon discovers that his powers are limited when he unsuccessfully tries to make Ada Price fall in love with him. She is no lamp or kitten!

As Fotheringay's reputation for miracles spreads, his boss and a banker try to acquire his services only for themselves in order to set up lucrative monopolies. When Fotheringay asks why he simply can't help everyone, he is told that things cannot be done that way because a world without need is only a dream.

Confused about how to use his power, Fotheringay asks the advice of Mr. Maydig, an advisor in religious and occult matters. At first, Maydig is credulous, but the appearance of a tiger in the parlor quickly convinces him that Fotheringay is the real deal. Acting on Maydig's suggestions, Fotheringay soon finds himself opposed by Colonel Winstanley, a boozing, blowhard military man whose solution to the Fotheringay problem is to shoot him.

Fotheringay foils Winstanley's plan, however, by wishing himself immortal. Further, he announces that a golden age is to begin that afternoon. True to his word, Fotheringay turns the Colonel's house into a palace with himself as all-powerful emperor. He takes Maggie as his queen and populates his world with pretty women. He then conjures forth the bankers, presidents, and bigwigs of the world and announces that from now on a common man will have power. Little men got very little when power was in the hands of the few, but that is about to change! War must end, he says, because you cannot shoot the truth! If some refuse to cooperate, Fotheringay promises that he will wipe them out with a word.

Wanting more time on this particular afternoon, Fotheringay orders that the "sun stop" as Joshua did in the Bible. Unfortunately, the earth stops rotating and everything on earth is flung into space. As he flies into sure oblivion, Fotheringay commands that he no longer have the power to work miracles and that the world return to its former state at the time he was given the power. The skeptical demigods are vindicated, but the Giver of Power reminds them that human beings were only yesterday apes. "Once an ape, always an ape," a demigod retorts. But the Giver replies that because human beings are godlike, they have the potential to gain wisdom along with power.

Adaptation

Wells' short story runs about seven thousand words; therefore, he considerably expands the story as a feature film adaptation. This he does by inventing a handfull of new characters: Ada Price, Maggie Hooper, Colonel Winstanley, and others. From the story comes, of course, the main characters of Mr. Fotheringay and Mr. Maydig, and the minor character of

Officer Winch. In the screenplay, Wells creates the demigods to account for Fotheringay's power, and he creates Colonel Winstanley, Major Grigsby, and the banker as personifications of Wells' philosophical enemies: capitalism and military conquest. The screenplay adapts all important elements of the story and ads quality elements needed for the film's feature length. All in all, this is a remarkably faithful adaptation.

Production and Marketing

The Man Who Could Work Miracles is the first of two collaborations between H.G. Wells and producer Alexander Korda, the other being *Things to Come. Man* was actually filmed first in 1936, followed by *Things*, but it was released after *Things* in 1937.

Hungarian-born Alexander Korda (1893–1956) is considered by many to be the man who saved British cinema. He formed London Films and made it successful with *The Private Lives of Henry VIII* (1932, with Charles Laughton). He then built Denham Studios and continued making fine and classic films for another twenty years.

British character actor Roland Young (1887–1953) headed the cast as George Fotheringay. Young made a career playing whimsical, diffident, and ineffectual characters. Among his other memorable films are *David Copperfield* (1934, as Uriah Heep), *Ruggles of Red Gap* (1934), *Topper* (1937), and *The Philadelphia Story* (1940).

Second-billed Sir Ralph Richardson (1902–1983) was one of Britain's most revered names on stage and screen. Among his many film successes are *Bulldog Jack* (1935), *South Riding* (1938), *The Four Feathers* (1939), *Anna Karenina* (1948), *The Fallen Idol* (1938), *The Heiress* (1939), *Richard III* (1956), *Oscar Wilde* (1960), *Long Day's Journey Into Night* (1962), *The*

Wrong Box (1966), and *Greystoke* (1984, for which he received an Academy Award nomination).

Ernest Thesinger (1879–1961) is best remembered today as Dr. Pretorius in *The Bride of Frankenstein* (1935), but he also brought his witty and sinister style to such fine outings as *The Old Dark House* (1932), *They Drive By Night* (1938), *The Man in the White Suit* (1952), and *Father Brown* (1954).

Appearing in small roles were George Sanders (1906–1972) and George Zucco (1886–1960). *The Man Who Could Work Miracles* features Sanders' first screen appearance. He would go on to star in such well-received films as *Lancer Spy* (1937), *The Saint* (series, 1939–1941), *Rebecca* (1940), *The Moon and Sixpence* (1942), *The Lodger* (1944), *The Picture of Dorian Gray* (1944), *A Scandal in Paris* (1946), *Forever Amber* (1947), *Lady Windermere's Fan* (1949), *All About Eve* (1950, for which he won an Academy Award), and *Village of the Damned* (1960).

Though George Zucco became typecast in horror/mystery films, he appeared in some memorable ones: *The Cat and the Canary* (1939), *The Hunchback of Notre Dame* (1939), *The Mummy's Hand* (1940), *The Adventures of Sherlock Holmes* (1940, as Moriarty), and others.

English character actor Edward Chapman (1901–1977) appeared in only a handful of films before *The Man Who Could Work Miracles*, but he would go on to make many fine films, including Wells' *Things to Come* (1936), *It Always Rains on Sunday* (1947) and *The Card* (1952).

American special-effects director Ned Mann (1893–1967) entered the film business in 1926 as an actor. He moved on to special effects, however, and perfected his methods over an impressive career which included such films as *Dirigible* (1930), *Madam Satan* (1930), *Deluge* (1933), *The Ghost Goes West* (1936), *Things to Come*

(1936), *The Thief of Bagdad* (1940), and *Around the World in Eighty Days* (1956). For *Deluge*, he constructed the New York City skyline that would be engulfed by a giant tidal wave. That skyline would be used again in *King Kong* (1933).

The Man Who Could Work Miracles received a big publicity push in both England and America. U.S. posters hyped "Roland Young in H.G. Wells' Comedy." This "film of imaginative comedy," as Wells described it, did well critically and financially.

Strengths

Though many positive things can be said about *The Man Who Could Work Miracles*, perhaps the highest compliment is that it is entertaining throughout. From the impressive opening credits to the ending, which brings us back to the picture's beginning, no one will be enticed to clock-watch. The demigods raise interesting questions about humanity's capacity to evolve responsibly, and the argument among themselves whet our appetite for a resolution. While Wells injects several of his socialist and anti-war ideas into the film, he is not heavy handed. For example, Fotheringay's foggy response to the banker and the businessman is handled humorously, as is the turning of the Colonel's weapon collection into farm implements. Of course, the comedy works partly because of the fine cast, Young and Richardson filling their roles perfectly. Young handles the transformation from timid salesman to frustrated tyrant believably, Richardson is humorously distasteful as the blow-hard Colonel, George Sanders is appropriately arrogant as a provocative demigod, and the usually urbane George Zucco successfully assumes a working class accent and demeanor as the Colonel's butler.

Wells' screenplay itself is excellent as he manages to adapt the short story faithfully without padding the film with irrelevancies to achieve feature length. He also successfully elevates the desire to entertain above the temptation to preach pro-socialist and anti-war perspectives. Viewers are certainly invited to consider such ideas, but they are not assaulted by them.

The film's musical score and cinematography are strong. Most memorable are the special effects of a tree blooming out of nowhere and the awesome spectacle of the end of the world. Though no special effects wonder, the sight of a befuddled bobby appearing in traffic out of nowhere on a crowded San Francisco street elicits a chuckle, as do many other endearing scenes.

The Man Who Could Work Miracles is a fine film indeed, the strengths strongly outweighing the weaknesses. So, will humanity eventually triumph over its shortcomings or will "once an ape, always an ape" prevail? Though generally pessimistic, the film leaves the door open for hope. Interestingly, it is Fotheringay's lack of scientific knowledge in foreseeing the consequences of his own actions that precipitates the end of the world. Wells seems to be saying that humanity must learn to harness power for construction rather than destruction. Humanity must allow knowledge and altruism to triumph over greed and callousness. Unfortunately, Fotheringay's general goodness is finally overpowered by the frustrations of dealing with self-centered power grabbers and money grubbers. Like the Time Traveller, the Angel (of *The Wonderful Visit*), Mr. Hoopdriver, Dr. Moreau, and Dr. Griffin, Fotheringay sets out to do good but finds himself under attack for his trouble. And like Moreau and Griffin, Fotheringay strives to be part of the solution but instead becomes part of the problem.

Weaknesses

One must be picky to identify obvious weaknesses in this film, but there are a few. Most obvious are the less-than-seamless special effects scenes in Fotheringay's room as the thrilled shopkeeper performs real magic tricks with the wave of his hand. Sometimes the split second between the stopped action and the appearance of some object is just noticeable enough to draw unwelcome attention. Another minor fault is Ernest Thesinger's tendency to overact, especially when projecting fear or amazement in close-up. But these flaws are minor and will not detract in any significant way from the film's overall effect.

Rating: 3½

7

The War of the Worlds (1898)

THE NOVEL

H.G. Wells seriously considered the possibility of life on Mars as early as 1893. According to Wells, a remark by his brother Frank suggested *The War of the Worlds* itself. While walking together on a peaceful day in Surrey, Frank wondered aloud what would happen if Earth were to be invaded by beings from another world. Perhaps the brothers had been discussing how the Europeans had discovered Tasmania and went about destroying its natives. Regardless, both brothers doubted that Earth could emerge victorious against such an invasion. At the time, Wells was writing short stories, but as he traveled the English countryside on his bicycle, he made geographical notes for what would become *The War of the Worlds*.

Later, Wells reported in *Strand Magazine*, Issue 59 (1920), that he tried to "keep everything within the bounds of possibility. And the value of the story to me lies in this, that from first to last there is nothing in it that is impossible." Be that as it may, most critics today believe that Wells had a tendency to make his early work seem more didactic than it really was. Wells was writing scientific romances, and he generally did not try for scientific accuracy in the tradition of Jules Verne. Still, *The War of the Worlds* is more potentially possible than any of his previous scientific romances. In addition, Wells ratchets up the level of violence. The skirmishes of *The Time Machine*, Dr. Moreau's vivisections, and the Invisible Man's "reign of terror" pale in comparison to the mass destruction and mutilations visited on humanity by the Martians.

Novel Scenario and Commentary

Toward the end of the nineteenth century, several English newspapers carry small accounts of a mass of flaming gas, chiefly hydrogen, originating on Mars and speeding toward Earth. Complacent humanity goes on its way, unconcerned and unaware that this seemingly innocuous event represents the beginning of the greatest danger ever to threaten the human race.

The narrator is told by his friend Ogilvy, an astronomer, about the approaching flash. Since he considers Mars uninhabited, Ogilvie suspects that a meteorite is approaching. Then the first "falling star" lands in the English countryside, creating a hole in a sand pit. In the pit lies a cylinder. A crowd gathers and notices that the cylinder is unscrewing. The cylinder is occupied by life!

As a larger crowd gathers, the top of the cylinder falls to the ground and a gray snake-like tentacle appears from within, followed by a grayish, rounded bulk rising slowly and painfully out of the cylinder. More monsters follow. A small group of men approach the pit waving a white flag, but a sudden flash of light shoots from the pit, destroying the "welcoming committee." The Martians possess a heat ray.

The narrator flees. A distant train passing convinces him that humanity has no idea what is happening. The narrator tries to warn people of the approaching danger, but they largely ignore him. He then returns home to his wife, momentarily calmed by the presumption that the Martians will be unable to leave the pit.

Meanwhile, however, the martians set about assembling giant tripods, walking engines of glittering metal capable of smashing everything in their path. Soon, more cylinders arrive on Earth, and the Martians open fire on English villages with their heat ray. The narrator and his wife borrow a horse and cart and flee the holocaust. Later, he drops her off with family in a nearby town and rides off to return the cart to its owner. As he drives through the stormy countryside, the horse bolts at the sight of an approaching tripod, spilling the narrator into a shallow pool of water. The tripod is joined by another, both controlled by Martians stationed in

Martian war machines attack in *The War of the Worlds* (1953).

the machine's heads. The narrator feels like a small animal that has just seen a steam engine for the first time.

The narrator learns from an artilleryman that the tripods are destroying England with their heat rays, wiping out troops of soldiers and artillery as though they were nothing. Later, the narrator finds out from his brother that London was at that time under heavy attack, and a warship called the Thunder Child was completely destroyed at sea by a Martian heat ray.

The narrator then holes up in a deserted house with a curate who thinks that the Martians are a punishment visited on humanity by God. The narrator does not share the curate's perspective but stays in the house with him since he knows nowhere safer at the moment. When a new cylinder falls near the house, the narrator and curate become prisoners in the wrecked kitchen for nine days. On the ninth day, the curate goes insane and tries to escape the house in order to preach the end times. Fearful of being discovered by the Martians, the narrator knocks the curate down with the butt of a meat-chopper. Then a metal tentacle slithers into the house and examines the head of the dead curate.

The narrator escapes into a coal cellar and closes the door behind him. Had the Martians seen him? The tentacle soon pushes open the door and slithers inside. As the narrator is on the verge of screaming, the tentacle, presumably to satisfy the Martians' curiosity, grips a lump of coal and withdraws. While the Martians are occupied, the narrator escapes.

The Martians have laid waste to the countryside. The narrator feels like one of the poor brutes dominated by humanity, like a rabbit, like an animal among animals under the Martian heel. Later the narrator comes upon a dusty, filthy man. It is the artilleryman again. But this time he is a man with a plan. "The war was never a war," he says, "no more than there is a war between human beings and ants. First, he says, the Martians will destroy all human weaponry and wreck the ships and railroads. Then they will probably make pets of some humans and teach them to do tricks. They might even train some humans to hunt the others. Humanity," he says, "must invent a life for itself underground so that people may breed and carry on guerilla warfare against the Martians. The weak will have to die and the strong must carry on." But the narrator soon realizes that the artilleryman's plans are folly, and the narrator staggers toward London in search of his wife.

When he enters the city, he hears a weird howling sound. Too exhausted to continue, he collapses in a pub and sleeps. When he wakes, he walks into the street and notices that the howling has suddenly ceased. The sound had come from the heads of the giant tripods. Now the death machines lay silent, the Martians dead. They have been slain by disease bacteria against which their systems were totally unprepared. They have been killed by the humblest things that God in his wisdom had put upon the earth.

When people begin their return to London, the narrator finds his wife unharmed. He concludes that the Martian invasion was not without benefit, for humanity has learned that the earth is not a fenced in and secure place, and they have learned that, faced with a common danger or cause, all men are brothers.

The narrator, the curate, and the artilleryman may be viewed as three stages in Wells' own development. The curate's scriptural response hearkens back to Wells' boyhood when he was under the thumb of his mother's version of Christianity. The narrator's intellectual and moral response parallels that of Wells at the time he wrote *The War of the Worlds*, and the artilleryman's survivalist-authoritarian response predicts the future H.G. Wells. Though Wells treats the curate without respect, the narrator himself is not anti-religious. He prays at times and uses Biblical allusions to describe the Martians' demise.

There are several ways to interpret *The War of the Worlds*. Certainly the book reflects common Victorian *fin de siecle* concerns—the possibility of foreign invasion and the fear of social dissolution—themes we see addressed in Wells' earlier *The Time Machine*. Darwinian and Huxlian influences are also present, especially Darwin's "survival of the fittest" and Huxley's insistence that because there is no guarantee of progress, Victorian England could ill afford complacency. Critic Mark Rose suggests that the vampiric Martians represent capitalist industrialist blood-suckers who pray upon society.

First published in serial form in 1897, *The War of the Worlds* went through several important revisions, culminating in the authoritative Atlantic edition of 1924 and the Essex edition of 1927. It received good reviews and is widely regarded today as one of Wells' finest novels.

THE FILMS

The War of the Worlds (1953)   Paramount, U.S.A. / Running Time: 85 minutes / Release Date: March 2, 1953

CREDITS: Produced by George Pal; Directed by Byron Haskin; Screenplay by Barre Lyndon, from the novel *The War of the Worlds* by H.G. Wells; Art direction by Al Nozaki and Hal Pereira; Astronomical art by Chesley Bonestell; Makeup by Wally Westmore; Cinematography by George Barnes; Special Effects by Gordon Jennings, Wallace Kelley, Chester Pate, Bob Springfield, Eddie Sutherland, Paul Lerpae, Aubrey Law, Jack Caldwell, and Ivyl Burks; Mattes and paintings by Jan Demila,

Irmin Roberts, and Walter Hoffman; Edited by Everett Douglas; Sound by Gene Garvin and Harry Lindgren; Sound edited by Lovell Norman; Music by Leith Stevens; Technical Advisor—Dr. Robert Richardson; Technicolor color consultant—Monroe W. Burbank; Assistant director—Michael D. Moore; Costumes by Edith Head; Set decoration by Sam Comer and Emile Kuri; Associate producer—Frank Freeman, Jr.

CAST: Gene Barry (Dr. Clayton Forrester), Ann Robinson (Sylvia Van Buren), Les Tremayne (General Mann), Robert Cornwaithe (Dr. Pryor), Sandro Giglio (Dr. Bilderbeck), Lewis Martin (Pastor Matthew Collins), Bill Phipps (Wash Perry), Paul Birch (Alonzo Hogue), Jack Kruschen (Salvatore), Vernon Rich (Colonel Hefner), House Stevenson, Jr. (General Mann's Aide), Paul Frees (Announcer and Opening Narration), Henry Brandon (Cop), Cedric Hardwick (Narrator), Carolyn Jones (Bird-brained blonde), Pierre Cressoy (Man), Nancy Hale (Young Wife), Virginia Hall (Girl), Charles Gemora (Martian), Walter Sande (Sheriff), Alex Frazer (Dr. Hettinger), Ann Codee (Dr. DuPrey), Ivan Lebedeff (Dr. Gratzman), Robert Rockwell (Ranger), Alvy Moore (Zippy), Frank Kreig (Fiddler Hawkins), John Maxwell (Doctor), Ned Glass (Well-dressed Man with Satchel of Cash), Russell Conway (Reverend Bethany), George Pal and Frank Freeman, Jr. (Bums Listening to Radio).

Film Scenario

It is the middle of the twentieth century. A fireball from the sky creates a crater near Linda Rosa, California, about thirty miles east of Los Angeles. A crowd gathers, and someone suggests that a group of scientists camping and fishing nearby be notified. Dr. Clayton Forrester, an astronuclear physicist, drives to the site and meets Sylvia Van Buren, a young woman who knows and respects his work, and her uncle, Pastor Collins. Forrester remarks that if the thing in the crater is a meteor it exhibits rather strange characteristics. The object in the crater is too hot to approach, so Forrester accepts an invitation to a square dance in town. That night, as the dance commences, three men camp near the crater to keep watch. They are startled to see the top of the "meteor" unscrew and a metal stalk rise up before them. The three men decide to approach the stalk with a white flag of peace. The metal stalk ticks and hisses. When it notices the men, it throbs and then destroys them with a heat ray.

When Forrester and the police reach the scene, they see the scorched outlines of the three men on the ground. The heat ray again strikes, destroying a car as it races away. Another cylinder falls from the sky, and Forrester and the police call for the military. When the military arrives, General Mann brings word that cylinders have fallen during the night in Santiago, London, and Naples. The Linda Rosa cylinder was the pilot ship. Planes drop flares over the crater for a better look, but the heat ray demolishes the planes, and all is quiet once again.

In the morning, Martian ships rise up from the crater. Pastor Collins goes out to meet them alone in an attempt to communicate. As he walks, he carries his Bible and quotes from the Twenty-Third Psalm. Before he can make contact, however, the heat ray destroys him. The military opens fire, and the Martian ships surround themselves with a transparent protective shield and proceed to wipe out soldiers and artillery. The war has begun.

The Martian ships are on the move, causing both humans and "lower" animals to flee in terror. Forrester and Sylvia take flight in a small army observation plane but soon crash. They make their way to a farmhouse where they fix something to eat and quietly talk. Sylvia relates that she feels like she did when as a little girl she got lost and took refuge in a church, praying that the person who loved her best would find her. It was Pastor Collins who found her, and now he is dead.

Suddenly a cylinder crashes into the farmhouse and Martian ships emerge to scout the area. Sylvia is startled to see a short, toad-like Martian move quickly past a window. Then a mechanical arm with a three-lensed viewing head slithers into the ruined farmhouse. Forrester chops the head from the arm, which slithers back into the ship. As Forrester and Sylvia wait for the Martians' next move, a long three-fingered hand grasps her shoulder. It is a Martian, and Forrester makes it cringe from the ray of a flashlight. He injures the Martian, which bleeds as it flees the farmhouse. Sylvia momentarily becomes hysterical, but Forrester brings her to her senses and suggests that they run.

Meanwhile the unstoppable Martians are destroying humanity around the globe. Large populations flee: "It was the beginning of the rout of civilization, the massacre of humanity." The White House authorizes use of an atomic bomb, but that too proves ineffective. As an analysis of Martian blood reveals, the only apparent weakness the invaders have is a weak immune system. Still, General Mann and Forrester try to remain hopeful.

A bus of scientists attempts to leave the chaos. Forrester becomes separated from the others when his vehicle is stopped and stolen by the mob. Society has dissolved, and panicked people fight each other for any means of leaving the city. The Martian ships move into Los Angeles, the heat rays destroying everything in their path. Forrester searches for Sylvia in the only place he thinks she would go: a church. Finally he finds her among others in a church, and they hug one another as death approaches.

Suddenly the destruction ceases and the city becomes quiet. The people leave the church to see the Martian ships grind to a halt. The same scene is repeated around the world. The Martians are dead or dying, the victims of bacteria, germs to which Earthlings had long been immune. The people had prayed for a miracle, and their prayers were answered.

Adaptation

In deviating from Wells' novel, Barre Lyndon's screenplay changes the setting from England to Southern California, U.S.A. This was because of the numerous UFO sighting reported there in the early fifties. Second, Lyndon deletes the curate and the artilleryman, allowing Sylvia to replace them as Forrester's focus companion. The narrator of the novel, by the way, is never named, and he is not a scientist as Forrester is. The narrator loses track of his wife early in the novel and is not reunited with her until the end. Pal wanted to follow this scenario, but production head Don Hartman insisted that audiences be appeased with a boy-meets-girl love interest. Later, Pal wisely repudiated this script change. The deletion of the curate and the artilleryman guts several of Wells' important themes—the ineffectual religious response and the survivalist (yet all too human) response to the possible destruction of humanity. Hollywood rarely encourages audiences to grapple with challenging ideas as part of their entertainment, and *The War of the Worlds* is no exception.

Lyndon's original screenplay featured a Burbank test pilot named Greg Bagley, who, as the son of a headstrong oil man, is engaged to Sylvia Delano, the arrogant daughter of an orange grower. Financial disagreements between the orange growers and the oil man lead to a Shakespearean Romeo and Juliet conflict. Pal liked that screenplay, but rejected it due to various technical reasons. Revisions led to the version that appears on screen.

In the film, the Martians are no longer tentacled gray bulks. They are somewhat smaller than human beings, and they have (three) fingers with suction cups, two arms, an over-sized head, and humanoid legs. On their face is a bulging three-lensed eye. Of course, there were no tanks or atomic bombs when Wells wrote the novel, but there were when the tale was filmed.

In many ways, Lyndon's screenplay is faithful to the novel. The curious crowds that gather at the crater site, the cold-blooded destruction of the initial peacemakers and the parson, the utter failure of the armed services, the fleeing mobs, the dissolution of society, and humanity's inability even to slow down the invasion are quite Wellsian. In both book and film we sense a strong atmosphere of impending doom. The fleeing animals in the film parallel the narrator's identification with the "lower" animals in the novel, emphasizing the theme of biological Darwinism. The bacterial demise of the Martians is also directly from the novel. Though Wells was an atheist, his narrator prays and implies that nothing but a miracle could have stopped the Martians. Still, Wells' main point is that progress is never assured. The Martians die as a result of their advanced science. Having destroyed bacteria on Mars, they evolve and lose their immunity and succumb to earth bacteria. The death of the Martians stands as a warning to Earthlings.

Production and Marketing

On the night of October 30, 1938, Orson Welles and John Houseman presented another episode of their struggling radio program *Mercury Theatre on the Air*. This night, they had chosen to dramatize H.G. Wells' *The War of the Worlds*. Instead of doing an obvious dramatization, Welles and Houseman wanted it done as a simulated live news broadcast. The result was a national panic as a musical program was interrupted to announce an invasion from

An original one-sheet poster for *The War of the Worlds* (1953)

outer space. People tuning in late had no idea that Wells' commentary was anything other than that of a newsman covering an alien invasion live. Without a doubt, the prospect of a Martian invasion proved frightening! So how could the cinema exploit that fact?

In 1925, Cecil B. DeMille planned an epic film based on *The War of the Worlds,* but the project was never realized. Undaunted, George Pal put *The War of the Worlds* on his agenda shortly after arriving at Paramount. He had won Academy Awards for his productions of *Destination Moon* (1950) and *When Worlds Collide* (1951). For further background on George Pal see Production and Marketing for *The Time Machine* (1960).

Pal had spent $186,000 producing *Destination Moon* and $936,000 for *When Worlds Collide.* Mostly due to the nature of its special effects, *The War of the Worlds* would require the substantial sum of $2,000,000. The special effects alone took six months, plus an additional two months for optical effects after regular shooting. No wonder about half the picture consists of some form of special effects. The cast worked a comparatively short forty days in the studio and on location in Arizona and Los Angeles.

The Martian was created by unit art director Albert Nozaki under the supervision of art director Hal Pereira. Nozaki built the Martian out of paper-mache and sheet rubber. He made arms that pulsated as a result of interior rubber tubing. Then he painted the whole creature lobster red. Though a great amount of work went into creating the Martian, it appears only for a fleeting few seconds in the film.

Sculptor, makeup man, and artist Charles Gemora (1903–1961), who had played a gorilla in *The Gorilla* (1939) and *At the Circus* (1939), operated the Martian while on his knees inside the suit. Later, the short-statured Gemora would don suits in films such as *Phantom of the Rue Morgue* (1954, again as a gorilla), *I Married a Monster from Outer Space* (1958), and *Jack the Giant Killer* (1962).

Pal went back to Wells for the model of the Martian crafts. Wells' crafts were mechanical tripods, but Pal decided on going electrical. The first plan was to generate a million volts of electricity down the legs of miniatures on the sound stage in order to create legs of pulsating static electricity. A high velocity blower would be used from behind to force sparks down the legs. The crew soon realized that, unfortunately, sparks from the million volts could fall about the stage, possibly killing someone or setting the studio on fire.

After the test opening scene, the crew gave up on the electrical legs. They scaled the machine down to one sixth regular size for the shooting and built three copper miniatures, forty-two inches in diameter, so as to retain the reddish hue. The result was flat, disc-shaped crafts with long necks. On the necks were a television-like scanner from which came the deadly heat rays. Fifteen hair-fine wires connected to an overhead device operated each machine. The triple-lensed scanner was actually thick plastic with hexagonal holes cut in, behind which were rotating light shutters which provided a flickering effect. To avoid a disconcerting effect as we get when wagon wheels seem to go faster and then slower when they conflict with a camera's shutter speed, the crew carefully regulated the shutter speed behind the head. The fire rays themselves were created by burning welding wire. A blow torch blew the melting wire outward.

More than one thousand sketches were prepared before shooting began, showing how the various special effects would appear. When shooting began on a rainy January day in 1952, the once rough sketches had become polished works of art inserted in the script to guide director Haskin and cinematographer Barnes.

In striving for believability, the crew constructed large, lifelike models of Los Angeles. The City Hall, for example, stood eight feet tall. To add believability to the evacuation scenes in Los Angeles, a camera crew rushed to a real traffic jam on the new Hollywood freeway. In addition, a check with Civil Defense Authorities allowed the crew to use the latest emergency techniques.

In the Los Angeles invasion, live action, special effects, and optical effects were extensively mixed. For example, the crew photographed a street on Paramount's back lot. They then matched the photo with a handful of ectachrome stills of Bunker Hill in downtown Los Angeles. These were then rephotographed on Technicolor film. Then, Paul Lerpae reduced a hand-painted eight by ten matte blowup of sky, background, flame effects, and Martian machines to regulation 35 mm film frame size.

The optical effects department painted between three and four thousand celluloid frames. The memorable scene of an army colonel being disintegrated by the heat wave required one hundred forty-four mattes of his inked-in body.

The scenes in which the army and Martians attack one another required great preparation. First, live action scenes were shot with cast and National Guard on location near Phoenix, Arizona. The outfit went through maneuvers for two days while cameras rolled. The special effects team then created matte shots of trees and a command post, as well as miniatures of a gully where the actors could hide. Finally the rays, explosions, and bright yellowish foreground explosions were inserted. At times, the crew made as many as twenty-eight different exposures to produce one color scene.

The atomic bomb explosion was engineered on the sound stage by powder expert Walter Hoffman, who placed colored explosive powders atop an air-tight metal drum filled with explosive gas. The ensuing mushroom cloud reached a height of seventy-five feet. Army clearance was needed for use of footage featuring the Flying Wing, which in the film drops the atomic bomb on the Martians.

Artist Chesley Bonestell, who had worked with Pal on *Destination Moon* and *When Worlds Collide*, produced the paintings of planets in our solar system shown during the prologue with voice over by Sir Cedric Hardwick. For further information on Hardwick, see Production and Marketing under *The Invisible Man Returns* (1940)

The Martian scream was produced by dry ice scraped across a microphone combined with a woman's high scream recorded backwards. The vibrating noise of the Martian machines was created by a magnetic recorder. The sound of the Martians' death ray was actually amplified chords struck on three guitars played backwards and reverbrated.

Since most of the film's budget went to special effects, Pal used no big names in his cast. Considered first was Lee Marvin, but eventually playing Dr. Forrester is the poised and debonair Gene Barry (1921–). At the time of *The War of the Worlds*, he had starred in *The Atomic City* (1952) and *The Girls of Pleasure Island* (1952). Barry would go on to appear in a few fine films such as *Red Garters* (1954), *Naked Alibi* (1954) and *Thunder Road* (1958), but he is best remembered today for *The War of the Worlds* and for starring roles on television series such as *Bat Masterson* (1958–1960), *Burke's Law* (1963–1965), and *The Name of the Game* (1968–1970).

Ann Robinson made her film debut in *The War of the Worlds*. She was finishing a stage production called *Wind Without Rain* when she took and passed a

Paramount screentest. To calm the studio's fears that her short hair style would date the picture, she reluctantly donned a wig with long curls. Miss Robinson said that everyone got along well on the set and that she had no particular memories. She did, however, speak with praise of those Martian war machines which tremendously impressed her. She was disappointed, though, because in some scenes the supporting strings are visible.

Paramount launched an impressive marketing campaign for *The War of the Worlds*, including a mammoth pressbook and a paperback tie-in of Wells' novel featuring cover art of the Martian war machines. Poster art and newspaper ads usually focused on the Martian three-fingered hand, reaching through space to terrify Earth. One rare half sheet poster fabulously depicted the Martian war machines in action.

A fire destroyed George Pal's collection of *War of the Worlds* memorabilia. What an attraction that material would be today! *The War of the Worlds* was re-released with Pal's *When Worlds Collide* in the late 1970s.

British playright and screenwriter Barre Lyndon (1896–1972) had distinguished himself as the author of *The Lodger* (1944), *The Man in Half Moon Street* (1944, based on his original play and later remade by Hammer as *The Man Who Could Cheat Death*), *Night Has a Thousand Eyes* (1948) and *The Greatest Show on Earth* (1951). He would go on to write the screenplay for Pal's *Conquest of Space* (1954), a much less successful film than *The War of the Worlds*.

One note of trivia: in the scene in which two bums are seen listening to a radio broadcast, those bums are George Pal and Byron Haskins in a scene lifted from *When Worlds Collide*.

Strengths

We must begin with the excellent special effects, almost all of which remain impressive and effective fifty years later. We might be able to see some strings in a scene or two, but we are usually too involved in the oncoming Martian invasion to notice. The solar system paintings are accurate and excellently rendered, the Martian hardware is awesome, and the miniatures dwarf all other 1950s efforts in quality. The film often takes on a newsreel quality, e.g. the shots of foreign nations under attack and the evacuation of Los Angeles.

Though some critics assail the film's decision to make the Martians appear invincible, this doesn't lessen the excitement and tension. Almost sure death does create tension and excitement. I cannot help but wonder what my reaction would have been had I watched every human attempt at stopping the Martians end in dismal failure. Would surrender be the answer? I don't think so. Few organisms surrender voluntarily to death. Here is where Wells' artilleryman would have come in handy. While his plan involved surrender to the Martians on the earth's surface, he envisioned guerilla resistance from below. Anyway, the Martian invasion gives humanity a taste of its own philosophy toward the rest of the animal kingdom—dominate and subdue, if not utterly destroy. If one can imagine how cows feel as they are herded into a slaughterhouse, then one can empathize with Forrester and Sylvia as they wait in the church for almost sure death at the hands of the Martians.

Some have criticized the screenplay in that Forrester spends what may be his last hours of life searching for a young woman that he only recently met. As Bill Warren points out in his book *Keep Watching the Skies!*, people do form close relationships during times of crisis, and isn't this a time of crisis? The relationship between Forrester and Sylvia is made believable in two scenes: In the first, Sylvia cradles Forrester in her arms after their plane crash. As the sounds of war reverbrate in the distance, he undergoes a re-evaluation of his life perspectives. He begins to change. Then, during breakfast in their soon-to-be-attacked house, Sylvia talks to Forrester of her childhood fears, and Forrester, possibly for the first time, understands real fear and connects on a primal level with another human being. Forrester is touched, and he cares. As Warren points out, Forrester, unlike most fifties science fiction film leading men, changes during the film. He begins as a self-absorbed scientist and ends as someone who cares about another human being as much as he cares about himself. Too much, too fast? Not under the circumstances. This is one of the film's many strengths. Chalk that up to a strength of Barre Lyndon's screenplay.

The War of the Worlds is an expert blending of sight and sound. Characterization does receive second billing, but, unlike several science fiction epics of the nineties, there is enough characterization there to make us care about the fate of the principle characters.

One repeated criticism of the film is its emphasis on religion. The Martians have already killed the three peacemakers who approached, but then they kill Pastor Collins, who represents no threat. Is this to show that the Martians are no closer to the creator, regardless of their technological superiority? The point is the Martians care not for religion, morality, or for anything else other than the power delegated to those with biological, evolutionary superiority. This is pure Wells! The scene is needed. It is a strength.

Now, as the film progresses, the only hope humanity has is God, and this production of *The War of the Worlds* implies

that God exists, and when weak believers are attacked by strong non-believers, God will intervene. But the ending is ambiguous. The screenplay sets up the notion that the Martians are biologically deficient due to advanced technology that destroyed all the harmful bacteria on their planet. The film finale gives us church bells ringing. Earthlings, and fifties audiences, accept the intervention of God, but did God intervene, or did humanity escape due to a biological miscalculation on the part of the Martians? The ringing bells reassure believers of the fifties, but the scientific explanation leaves the possibility of another alien invasion made stronger by knowledge of the Martian failure. Though Wells was an atheist, the narrator of *The War of the Worlds* prays, and from a believer's perspective, his prayers are answered. The film preserves this ambiguity.

The War of the Worlds is one of the five best science fiction films of the 1950s, as well as one of the top fifteen science fiction films of all time. Wells is generally well served by the production. Pal and Haskins turn a great novel into a great film, and Wells would be suitably impressed by the outcome.

Weaknesses

The only real weakness of the film was budgetary. Paramount could not afford a top-notch cast. Ann Robinson became a better actress than she was in *The War of the Worlds*, but at that time she turned in a mediocre performance. For example, when she connects Pastor Collins' rescue of her as a child in the church with his recent death, she responds as though directed to feel first awareness and then sorrow. In other words, she goes through the paces. That scene, by the way, was the one Robinson did with Barry as her screen test for the film.

Gene Barry was never a great actor,

but he was usually a good one. *The War of the Worlds* was one of his first starring efforts, and he isn't bad. For example, his transition from self-centered scientist to love-driven human being is impressive. Still, it is weakness for *The War of the Worlds* that he is better on television as Bat Masterson and Amos Burke.

The screenplay offers some effective humor, but when General Mann opines from his foxhole that the Martians will probably move at dawn, we immediately, and inappropriately, think of Indians moving against the U.S. cavalry. Science fiction should move us conceptually forward, not backward.

As Michael Wolff points out in a *Starlog* article, the film suffers from a few inconsistencies, errors, and anomalies. For example, why do the Earthlings immediately assume that the cylinder is from outer space in general and from Mars in particular? There is no scientific corroboration for that conclusion in the film. Since the aliens come prepared with protective shields around their ships, why do they fail to wear personal protective gear on occasions when they disembark and explore? They don't even wear run-of-the-mill spacesuits! When the armed forces drop an atomic bomb on the ships, the radiation does not damage the ships because it cannot penetrate the protective shields. Still, we know sunlight can penetrate the shields because we can not see the ships within—and if sunlight can penetrate, so can atomic radiation. But these are small matters indeed.

Rating: 3½

8

The First Men in the Moon (1901)

THE NOVEL

Following the success of *The War of the Worlds*, H.G. Wells published *When the Sleeper Wakes* (1899) and *Tales of Space and Time*. In 1900 he built Spade House in Sandgate, Kent, and published *Love and Mr. Lewisham*, which he had completed the previous year. Wells' first child, G.P. ("Gip") was born in 1901, the same year he published *The First Men in the Moon*.

Jules Verne had published a moon voyage novel in 1865, but Wells was unimpressed by the story's lack of scientific foundation. Wells originally serialized *The First Men in the Moon* in the *Strand* as three unconnected short stories. When the editor asked Wells for an extension, he complied and produced seven more chapters, and later even more. The original mood was less serious than the resulting 1901 novel.

In his preface to the novel for the later Atlantic Edition, Wells called *The First Men in the Moon* "an imaginative spree," that was probably his best scientific romance.

Novel Scenario and Commentary

Scientist Cavor convinces his neighbor, Bedford, the novel's narrator, to accompany him on a trip to the moon. Cavor has discovered a substance named Cavorite that can screen out the force of gravity just as other substances can screen out light or heat. The two men leave Earth in a spherical vehicle covered with adjustable screens of Cavorite.

The travellers land on the dark, cold moon during the night and have to wait until daylight to begin investigations. When the lunar day arrives, what once looked like mounds of snow turn to mist at the touch of a sunbeam. The arctic character of the moon is transformed by the sunlight, and exotic plants begin to grow, their life cycle apparently corresponding to the lunar day. Since growing plants signify oxygen, the travellers leave their sphere to investigate the new environment. On the moon's surface, lack of gravity allows them to cross long distances at a skip as they marvel at the plush vegetation growing up all around them.

They stop to rest a few minutes and suddenly realize with terror that the sphere has disappeared. Then they feel a dull pounding beneath their feet. As one strange experience follows another, the travellers are stunned by the sight of an enormous moon-calf. Even more strange, behind the moon-calf walks a humanoid ant creature, herding the moon-calf before it. Cavor explains that the ant-man is a Selenite.

The travellers soon discover an open lid in the moon's surface that leads down into blackness. Cavor speculates that the Selenites must live in this cavern during the night and emerge during the day.

After lunching on a mushroom, the travellers become drugged and are taken captive by several Selenites. They awake in a cavern, chained together. They are fed by the Selenites, unchained, and goaded into a larger chamber. There they see a machine for making liquid light. Bedford breaks his chains and strikes one of the guards, who is sent spinning. The flimsy Selenites prove no physical match for the travellers, who escape into some other part of the underground dwelling. From behind a ledge they watch as Selenites butcher a moon-calf. Soon the travellers are pursued by spear-carrying Selenites intent on their destruction. Again, however, the Selenites prove relatively ineffective against the stronger and quicker Earthlings. Fleeing once again, the travellers emerge from a tunnel into the sunlight of the surface.

The two men become separated, and Bedford finds the sphere. Unable to locate Cavor, Bedford leaves the moon for Earth just as terrible nightfall descends upon the moon's surface. Months after returning to Earth, Bedford receives word from a Dutch scientist about messages being received from the moon. The messenger is Cavor, who describes a great lunar sea and an immense network of caverns in the moon. There is the Grand Lunar, the master of the moon, who has questioned Cavor about the governments of the Earth and about war. Cavor, however, realizes that he was wrong to inform the Grand Lunar of Earth's warlike tendencies and his messages immediately cease—to be replaced by endless silence.

In *The First Men in the Moon*, Wells returns to concerns he raised in *The Time Machine*. Like the Morlocks, the Selenites dwell underground and go to the surface out of necessity or when weather conditions allow. The Morlocks represent the result of evolution on uncontrolled masses of workers. The Selenites, however, are different because the Grand Lunar has matters well under control. The Selenites are "educated" to perform some specialized task in the moon's economy. They are kept ignorant of general knowledge. They are workers controlled by scientific management in Saint-Simon's world industrial state. They are the means of specialized production envisioned by Auguste Compte when he wrote that in the future there will be no immoral concept of individual rights, only duties, no private persons, only state functionaries at various levels. After the pessimistic thinking that foundationed his previous scientific romances, Wells intends the managed lunar society to reflect a sort of possible utopia. *The First Men in the Moon* is a transitional novel. It ends Wells' early pessimistic period and begins a period of optimism based on hopes of scientific management.

Again Plato's influence is evident. In the *Republic*, Plato called for Guardian teachers, whose function is propaganda, and Guardian soldiers, whose function is coercion. The citizens are the producers, and their function is obedience. The guardians operate according to wisdom and force, and the citizens operate according to desire. Wells modifies this system in the light of Saint-Simon, bypasses the Marxist ideology of the Soviets, and suggests what he would call The

Council of World Direction in *The Shape of Things to Come*, which we will discuss further when considering that particular novel and the film it generated.

THE FILMS

Le Voyage dans la Lune (1902) aka *A Trip to the Moon*, aka *A Trip to Mars*

Star, France / Running Time: 21 minutes

CREDITS: Produced and Directed and written by Georges Méliès, inspired by *From the Earth to the Moon* by Jules Verne and *The First Men in the Moon* by H.G. Wells.

CAST: George Méliès (Professor Barbenfouillis), Victor Andre, Bleutte Bernon, Depierre, Farjaux, Corps de Ballet du Chatelet.

Film Synopsis

The Scientific Congress of the Astronomic Club accepts Professor Barbenfouillis' plan to explore the moon. After a large gun or cannon is cast in the foundry, the astronauts enter a space shell and are fired by the cannon into space. The shell lands directly in the right eye of the Man in the Moon. The astronauts leave the shell and observe the Earth from the Moon. A snowstorm starts, and the astronauts take refuge in a crater leading to the interior of the moon. There, they find a grotto where giant mushrooms grow. To their surprise, they are taken captive by Selenites, who take the astronauts before their King. The astronauts escape and realize that they can easily overpower the Selenites, who vanish into smoke when struck. The astronauts find their shell again and literally drop off the edge of the moon and down into Earth's sea. They marvel at the wonders of ocean life, are rescued by ship and returned to Paris. The returning heroes are treated to a parade and decorated by the Mayor, who honors them with a commemorative statue.

Adaptation

The first part of the film is fairly true to Verne's novel in which astronauts enter a shell and are fired to the moon by a giant cannon. From that point, the plot is that of *The First Men in the Moon*. We get Wells' lunar snowstorm, moon crater, underground caverns, mushrooms, Selenites, and the moon king. The celluloid Selenites prove no more a match for the Earthlings than did those of Wells' novel. In fact, Méliès' Selenites vanish in a puff of smoke when hit (or when bodyslammed, as occurs on one occasion).

While Wells took great pains to make his novel scientifically accurate, the film exhibits no such interest, and, of course, none of Wells' social concerns find their way into this 21 minute silent film. For Méliès, all is fun and fantasy.

Production and Marketing

French director Georges Méliès (1861–1938) produced the cinema's first trick films. While the pioneering Lumiere brothers were content showing workers emerging from a factory or with one minute comedies, Méliès, a former stage magician, was the pioneer who best showed how cinema could bring the magical and fantastical to life. Some of his earliest works included *Une Partie de Cartes* (1896), *The Artist's Dream* (1898), *The Dreyfuss Affair* (1899), *Cinderella* (1899) and *Indiarubber Head* (1900), but it was *Le Voyage dans le Lune* that broke remarkable new ground. First, the film runs about 21 minutes, compared to the one or two minute running times of its contemporaries. As such, it is the cinema's first science fiction epic. And contemporary audiences were astonished.

The film was first shown publicly in a small film theater on the fairgrounds of the Place du Trone in Paris. Méliès himself quickly produced a poster featuring the man in the moon with the shell penetrating his eye. Prints of the film quickly spread from Europe to America where it was pirated as *A Trip to Mars*. Thereafter, Méliès took pains to copyright his films.

Méliès went on to direct and produce many more magical films before his era of dominance ended about 1907. His most notable film after *Le Voyage dans la Lune* is undoubtedly *The Conquest of the Pole* (1912), which contains one of the most grotesque scenes in the silent cinema.

Before England produced a version of *The First Men in the Moon* in 1964, apparently a version of the novel was released in 1919. According to John Baxter's book, *Science Fiction in the Cinema*, the film, which added a love triangle, was criticized by one contemporary viewer for its "inadequate" special effects work.

Strengths

Méliès lets us know early that his film is a comedic fantasy. The sets, which we study with admiration, are obviously sets, yet the illusion of depth and contrast is maintained throughout. After the blastoff, the camera takes us increasingly closer to the moon until we are inventively shown the face of the man in the moon. The shell plunging into the moon's eye remains the film's most memorable moment. The "undersea" and moon cavern sets are appropriately otherworldly, and the Selenites are interesting and Wellsian enough.

Méliès keeps matters light as chorus line dancers perform at the shell's launching. Later, as the astronauts try to sleep on the moon's surface, girls' faces appear in the stars overhead, an old man peeks out from behind Saturn, and a chorus girl sitting on a crescent precipitates a snowstorm! The battle with the Selenites has all the thrills of a modern pro wrestling match, including a moment when an astronaut bodyslams the lunar king!

In *Le Voyage dans la Lune*, George Méliès uses everything at the disposal of a turn-of-the-century producer/director, and he uses it all inventively to offer up a quite entertaining science fiction romp. The pace is fast, the visuals are always engaging, and what the cinema might later visually achieve is promised here in miniature. This film was *the* undisputed classic of its decade, and it remains engrossing even today.

Weaknesses

It is not quite fair to judge Méliès by today's standards, but we can see in his films a tendency to let trick photography carry the entire production. This was true, of course, of other directors at the turn of the century. Later, Méliès' reliance on trick photography fell into disfavor when studios began adding character development and ideas to their plots. Obviously, Méliès had little time to develop character or examine ideas, but his approach can to some extent be viewed as a harbinger of what has happened in recent decades when special effects have tended to be the *raison d'etre* of high-budget, low-imagination science fiction films.

Rating: 3

The First Men in the Moon (1964)
Columbia, Great Britain/ U. S. A. / Release Date: August 4, 1964 (Great Britain) / Running Time: 102 minutes

CREDITS: Produced by Charles H. Schneer; Associate Producer—Ray Harryhausen; Directed by Nathan Juran; Screenplay by Nigel Kneale and Jan Read, from the novel by H.G. Wells. Cinematography by Wilkie Cooper; Special Effects by Ray Harryhausen; Music by Laurie Johnson; Production Manager—Ted Wallis; Art Direction by John Blezard; Edited by Maurice Rootes; Technical

Staff—Les Bowie and Kit West; Camera operated by Harry Gillam. Assistant Director—George Pollard; Continuity by Eileen Head; Sound recorded by Buster Ambler and Red Law; Title designed by Sam Suliman; Technical Advisor—Arthur Garratt; Filmed in Dynamation; Lunacolor by Pathé.

CAST: Edward Judd (Arnold Bedford), Lionel Jeffries (Cavor), Martha Hyer (Kate Callender), Erik Chitty (Gibbs), Betty McDowall (Maggie), Miles Malleson (Registrar), Lawrence Herder (Glushkov), Gladys Henson (Matron), Marne Maitland (Dr. Tok), Hugh McDermott (Challis), Gordon Robinson (U.N. Astronaut Martin), Sean Kelly (U.N. Astronaut Col. Rice), John Murray Scott (U.N. Astronaut Nevsky).

Film Synopsis

A successful United Nations landing on the moon finds evidence of an earlier landing. U.N. Moon Project representatives investigate and find aging Arnold Bedford, who insists he made the moon journey 65 years before. Bedford tells his story:

In 1899, in a small Kentish village, Bedford and his fiancée Kate Callender meet Joseph Cavor, a research scientist who has created Cavorite, an anti-gravity substance which he plans to use on a trip to the moon. Bedford, an aspiring playright, agrees to accompany Cavor to the moon in hopes of gaining riches.

Cavor constructs a sphere for space travel and walls it with Cavorite. When he and Bedford are awaiting take-off, Kate enters the sphere complaining about a court summons and is trapped inside when the sphere explodes through the cottage roof toward the moon.

On the moon, they enter an underground crater and are greeted by Selenites, a race of ant-like humanoids. Bedford suggests that they fight to survive, but Cavor warns against teaching force and violence to the Selenites. The Selenites attack, and Bedford responds with force.

Upon escaping to the surface, the astronauts discover that their sphere, along with Kate, has been dragged through a massive door leading to the moon's interior. Forcing their way inside, they begin a search for Kate and the sphere. Unfortunately, they encounter a giant moon beast, a Gastropod, instead. The Gastropod attacks, and Cavor is captured by a group of Selenites carrying a strange electrode device. With the device, the Selenites destroy the attacking moon beast with deadly electrical arcs.

Bedford rescues Kate and they watch in secret as Cavor is brought into a giant hall to meet the Grand Lunar. The Grand Lunar is fearful that other Earthlings will come to the moon and use violence against them. Cavor assures him that this can be prevented because he, Cavor, is the only person who knows the secret of Cavorite. Knowing that they will never be allowed to return to Earth, Bedford attacks the Grand Lunar and tries to leave with Cavor. Cavor, scientist till the end, refuses to go. Bedford and Kate enter the sphere while fending off an army of Selenites. Moments later they break through the moon's crust and fly into space.

Back to the present, television reports that the U.N. astronauts have entered the crystal caverns; they find no signs of life or danger, only contamination and decay. Bedford thinks he knows why the moon's inhabitants are all dead. "Poor Cavor," Bedford says. "He did have such a dreadful cold."

Adaptation

Nigel Kneale and Jan Read stick closely to Wells' plot. Of course, the Wells novel has no modern day space landing, but the update works. The addition of Kate Callender adds a bit more human interest for theater audiences, but she is nowhere to be found in Wells' novel. In the film's pressbook, Producer Schneer explains: "I had to be a little more thoughtful than Wells. In this day and age, it's not so surprising that a woman should be an interplanetary traveler, since we already have a woman cosmonaut. In all other particulars, we stick to the theme of the book." The only trouble is that the female travels in 1899, not in 1964, when her appearance in space would have been more explainable. Regardless, she is there by accident. No, she is in the film simply to meet audience expectations. The film does include such staples from the novel as Cavorite, the sphere, the crystal caverns, strange vegetation, the Selenites, the Grand Lunar (though in the novel we only hear reports of him), and the Gastropod, which seems to be a violent stand-in for Wells' docile Moon-Calf.

While the film stays close to the Wells plot, it avoids any contact with Wells' ideas. None of HGW's socio-political concerns see celluloid life. Cavor is remarkably like Well's humorous hero scientist who wants to know for the sheer joy of knowing. Bedford, on the other hand, is on the trip to line his pockets. The film does little to approve of Cavor's motives over those of Bedford. Also, the film does nothing with the nature of society on the moon and the breeding of Selenites to fill various social functions.

Production and Marketing

The production star of *The First Men in the Moon* is obviously Ray Harryhausen (1920–), the creator of dynamation.

Edward Judd and Lionel Jefferies fight off Selenites in this lobby card scene from *The First Men in the Moon* (1964).

Among Harryhausen's pre–*First Men in the Moon* special effects films were *Mighty Joe Young* (1950), *It Came from Beneath the Sea* (1952), *Twenty Million Miles to Earth* (1957), *The Seventh Voyage of Sinbad* (1958), *The Three Worlds of Gulliver* (1960), and *Jason and the Argonauts* (1963). Harryhousen had to do six months of pre-production work on *The First Men in the Moon*, plus another four months after the twelve weeks of filming. In the film's pressbook, Harryhausen commented on the challenge he faced: "There is no quick way of doing my job. One needs unlimited patience and first class assistants. Everything had to be minutely planned and scaled and there were hundreds of color and matching tests to be done." He and art director John Blezard created the complete lunar world and all of its inhabitants, except for the Selenites. Rather than construct and animate humanoid insects, Harryhausen broke with his usual approach and reluctantly used children in suits. He also had a problem with panevision because it required a special lens which squeezed and distorted the images. When shot through a similar lens, the images would then expand to original size. Since all of this caused rear projection problems, Harryhausen redesigned the picture and used more traveling mattes and less rear projection, an approach that hampered his flexibility.

Austrian director Nathan Juran (1907–) is a study in contrasts. As an art director he won an academy award for his work on *How Green Was My Valley* (1941). After becoming a director of action films he orchestrated *The Black Castle* (1952), a mediocre gothic thriller with Boris Karloff and Lon Chaney, Jr.. He directed future United States President Ronald Reagan in *Law and Order* (1953) and *Hellcats of the Navy* (1957). He also helmed the garden variety big bug picture, *The Deadly Mantis* (1957), and, under the pseudoname of

Nathan Hertz, the cult classic *Attack of the Fifty Foot Woman* (1958). Otherwise, he worked with Ray Harryhausen in *Twenty Million Miles to Earth* and *The Seventh Voyage of Sinbad* before finishing his career making the uninspired *The Boy Who Cried Werewolf* (1973).

Script writer Nigel Kneale (1922–) was best known for the BBC serials about Professor Quatermass, all of which were eventually filmed by Hammer.

British actor Edward Judd (1932–) had appeared in *The Day the Earth Caught Fire* (1961), one of the Sixties' best science fiction films, as well as *Stolen Hours* (1963) and *The Long Ships* (1963). He would later lend his talents to such British horror/adventure films as *Island of Terror* (1966), *The Vengeance of She* (1968), and *Vault of Horror* (1973).

Before *First Men in the Moon*, bald British character actor Lionel Jeffries (1926–) had played in such fare as *Stage Fright* (1950), *The Nun's Story* (1958), *Two-Way Stretch* (1960), and *The Trials of Oscar Wilde* (1960). He continued acting in such well-received pictures as *The Spy with a Cold Nose* (1967) and *Camelot* (1967). He finished his distinguished career as a director.

Martha Hyer (1929–), a lovely leading lady of the fifties, had appeared in routine films, many of them Westerns. She did, however, earn an Academy Award nomination for her performance in *Some Came Running* (1959), a film based on James Jones' novel. Her acting career continued successfully into the seventies.

Columbia aggressively promoted *The First Men in the Moon* with a Ballantine paperback tie-in, a Gold Key comic book tie-in, a float in the Macy's Thanksgiving Day Parade, and newspaper ad mats, open-end radio interviews, and television spots featuring Colonel John "Shorty" Powers, the "voice of Mercury Control." Posters and ads had Powers saying, "For

Selenites climb the sphere as Edward Judd and Martha Hyer try to escape in this lobby card scene from *The First Men in the Moon* (1964).

space-age screen excitement, don't miss H.G. Wells' astounding 'First Men in the Moon.' It's Definitely all systems go!" Columbia also urged theater owners to exploit toy tie-ins as Christmas season approached.

The First Men in the Moon was a critical and financial success, and the name of H.G. Wells was carried triumphantly into the sixties space age.

Strengths

Without a doubt, the film's greatest strength is the special effects work of Ray Harryhausen and crew. The color and construction of the moonscapes, the moon interiors, and the vast expanse of outer space are all impeccably rendered. Also nice is

Wilkie Cooper's photography of the delightful English village.

The updating of the film to 1964 is very effective as it allows full exploitation of Wells' novel in a relatively believable way.

Lionel Jeffries, suitably comical and sympathetic as Dr. Cavor, is very much like Wells' creation. Edward Judd provides the muscular masculinity and does well as both young Bedford and old Bedford. Martha Hyer, lovely as usual, carries off her role charmingly.

The film is well-paced and suitable for family viewing, all of which aided its success in 1964. Though intentionally comical, the general mood is appropriately serious. *The First Men in the Moon* is an enjoyable motion picture, a delightful way to pass 102 minutes. It does not bear repeated viewings, but it was never made to do so. It still holds up today on the level of entertainment.

Weaknesses

For all of its strengths, this film is a comic book version of Wells' novel. It is 100% physical and 0% cerebral. It is a sixties popcorn movie. While generating great fun, it fails to address challenging themes suggested in the novel. Kneale's other screenplays do not shy away from such possibilities, but this one does.

Compare and contrast Cavor with other Wells scientists: the Time Machine narrator, Dr. Moreau, and Dr. Griffin. It has been argued, as with Leon Stover, that Wells was largely sympathetic with his fictional scientists. *The Time Machine* narrator was misunderstood by the romantically inclined Filby, who mistakenly appears to most readers and filmgoers as Wells' mouthpiece. Dr. Moreau was misunderstood by Prendick, who mistakenly appears to most readers and filmgoers as Wells' mouthpiece. Dr. Griffin was misunderstood by Kemp, who appears to most readers and filmgoers as Wells' mouthpiece. In the case of Moreau and Griffin in particular, Wells was ambivalent. He knew that the future depends on scientists governing and planning the future of humankind, but he was not pleased with this fact. If only humanity could govern itself! But Wells was becoming increasingly certain that it could not.

The production of the Selenites as producers in a utopian society both appealed to and appalled Wells. Plato called for the Guardians to educate, evaluate, and then assign the people to the positions for which nature most prepared them. In *The First Men in the Moon*, Wells explores the possibility of Scientific Elite that judges what society needs and then produces beings to fill those slots contentedly. Such a process de-humanizes the beings, but can human beings uneducated by the Elite be trusted to act in the best interests of humanity? Wells says NO! *The First Men in the Moon* is an attempt by Wells to explore this problem. None of this exploration, however, is taken up by the film. This is true of most Wells-based films. Still, we must evaluate the film on its own merits.

Rating: 3

9

"The Story of an Inexperienced Ghost" (1902)

THE SHORT STORY

In 1901, Wells began his flirtation with the Fabian Society, a group devoted to the spread of socialism through cultural persuasion. "The Story of an Inexperienced Ghost," which appeared in the *Strand* in 1902, shows no sign of the author's developing Fabian interests. In fact, this humorous story is rarely mentioned by Wells scholars. It is a piece of fluff, a short trip along a tributary of the river that was pushing Wells' writings into an increasingly didactic direction.

Short Story Scenario and Commentary

At the Mermaid Club, Clayton entertains his friends with the story of how he recently "caught" a ghost but decided to release it. Clayton says he never believed in ghosts until he encountered one in the dead of night in a hallway of the Mermaid Club. The club was empty, and Clayton came upon the ghost quite unexpectedly. The ghost immediately struck Clayton as weak, a person who was probably weak in life. The ghost, young, lean and poorly dressed, tried to frighten Clayton by going "Boo-oo," but Clayton responded "Boo—be hanged!" The ghost was very disappointed.

Clayton established that while the business of ghosts is to haunt, this particular ghost had no business at the Mermaid Club. Clayton then asked how the apparition happened to get there. The ghost then related how as a senior English master in a London private school, he was killed as a result of a silly accident and learned how to return to Earth as a ghost by moving his arms in certain patterns. Unfortunately, the ghost forgot the arm movements that would return him to the land of the dead.

Finally, the ghost thought he remembered the right series of gestures and asked Clayton to turn his head as the ghost performed them. Clayton turned, but watched the ghost's performance in a mirror. The ghost disappeared, and Clayton retired to bed.

Clayton tells his friends that he believes he could reproduce the gestures right then and there in the Mermaid Club. He is encouraged by most, but warned by one friend not to repeat the gestures because they could lead to death. Clayton stands, gently swaying, waving his arms in the proscribed manner. Moments later, he falls dead, his soul apparently removed to that kingdom beyond mortal existence.

The story is well-written and worth reading. It is fluff, but it is worthwhile fluff. Wells gets in a dig at the private (public, in the American context) school master for whom Wells held little admiration. A flesh and blood fool becomes a ghostly fool: Inexperienced, yes—but also considerably dense. But what of Clayton? Is he discernibly brighter? No, this upper class blowhard meets the same fate as the inexperienced ghost: Death by foolishness.

THE FILMS

Dead of Night (1945) Ealing, Great Britain / Running Time: 102 minutes (complete film) / Release date:

CREDITS FOR "THE INEXPERIENCED GHOST" SEQUENCE: Directed by Charles Crighton; Produced by Micahel Balcon; Screenplay by Sidney Cole and John Croydon, from situational material by H.G. Wells. Edited by Charles Hassey; Cienematography by Jack Parker and H. Julius.

CAST FOR "THE INEXPERIENCED GHOST" SEQUENCE: Basil Radford (George Parratt), Naunton Wayne (Larry Potter) Peggy Bryan (Mary Lee).

Film Synopsis

Dead of Night is a five-story omnibus. In the first story, a driver suffers a racing accident and later envisions a hearse waiting in the hospital courtyard. The hearse driver says, "Just room for one inside, Sir." When the patient leaves the hospital, he starts to take a bus but recoils in fear when the bus driver, who drove the hearse in the vision, says "Just room for one inside, Sir."

The bus leaves without the man and crashes. All aboard are killed.

In the second story a girl plays a game of hide and seek in an old house and hears weeping in a room. She finds a distraught boy who claims that his sister wants to kill him. The girl later finds that the boy was murdered years ago. She has seen a ghost.

In the third story, a woman presents her fiancé with a mirror that proves to be haunted. The fiancé becomes possessed by the spirit of a murderer and is driven to kill his new wife. The breaking of the mirror saves the couple.

The fourth story is "The Inexperienced Ghost," based on the H.G. Wells story. Potter and Parratt, deadly golf rivals, are both in love with Mary. Since she cannot decide which to marry, the golfers decide the matter by playing a game of 18 holes, the winner to wed. When Potter loses, he drowns himself in the golf course lake. Parratt weds Mary and takes up golf again. At the lake, Parratt hears Potter's voice. This, of course, ruins Parratt's game. Later, Parratt sees Potter's ghost in the clubhouse and orders drinks for both. Potter's ghost accuses Parratt of cheating and orders him to give up Mary and then give up golf. When Potter tries to return to the land of the dead via certain hand gestures, he finds that he has forgotten the formula that allows him to vanish. Apparently he is too inexperienced a ghost to be out haunting. In an effort to help, Parratt performs the gestures and vanishes. The ghost now has Mary to himself.

In the final story, a ventriloquist is driven mad by a dummy with a mind of its own.

Adaptation

Wells' idea of an inexperienced ghost that cannot vanish is the foundation of the golf segment in *Dead of Night*. In the film, Clayton becomes Parratt and the nameless ghost becomes Potter. In the story neither are identified as golfers and there is no romantic rivalry. Though both story and film segment are humorous in tone, the only plot similarities are the failure of the ghost to vanish and the subsequent disappearance of the other fellow when he tries the gestures.

Production and Marketing

Dating back to the silent horror cinema, the horror omnibus was nothing new to 1945 audiences. Director Charles Crichton (1910–1999), however, was fairly new to directing. Having begun as an editor, he helmed *For Those in Peril* in 1944 and from there went on to direct the "golfing" sequence for *Dead of Night*. He would later direct such notable films as *Hue and Cry* (1946), *The Lavender Hill Mob* (1951), *The Titfield Thunderbolt* (1953), and *A Fish Called Wanda* (1988), which he wrote, and for which he received an Academy Award nomination.

Basil Radford (1897–1952) was a light character comedian. He and Naughton Wayne (1901–1970) became popular portraying Englishmen abroad, a collaboration that fueled *The Lady Vanishes* (1938), *Night Train to Munich* (1940) *Crooks' Tour* (1941), *Next of Kin* (1942), and *Millions Like Us* (1943).

Dead of Night was aggressively hyped in England and the United States. American posters quote Walter Winchell saying "A thriller ... the critics hugged it!" Another catch phrase screamed "Like nothing in this world you've ever thrilled to before!"

Strengths

With a source as insubstantial as Wells' "The Story of an Inexperienced Ghost" and a screenplay that adds only romantic rivalry to the plot, the greatest strength of the segment becomes the lead actors, Basil Radford and Naunton Wayne. They had proven a humorous mix in several previous collaborations. Radford at one point chastises Wayne for haunting before he is experienced, and Wayne utters the line, "Because a chap becomes a ghost, it surely doesn't mean that he ceases to be a gentleman." All so very British!

Director Crighton adequately guides the affair, but we see little of the flair he would demonstrate in later years after gaining experience.

Weaknesses

This sequence would have worked better in a comedy omnibus. In *Dead of Night* it serves only to break any mood established by previous episodes (which isn't much). Since this is a fairly tepid horror film, comic relief is not needed and is, therefore, most unwelcome.

Dead of Night is an overrated horror film. The best segments are those featuring the haunted mirror and the ventriloquist. The other horror segments are too weak, more like the lesser television episodes from *One Step Beyond*. The Wells segment doesn't belong and actually detracts from the film.

Rating for Dead of Night: 2½

Rating for "Inexperienced Ghost" Segment: 2

10

The Food of the Gods (1904)

THE NOVEL

In 1902, Wells published *The Sea Lady*, a light romance about a mermaid who comes ashore and becomes emotionally involved with several human beings. In February of 1903, he joined the Fabians, with whom he had been associating since 1901. His debut address to the group included the reading of his essay "The Question of Scientific Administrative Areas in Relation to Municipal Undertakings," in which he argues that local areas of government were too small and ineffective for modern conditions. Local and national boundaries must be put aside and the world placed in the hands of scientific managers. Such socialistic concerns provide the foundation for *The Food of the Gods*, a satire on the administrative ineffectiveness characterizing the world as Wells knew it at the turn of the century.

Novel Scenario and Commentary

Mr. Bensington and Professor Redwood invent a remarkable substance that changes the growth pattern of any living thing. If administered in the early stages of life, the organism can grow to six or seven times its normal size. They call the substance Herakleaphorbia, but it soon becomes known as "boomfood." At their experimental farm near Urshot, Kent, the pair experiment on baby chicks. Boomfood is successful in producing very large chicks, but as a result of Redwood's carelessness, other organisms feed on it. Soon reports come from Kent of giant wasps, giant chickens, giant rats, and giant plants. Cossar, an engineer friend of the scientists, takes the responsibility of hunting down the giants and killing them.

When Redford feeds boomfood to his sickly grandson, Cossar uses it to plan a race of super humans, and when Mrs. Skinner, the caretaker's wife, feeds it to her young grandson Caddles, it becomes clear that the experiment is becoming dangerously out of hand. It seems that the substance stays active when passed on from one life form to another, and whatever eats the food must continue eating it in order to live.

About twenty years pass and there exist about sixty male human giants. A giant princess, unaware of the males, exists in a foreign land. Because the giants must eat enormous amounts of food and ruin the roads just by walking on them, the normal locals become angry and demand action from their politicians. The giants are soon forbidden to use the roads and are severely limited by laws. Caterham, an activist politician, works to destroy the giants.

Caddles, who was raised in an orphanage, can find no other children his own size to play with and is finally placed in a chalk quarry that he works singlehandedly for the profit of a rather nasty philanthropist. As Caddles grows up, he tires of working perpetually for food and clothes and begins to wonder why others deny him access to the world beyond the quarry. Meanwhile, Cossar's giant sons are becoming troublesome adolescents and Redwood's son meets the giant princess.

Caddles rebels and enters the town, where he is shot to death on orders of the newly elected Caterham government. What's more, the people know that young Redford and the princess will soon have offspring, endangering life as rural England has known it. War breaks out between the people and the giants. The giants reject offers by the government that would preserve the life of the giants while allowing their race to eventually become extinct. The giants envision a world under their control which will be fairer and less violent than ever before. Therefore, they recommend that boomfood be made available to everyone so that all can share in this better future. The novel's end suggests that progress and growth will not be stopped and that a superior race will soon rule the world.

Unlike Wells earlier romances, *The Food of the Gods* is optimistic. Once the revolution is started, it will not be stopped. That which is provincial, near-sighted and weak will end. Mankind will not end as *The Time Machine* fears, changes will occur as Dr. Moreau hoped, and regardless of backlash and fear, the courage of our Griffins and Cavors will bear fruit. As usual, though, Wells is somewhat ambivalent about this glorious future. His descriptions of rural England as he knew it as a youth are nostalgic and positive. It seems, however, that such simplicity must be sacrificed if humankind is to advance.

Critical opinion of the novel is divided. Few deny that *The Food of the Gods* contains some of Wells' best and tightest writing, yet it also introduces a tendency to preach that would increasingly infect much of his subsequent work.

As in his previous novels, Wells lauds courageous science while castigating the science establishment and its close-minded membership. Boomfood is socialism, the revolution that cannot be stopped. Eventually, it will overcome the reactionary Caterhams of the world and transform human life. It is obvious that giants and pygmies cannot share the world. One or the other must go, and Wells hopes and predicts that humanity has within itself the courage to think big.

THE FILMS

Village of the Giants (1965)   Embassy, U. S. A. / Running Time: 82 minutes / Release Date: September 30, 1965

CREDITS: Produced and Directed by Bert I. Gordon; Screenplay by Alan Caillou; Original Story by Bert I. Gordon, based on the novel *The Food of the Gods* by H.G. Wells; Music composed and conducted by Jack Nitzsche; Cinematography by Paul C. Vogel; Art Direction by Franz Bachelin; Set Decoration by Bob Benton; Special Effects by Bert I. Gordon and Flora Gordon; Edited by Jack Bushelman; Makeup by Wally Westmore; Process Photography by Farciot Edouart; Assistant Director—Jim Rosenberger; Production Manager—Frank Caffey.

CAST: Tommy Kirk (Mike); Johnny Crawford (Horsey), Beau Bridges (Fred), Ronny Howard (Genius), Joy Harmon (Merrie), Bob Random (Rick), Tisha Sterling

(Jean), Charla Doherty (Nancy), Tim Rooney (Pete), Kevin O'Neal (Harry), Gail Gilmore (Elsa), Tony Basil (Red), Hank Jones (Chuck), Jim Begg (Fatso), Vicki London (Georgette), Joseph Turkel (Sheriff), Beau Brummels, Freddy Cannon, and Mike Clifford as themselves.

Film Synopsis

A gang of eight beer-drinking, rock-dancing teenagers smash up their car on the outskirts of small Hainesville. In town, teenagers Nancy and Mike are astonished when Nancy's kid brother, Genius, invents a substance called Goo in his cellar laboratory. Soon the family dog, a cat and several pet ducks grow six times their normal size. Nancy and Mike immediately realize the commercial possibilities.

That night, Mike and Nancy attend a local dance, where they are joined by their friends Horsey and his girl, Red. At the same time, the gang of eight arrive, looking for a good time. When the oversized ducks enter the dance and take part in the fun, the gang learns about Goo and decides to steal it.

Following the theft, Fred and the gang break into a deserted theatre and "take" Goo, after which they grow to a height of about twenty or thirty feet. They, too, see potential use for Goo! After playing some pranks, the giant teenagers plan to get the Goo formula from Genius. The Sheriff tries to control the gang to no avail. They hold his daughter hostage, demand rules and regulations for all adults in the town, and generally bully the community.

Mike unsuccessfully tries to fight Fred in a "David and Goliath" match-up, and the teenagers of Hainsville fail to stop the giants. At last, Genius concocts a unique gas that, when inhaled, shrinks the giants back to normal size. The gas works, the gang of eight leave town, and Mike and Nancy rejoice that life will now return to normal.

Adaptation

Village of the Giants is a clever adaptation of H.G. Wells' novel. In both versions, we have science creating a substance that produces giantism in organisms that eat it. The first "subjects" are animals. When humans eat the substance, real problems develop. The young people in Wells' novel, tired of adult restrictions and control, use their size to seize power. In both book and film, local officials are unable to contain the situation.

Besides the film's obvious deviations from the novel in terms of setting and period, the film strays most from Wells in its overall message. Wells tries to show that a better future is inevitable and that the status quo cannot stop progress. Gordon, on the other hand, concludes that the giants are just as bad, if not worse, than the status quo they rebel against. Wells leaves us to contemplate the coming of a brave new world while Gordon assures us that, while kids will be kids, the established order should and will prevail.

Production and Marketing

Writer, producer, and director Bert I. Gordon (1922–) established himself as a successful low budget science fiction auteur with such films as *Serpent Island* (1954), which features a giant serpent, *King Dinosaur* (1955), which features a giant lizard, *The Beginning of the End* (1957), which features giant grasshoppers, *The Amazing Colossal Man* (1957), which features, obviously, a giant man, *The Cyclops* (1957), which features a giant cyclops, *Attack of the Puppet People* (1958), which surprisingly features the ultra small, *War of the Colossal Beast* (1958), which reprises the colossal man, and *Earth v.s. the Spider*

Ad art for *Village of the Giants* (1965)

(1958), which features a giant spider. The best of these pictures is probably the last. Certainly, Gordon had produced his share of giants before adapting H.G. Wells in 1965.

According to the film's pressbook, Gordon had a great belief in young people and wanted to serve youth in his film. The victorious young people, however, are those who defend the status quo.

Gordon achieved the desired special effects by duplicating each set in which the giants appear, making each one slightly smaller. He also matches blow up animals with regular footage to create the effect of giantism.

The focus of exploitation, however, was neither Gordon nor H.G. Wells. It was the young thespians. Former Disney actor Tommy Kirk (1941–) was a well-known quantity having starred in such pleasing fare as *Old Yeller* (1957), *The Shaggy Dog* (1959), *The Swiss Family Robinson* (1960), and *The Absent-Minded Professor* (1960). He graduated from the child to teenage market in 1965 with *Mars Needs Women* (1964), *Village of the Giants*, and *How to Stuff a Wild Bikini* (1965). He hit his professional nadir in the Seventies with such films as *Blood of Ghastly Horror* (1972). As a homosexual, Kirk had it rough growing up and working under family-oriented Walt Disney. Nevertheless, his performances were always solid and enjoyable.

Several young performers in *Village of the Giants* followed their parents into the film industry. Beau Bridges (1941–), son of Lloyd Bridges, had appeared in films such as *Force of Evil* (1948) and *The Red Pony* (1949). He also worked in television shows such as *Sea Hunt* (which starred his father), *Ensign O'Toole, Ben Casey, Dr. Kildare, Mr. Novak, Eleventh Hour*, and *Combat*. His career would blossom, and he would be a successful leading man for the next four decades.

Tisha Sterling, daughter of Robert Sterling and Ann Sothern, had appeared in television episodes of *Alfred Hitchcock Presents, Mr. Novak, The Donna Reed Show*, and *Dr. Kildare*. She continued to work mainly on television and in minor motion pictures.

Tim Rooney, son of Mickey Rooney, appeared on television in *The Colgate Comedy Hour* and as a regular on *Mickey Mouse Club*. His first film role was in *King of the Roaring Twenties*. Though triumphing over polio as a child, he was unable to triumph over Hollywood and soon chose another line of work.

Like Rooney, Johnny Crawford (1946–) had also begun as a Walt Disney Mouseketeer. He played in several films, made a few hit records in the Sixties, and is today best remembered for his co-starring role on television's *The Rifleman*. Today, he concentrates on singing and leading his own band.

Perhaps the most successful of all the film's young stars is Ronny Howard (1954–). Ron was appearing as little Opie on television's *The Andy Griffith Show* when signed to co-star in *Village of the Giants*. Ron went on to appear in such films as *American Grafitti* (1973) and *The Shootist* (1976), as well as co-starring in television's popular *Happy Days*, but he quickly graduated to become a successful director, screenwriter and producer.

Composer Jack Nitzsche (1937–) composed the film's musical score. He would go on to pen music tracks for such films as *The Exorcist* (1973), *One Flew Over the Cuckoos Nest* (1973), and *Stand By Me* (1986).

Village of the Giants was clearly marketed as a youth exploitation film, one of many produced in the late fifties and sixties. A pressbook ad claims that the film "literally jumps with music and dance." And it does, as the popular Beau Brummels, Freddie Cannon, and Mike Clifford perform catchy tunes while scantily clad girls shake bootie to all the latest dances. A bit of clever hype suggested that the theatre sponsor a "Smallest and Tallest Dance Contest" at which the tallest and shortest couples would win prizes. The pressbook also encouraged exhibitors to approach supermarkets, ice cream parlors, and furniture stores with various promotions to hype the film. Rather eye-catching is the film's poster art, which features a trepidacious Johnny Crawford hanging from the bra straps of a teenage female giantess. Catch lines scream: "It's the teen scene you've never seen! Teenagers zoom to supersize ... and terrorize a town! It's what happens when their sounds, their dances, their loves, their rebellions explode—30 feet tall!"

Strengths

In a film such as *Village of the Giants*, if the special effects fail, everything fails. In this case, Bert I. Gordon is up to the task. They are primitive compared to today's special effects, but they are good for the sixties and must therefore be considered a strength even today.

The film's premise is interesting. What would happen if youth could take over? Would they usher in an age of greater understanding and fairness, or would they botch things as much as their parents did? *Wild in the Streets* (1968) would investigate this theme in a different context, but in both cases the prognosis is negative.

Jack Nitzsche's musical score is one of the film's greatest strengths. It is a powerful score with an underlying mood of menace. Perfect! Also helping the film is the rock music by celebrities The Beau Brummels, Freddy Cannon, and Mike Clifford. It isn't the greatest music in the world, and it isn't their hits, but compared to similar scores in other teen exploitation

pictures, this score literally, and figuratively, rocks.

Of course, the sixties saw the rise of America's drug culture, and Gordon chooses to include subtle drug related propaganda in the film. For example, though Goo resembles ice cream, the teenagers "take" it. "Take" is usually the term used to describe the injesting of drugs, not the consuming of foods. The gang dares Fred to take Goo. As a result of peer pressure he does, and the others follow. Like Adam and Eve, the giants are ashamed of their nakedness, but cloth from old theatre costumes soon allows them to stroll about in their new Eden. But can society really stomach identification cards and curfews for adults? Since the results are negative, Gordon is making a conservative statement about drug use and teenage delinquent culture (which he goes out of his way to portray as a minority among teenagers). Is this reaction a strength? It probably isn't if you are a New World Wellsian, but it is if you are a social conservative.

It is hard to judge the film's acting performances. For the most part, the whole affair is light, even comedic. There is a sense of pervading unreality common to the sixties. Giant ducks invade a dance and young people are amused, but not startled. Life goes on as long as the music does, and Gordon maintains this aura of fantasy throughout the film.

By the way, it may be a small matter or even an inside joke, but Gordon disposes of a giant spider in this film as he did in his *Earth v.s. the Spider*—with electricity.

Weaknesses

Though the *raison d'être* for this film is youth exploitation, the hedonistic dancing scenes just go on too long. This kind of padding hurt many teen exploitation films of that era.

While special effects are one of this film's strengths, a few such efforts are weaknesses. For example, when we get shots of Fred's giant bare legs, they are obviously wooden. And when the giants shrink they simply sink vertically without any accompanying change in volume. Another problem is the slow motion, exaggerated movement of the giants which renders them much less menacing than they might have been had they been able to move at regular speed.

This brings up another weakness. The giants are never the terrifying threats they might and should have been. They hole up in a theatre and only venture out to dance and bully the populace. Well, maybe, as the pressbook suggests, they are really good kids at heart, but the film suffers as a result.

The bottom line is that this is an entertaining film. You have to be in the right mood to watch it, but it does what it set out to do, and it is what it set out to be. It is dated today, but it still has the power to deliver a few laughs and keep us at least minimally involved from start to finish. As a Wells picture, it adopts his premise but reaches an altogether opposite conclusion. It is an exploitation film that ultimately caters to the status quo.

Rating: 2½

The Food of the Gods (1976) American International, U.S.A. / Running Time: 89 minutes / Release Date: June 9, 1976

CREDITS: Produced and directed by Bert I. Gordon; Screenplay by Bert I. Gordon, based upon a portion of the novel by H.G. Wells; Music by Elliot Kaplan; Unit Production Manager/First Assistant—Flora Gordon; Executive Producer—Samuel Z. Arkoff; Assistant to Producer—Eunice Forester; Executive Production Supervisor—Elliot Schick; Edited by Corky Ehlers; Canadian Production coordinated by Jacques Khouri and Carol Gordon; Cinematography by Reg Morris; Makeup by Phyllis Newman; Special Visual Effects by Bert I. Gordon; Art Direction by Graeme Murray.

CAST: Marjoe Gortner (Morgan); Pamela Franklin (Lorna Scott); Ralph Meeker (Bensington); Ida Lupino (Mrs. Skinner); John Cypher (Brian), Belinda Balaski (Rita), Tom Stovall (Thomas), John McLiam (Mr. Skinner).

Film Scenario

Canadian football players Morgan, Davi, and Brian go deer hunting on a lonely island off the coast of Canada. Davis is attacked by giant wasps, and his partners find him dead and hideously swollen. Not having seen the wasps, Morgan seeks help at a nearby farm, but soon finds himself battling giant chickens. Escaping with his life, Morgan finds a Mrs. Skinner barricaded in her house. When questioned, she explains that she and her husband discovered a strange substance oozing from the ground on their property. They found that when mixing the substance with meal, the chickens would eat it. While no changes occurred in the adult chickens, the little chicks grew to enormous size and soon ate the adults. Mr. Skinner has gone to the mainland to sell the rights to his "food of the gods." When Morgan sees overturned cans of FOTG, he realizes that creatures in the pest-ridden storeroom are feasting on the food.

Mr. Skinner never makes it home that night. Rather, he falls victim to giant rats on the road leading to the farm. The next day, dog food company owner Bensington and his pert biologist Lorna Scott make a visit to the farm. Bensington demands that Mrs. Skinner sign over the rights to the food as Mr. Skinner had agreed to do, but Mrs. Skinner wants to wait for her husband's return. Since she

Marjoe Gortner fires at giant rats as Pamela Franklin raises her arm in fear in this lobby card scene from *The Food of the Gods* (1973).

was revolted by giant worms the previous night, she is becoming fearful for her husband's safety.

Morgan and Brian want to destroy the food of the gods, but Bensington insists on marketing it for big profits. Lorna becomes fed up with Bensington's greed and callous behavior and latches on to Morgan, who goes on an expedition to destroy a giant wasp nest. Having burned the nest, Morgan encounters Brian and Rita, whose recreation vehicle has been invaded by giant rats. Rita is very pregnant, and Morgan takes the two to the farmhouse.

It seems that the rats are being led by a white rat of superior intelligence. Morgan and Brian succeed in drowning some of the rats, but the rest head for the farmhouse where Mrs. Skinner and Bensington

fall victim to their voracious appetite. Morgan and Brian return to the farmhouse, which the rats are placing under siege. During the chaos, Rita delivers a boy, with Lorna's encouragement. Morgan and Brian blow up a dam and release torrents of water. As the rats drown below, Morgan, Brian, Rita, and Thomas make a last stand on the farmhouse roof. The white rat crawls to the roof but is killed when Morgan beats it back into the water. Finally all is quiet. The rats and, apparently, all other forms of giantism are dead.

With the closing credits, however, some of the food finds its way to a dairy farm and into the diet of cows. The cows give milk, and school children drink the milk. Perhaps nature is not yet finished rebelling against mankind.

Giant rats exterminate Ralph Meeker in this lobby card scene from *The Food of the Gods* (1973).

Adaptation

As the credits say, *The Food of the Gods* is based upon a portion of the H.G. Wells novel, namely the early chapters. In his autobiography, Wells noted that "Nobody saw the significance of [the novel], but it left some of its readers faintly puzzled. They were vastly amused and thrilled by my giant wasps and rats, but young Caddles was beyond them." Bert I. Gordon had experimented in a rather un-Wellsian way with the idea of giant adolescents in *Village of the Giants*, but here he concentrates on those giant wasps and rats that so engrossed Wells' readers. HGW's initial concern had been with socialism and political control, and Gordon's con-

cern in *Village of the Giants* was the sixties issue of teenage rebellion. The seventies saw an increasing interest in ecology, so Gordon's *The Food of the Gods* focused on that. Except for the idea of giant creatures attacking mankind, little of Wells' novel remains except for the final frame's hint that human children may soon grow as a result of the food. What will happen then? Just remember what happened to those adult chickens when their chicks became giants.

Production and Marketing

After producing and directing *Village of the Giants*, Bert I. Gordon strayed from science fiction for a decade and made what is probably his best film, *The Mad Bomber* (1975). After *Food of the Gods*, Gordon was not finished with H.G. Wells. The following year he would adapt Wells' short story "The Empire of the Ants." For an account of Gordon's work prior to *The Food of the Gods*, see the production and marketing section of *Village of the Giants*.

Gordon assembled a strong cast for *The Food of the Gods*. Marjoe Gortner (1944–) began life as child evangelist. After a 1972 biographical documentary, he turned his acting talent to the silver screen. Before being hired by Gordon, Marjoe appeared in the television movie *The Marcus Nelson Murders* (1973), which launched Telly Savalas as Kojak, and he received good reviews for his work in *Earthquake* (1974). After 1976, he appeared in many minor action films and the television series *Falcon Crest* (1986–1987).

Pamela Franklin (1949–) made her film debut in *The Innocents* (1961), probably the greatest ghost entry ever made. She went on to appear with Bette Davis in *The Nanny* (1965) and with Marlon Brando in *The Night of the Following Day* (1968). She also wowed critics with her strong performance in *The Prime of Miss Jean Brodie* (1969). Otherwise, Franklin starred in a number of minor horror films, the best being *The Legend of Hell House* (1973).

Veteran leading man Ralph Meeker (1920–1988) came to *The Food of the Gods* near the end of an outstanding career that included such memorable films as *Teresa* (1951), *Kiss Me Deadly* (1955, as Mike Hammer), *Paths of Glory* (1958, directed by Stanley Kubrick), *The Dirty Dozen* (1967), and *The Detective* (1968).

The biggest name to appear in *The Food of the Gods* was Ida Lupino (1914–1995), the wife of actor Howard Duff, who built a long career with praised performances in such hits as *The Adventures of Sherlock Holmes* (1939), *The Light That Failed* (1940), *They Drive By Night* (1940),

High Sierra (1941), *The Sea Wolf* (1941), *Ladies in Retirement* (1941), *The Hard Way* (1942), *Devotion* (1946), and *Roadhouse* (1948). Lupino also blazed the way for other talented women by capably directing many films and television episodes.

Gordon filmed on Bowen Island, but weather did not cooperate. Despite the beautiful natural photography, Gordon and crew were plagued by record blizzards, hail storms and rain. Gordon joked that his next film would not be shot on Bowen Island! According to the pressbook, the crew came under scrutiny by local law enforcement when a giant rat was reported gnawing on cauliflower in one of the fields. The creature was soon identified as a South American rodent called a capybara. Cleared of allowing a giant rat to escape, Gordon joked that his rats would never eat cauliflower. Said Gordon, "They stick to actors." Nevertheless, the rats were unwilling to swim to get at the actors. Rats do swim, but the ones in the film were reluctant and had to be coaxed across the water.

Impressive posters for the film feature a giant rat on a tree limb attacking a prostrate girl. Catch phrases included the following:

"H.G. Wells, the master of science fiction, tells his most frightening story of a doomed civilization fighting for life against an ecology gone berserk."

"H.G. Wells predicted rocket ships and space travel in 'Things to Come' ... nuclear energy and the atom bomb in 'The Time Machine.' Now ... the master of science fiction, tells his most frightening story... Was he right again?"

Exploitation ideas (or "food for thought") were pretty lame. Of course there was the obligatory library tie in exploiting H.G. Wells. But how about a Disk Jockey Chili Cook-Off during which fans would cheer for their favorite DJ's chili that tastes most like the food of the gods? Exploitation went downhill from there.

Strengths

Though they don't compete with today's special effects, those of Bert I. Gordon are impressive for their time. Although not a great improvement over *Village of the Giants*, Gordon's rats crawling about models and his rodent close-ups work pretty well. His wasp work is serviceable, though less impressive.

It is hard to fault the cast. Gortner gives a memorably manic performance, and Meeker delivers the film's best performance as the greedy businessman. Franklin is fine as the love interest, and Ida Lupino has a good death scene as a rat devours her innards.

Cinematography is excellent. There are pleasing shots of Canadian greenery that contrast with the man-instigated horrors of the food of the gods. Lupino at one point prays, "Oh, God! I won't sin again, never. Just don't let no rats eat us. Please God!" Of course, her prayer is not granted. The rebellion of nature is just as much God-directed as the human response. Hence, the main conflict of the film.

Humanity wins, but Morgan knows that humanity must reform. It cannot walk in the footsteps of Bensington if it is to survive. The final threat is the contamination of human children. Too bad there wasn't a sequel in which giant children eat their parents!

The film is fast-paced. Few will be bored as the story unfolds, and the characters are engaging.

Weaknesses

Rats are obviously harmed in the filming of this picture. Gordon could not have gotten away with what he did here if today's laws were in effect. It is painful to watch live rats bloodied and drowned in the making of a motion picture designed to entertain.

By today's standards the special effects look a bit weak. So, the special effects that were a strength in 1976 are a weakness in 2000.

This film's biggest problem is its script. Gordon apparently spent much more time on special effects than on the screenplay. Could he (should he) not have put a little more effort into character development beyond the stock lines and responses we get in the film?

In some ways, *The Food of the Gods* should have been a prequel to Gordon's *Village of the Giants*, but had it been so in the early sixties, I don't think the results would have been very satisfying. It would have been just another "big creature" feature. I don't think Gordon ever really understood what Wells was getting at in his novel. If he did, he chose to ignore it in order to deliver exploitation material for American mass teenage audiences. Still, *The Food of the Gods* is an entertaining picture on its own merits. What Gordon sacrifices in screenplay he makes up for in pacing. Does he adequately serve Wells? No, but that was never his purpose.

Rating: 2½

11

"The Empire of the Ants" (1905)

THE SHORT STORY

Though Wells published his short story "The Empire of the Ants" in the *Strand* in 1905, he may have begun it or even written it as early as 1894. In that year Wells published the essay "The Extinction of Man," in which he warned that "In the case of every other predominant animal the world has ever seen ... the hour of its complete ascendancy has been the eve of its entire overthrow." If complacency can kill in the form of a Martian invasion, it can also kill in the form of other earth species. Wells also visited the theme in "The Sea Raiders" (1896), in which octopus-like creatures invade the south coast of England, and in "Valley of the Spiders" (1903), in which three men, riding in pursuit of a girl, are attacked by giant spiders floating on gossamer webs.

Short Story Scenario
and Commentary

The Brazilian gunboat *Benjamin Constant* acts on orders to investigate reports of an ant plague. Brazilian captain

Gerilleau and English engineer Holloyd discuss what they have been led to expect: ants about two inches long, carnivorous, and equipped with poisonous stings. There are hints that the ants might even be intelligent. When their gunboat enters the jungle area, Gerilleau and Holloyd discover no signs of human life. Soon they come upon a small derelict vessel overrun by black ants that, unlike normal ants, move deliberately. Having established that the crew is dead, Gerilleau orders Lieutenant da Cunha and sailors to board the boat. The Lieutenant argues vehemently against such an action, but Gerilliau threatens him with court martial if he resists orders. The angry and reluctant Lieutenant goes aboard the vessel, but is soon poisoned by the ants and dies. Because these intelligent ants are apparently able to use fire and tools, they thwart every attempt by Gerilleau to turn them back. The narrator declares that by 1920 the ants will be halfway down the Amazon, and by 1950 or 1960 they will strike Europe.

THE FILMS

Empire of the Ants (1977)   American International, U. S. A / Running Time: 91 minutes / Release Date: June 30, 1977

CREDITS: Produced and Directed by Bert I. Gordon; Screenplay by Jack Turley; Story by Bert I. Gordon, based on a story by H.G. Wells; Assistant to Producer/Director—Cariline Anne Davis; Unit Production Manager—Neil A. Machlis; Cinematography by Reg Morris; Edited by Michael Luciano; Publicized by Julian F. Myers; Ant Consultant—Dr. Charles L. Hogue; Special Visual Effects by Bert I. Gordon; Special Effects by Roy Downey; Costumes by Joanne Haas; Makeup by Ellis Burman; Production Assistant—Mark Perry; Post Production Supervisor—Salvatore Billitteri.

CAST: Joan Collins (Marilyn Fryser), Robert Lansing (Dan Stokely), Edward Power (Charlie Pearson), John David Carson (Joe Morrison), Jacqueline Scott (Margaret Ellis), Albert Salmi (Sheriff Art Kinkaid), Pamela Shoop (Coreen Bradford), Robert Pine (Larry Graham), Brooke Palance (Christine Graham), Harry Holcombe (Harry Thompson), Irene Tedrow (Velma Thompson), Jack Kosslyn (Thomas Lawson).

Film Synopsis

Marilyn, an aggressive land developer, is trying to sell an area of reclaimed swamp land in the extreme southeastern United States as an exclusive residential district. She leads a boatload of prospective buyers to the site, with the help of charter-boat captain Dan and Marilyn's assistant Charlie. Unknown to the group, bulldozer operators had ruptured a large can of atomic waste that had drifted ashore. A colony of ants has fed on the substance and grown to the size of tigers.

Marilyn's gala sales outing is disrupted when two of her guests are attacked by giant ants. Suddenly Dreamland Shores becomes a nightmare. Dan's boat is burned, and everyone flees into the swamp to find the stream that leads to a nearby town. Several former-prospective buyers fall to the ants in the process. The remaining survivors, Marilyn, Dan, Charlie, Margaret, Joe, and Coreen, head upstream in a rowboat, still under attack by the ants.

Arriving at the town, the survivors appeal to local sheriff Art Kinkaid for help. When he doesn't help, they suspect that the whole community is under the ants' control. Their worst suspicions are realized when the ants herd them into a nearby sugar refinery where a Queen Ant takes over human minds by emitting a pheromone gas. Dan enters the control chamber but fights back against the Queen Ant with a flare. Soon all hell breaks loose, and the survivors flee the sugar refinery. Joe guides a tanker truck full of highly inflammable contents into the sugar refinery, destroying the Queen Ant and the ants' center of control. Marilyn becomes ant food, and the remaining four survivors take a speedboat to safety.

Adaptation

Turley's screenplay changes the setting from Brazil to the southeast United States. In fact, except for the broad thematic possibility that ants might someday replace human beings as the dominant species, Gordon adapts almost nothing specific from Wells' short story. For example, no character in the film has a counterpart in the story. In the sixties, however, Roger Corman directed a number of Poe-inspired American International films which often wandered far from their original sources but conveyed Poesque themes. Gordon seems to do the same here. The Wellsian theme Gordon incorporates into *Empire of the Ants* is that of anti-capitalism.

Marilyn Fryser is a bullying feminist capitalist, and her assistant Charlie is one

...for they shall inherit the earth!
...SOONER THAN YOU THINK!

H.G. WELLS'

Empire of the Ants

Samuel Z. Arkoff presents a Bert I. Gordon film "Empire of the Ants" released by American International Pictures

starring

JOAN COLLINS · ROBERT LANSING · JOHN DAVID CARSON

co-starring

ROBERT PINE · EDWARD POWER · ALBERT SALMI · JACQUELINE SCOTT · PAMELA SHOOP

executive producer   screenplay by   screen story by   based on the
SAMUEL Z. ARKOFF · JACK TURLEY · BERT I. GORDON · story by H. G. WELLS
produced & directed by BERT I. GORDON · color by Movielab · a cinema 77 film
Music by DANA KAPROFF   Classic edition by Tempo Books, paperback by Ace Books.

PG PARENTAL GUIDANCE SUGGESTED
SOME MATERIAL MAY NOT BE
SUITABLE FOR PRE-TEENAGERS

of the film's most unlikable characters. Dan, whose point of view we come to trust, tells Margaret that he would not invest in the property and that the guests are being "taken." Margaret confesses that she was fired from her secretarial position with little compensation after years of service. Corporate capitalists are under attack in this film, as they are in many of Wells' writings.

Production and Marketing

Empire of the Ants is director Bert I. Gordon's third H.G. Wells adaptation. For background information on Bert I. Gordon, see *Village of the Giants* and *The Food of the Gods*.

British leading lady Joan Collins (1933–) had appeared in a broad assortment of international films before traveling into the swamp with Bert I. Gordon and crew. Among her films were *The Virgin Queen* (1955), *The Girl in the Red Velvet Swing* (1955), *The Wayward Bus* (1957), *Rally Round the Flag Boys* (1958), *Tales from the Crypt* (1968), and *Tales That Witness Madness* (1973). She is probably best known today for her starring role in the popular television soap opera *Dynasty* (1981–1989).

American leading man Robert Lansing (1929–1994) played rugged roles throughout the sixties and seventies in such films as *The 4D Man* (1959), *A Gathering of Eagles* (1963), *Under the Yum Yum Tree* (1964), and *The Grissom Gang* (1971). He also starred in three action-oriented television series that never lasted more than a season: *87th Precinct* (1961), *12 O'Clock High* (1964), and *The Man Who Never Was* (1966). Later, he was a denizen of such forgettable horror films as *Scalpel* (1976), *Island Claws* (1980), and *The Nest* (1988).

American character actor Albert Salmi (1928–1990) had appeared in many action-oriented pictures such as *The Unforgiven* (1959), *Wild River* (1960), *The Ambushers* (1967), *The Deserter* (1970), and *Lawman* (1971). The most notable film to display his talents is probably *The Brothers Karamazov* (1958). Salmi also starred in two television series: *Daniel Boone* (1963) and *Petrocelli* (1973). He made headlines in 1990 when he committed suicide after killing his terminally ill wife.

The pressbook and advertising aids for *Empire of the Ants* highlighted the name of H.G. Wells. A special "Facts" one-sheet poster screams:

> DON'T YOU BELIEVE IT!! Of all history's prophets, none has a greater degree of credibility than H.G. Wells with his predictions of moon-landings, ray guns, sonic signaling devices, etc. Because of his record, it becomes impossible to ignore prophesies and topics chosen by Wells for the subjects of his writings. The unlikely subject of giant rampaging ants the size of tigers was chosen by Wells for his story "Empire of the Ants." Ants, in addition to their aimless, endless wanderings along sidewalk cracks are most frequently encountered as pests at picnics and in sugar bowls. Are they merely a nuisance rarely worthy of any great concern on our part? DON'T BELIEVE IT ... FOR THEY SHALL INHERIT THE EARTH!!!!"

One promotional idea suggested a library display because "H.G. Wells is known as one of the greatest and most prolific authors of all time. His imaginative novels were the forerunners of the entire science-fiction field. Countless movies and television plays have been based on his works. They are considered to be classics and are used in many English classes."

Sticking with the literary theme, Ace

Opposite: Advertising art from *Empire of the ants* (1977)

published an illustrated tie-in Paperback, written by Lindsay West, which featured cover ad art of a woman frantically crawling away from an attacking giant ant, and Tempo published a Classic edition featuring the Wells short story.

Other promotional ideas suggested setting up ant farms in the theater lobby, building a giant ant on a flatbed truck and driving it around town as a loud-speaker emits horrific ant sounds, and holding a "largest ant" contest.

Pressbook publicity hyped the conditions under which the film was shot on location in "remote areas of Florida, including Lake Okeechobee in the Everglades." According to publicity, stars Collins and Lansing fed bagels and marshmallows to alligators that infested the swamp during production. "I've got scars all over," said Joan Collins. "Even at that, I'm lucky. Bert asked us to do things that actors usually don't. We were hip-deep in swamps. We did scenes where real, untamed alligators were within twenty feet. We were literally eaten alive by swamp fleas and mosquitoes. And that was only a small part of it!" Well, as Klaus Kinski once said, "Making movies is better than cleaning toilets.

Strengths

Empire of the Ants benefits from a strong leading cast and some impressive location cinematography. The interaction of characters, particularly of Fryser, Stokely, and Ellis, while not rivaling that of the best character-oriented pictures, keeps our attention. The characters could have kept our attention even better had their dialogue been stronger.

The pressbook-hyped Matex Prism Lens invented by Gordon shows 33 views of the same scene simultaneously, allowing audiences to see the action through the eyes of the ants. While nothing astounding, the effect is neat and adds to the film rather than detracts.

Though it depends on one's political ideology, the reduction of Marilyn Fryser from a controlling, full-of-it feminist to a frightened, whimpering woman in Dan's arms is a strength. Fryser is the high-powered feminist, bossing around her male help. Her power is artificial, however, all socially constructed by the politically correct seventies environment. When the artificial constructs of a feminized America are destroyed by the ants, Fryser is helpless. As they go by boat for help, Fryser complains to Dan, who is rowing the boat. He asks her if she would like to row. That shuts her up. Later she whimpers in his arms as the ants draw nearer. In the state of nature, Fryser is reduced to her natural state, and Dan, who is her underling in feminized America, rises to the helm as a result of his natural abilities. On the other hand, Margaret Ellis has been wrongfully exploited and abandoned by that part of America dominated by males, and she certainly deserved better. So Gordon is not offering an anti-feminist diatribe. He shows both sides, and that is a strength.

Weaknesses

The special effects are no advance over those employed in Gordon's *The Food of the Gods*, in which he simply enlarges the monsters and superimposes them on footage. In fact, there is little advance here over what Gordon was doing in the late fifties. Just substitute ants for rats, spiders, and colossal men and you have the idea. *Star Wars* made the special effects of *Empire of the Ants* pale by comparison, though to be fair, Gordon didn't work with the *Star Wars* budget.

While the main cast is strong, the farther down the cast list a name appears, the less impressive the acting is. Unfortunately, this is a film that can use all the help it can get, and much of the cast provides nothing special. Jack Turley's dialogue doesn't help any either.

The storyline itself is something out of the late fifties. The idea of ants controlling humans via activities at a sugar refinery is very weak. The seed pods of *Invasion of the Body Snatchers* are better. And the Queen Ant, which is rather ridiculous, would have looked just as ridiculous twenty years earlier.

Though it owes almost nothing to H.G. Wells, *Empire of the Ants* is passable summer drive-in fare. The trouble is, there aren't very many drive-ins anymore, and this picture would either be laughed off the multiplex screen today or make a fortune as camp. Regardless, the theme of giant ants threatening mankind was handled better in *Them!* (1954).

Rating: 2

12

Kipps (1905)

THE NOVEL

The same year that H.G. Wells published "The Empire of the Ants," he published the novels *A Modern Utopia* and *Kipps: The Story of a Simple Soul*. In the former, Wells follows in the footsteps of Plato, Thomas More, Francis Bacon, E. Zamyatin, Edward Bellamy and others in laying out a blueprint for the perfect political/economic state. The latter novel was conceived in 1898 while Wells was recovering from a kidney ailment. Wells conceived the novel first as a Dickensian tome to be titled *The Wealth of Mr. Waddy*. Mr. Waddy, Kipps' benefactor, was to be the novel's central character, but sometime between March, 1899, and April, 1900, Wells changed gears. As the novel grew, it became clear that major cutting was required. The gestation period for *Kipps* (seven years) proved longer than that for any other Wells novel except *The Time Machine*. The final result was *Kipps*, a novel intended as a bit of comic relief after *Love and Mr. Lewisham* (1900). All the while, Wells continued to expand his number of literary and political friends.

Novel Scenario and Commentary

Young Arthur Kipps knew that circumstances surrounding his birth were mysterious. His mother had apparently disappeared, leaving Kipps in the care of his aunt and uncle with a small sum set aside for his education. He receives some awful, ineffective schooling and when on vacation is forced to be "proper" by his aunt. He does find pleasure, however, in his friendship with the "lower class:" Pornick and his sister Ann. One day he and Ann tear a sixpence note in half, each keeping one part. Kipps is in love with Ann, but soon he is sent away to be a draper's apprentice. The Pornicks soon move away also and Ann goes into domestic service. Seven dull years pass, and Kipps is given a position in the firm at twenty pounds a year. Though he gets engaged several times just because his acquaintances do, his first real infatuation after Ann is Miss Helen Walsingham, a middle-class "lady" who teaches woodcarving. Of course, he feels clumsy and unworthy in her presence, and she largely ignores him.

Fortunes change for Kipps when he learns that he was the illegitimate son of a wealthy man whose father would not allow him to marry Kipps' mother. Kipps' grandparents are dead, but the grandfather agreed shortly before passing away to allow Kipps to inherit the family fortune and a fine house.

Newly rich, Kipps initially wants to learn only about the world he knows so little about. He is hounded by charities, and his friend Chitterlow persuades him to buy a quarter interest in a play which he is writing. Kipps' uncle invests the young man's money in antiques.

Now a wealthy man, Kipps again meets Helen Walsingham. This time, Helen responds differently, promising to teach Kipps the ways of the world and maneuvering him into proposing to her. Thereafter, she dominates Kipps' life regarding speech, dress, manner, attitudes, etc., and soon he tires of the whole thing. She even persuades him to replace his former solicitor with her brother, who has just opened an office.

While visiting his aunt, Kipps meets Ann Pornick again. She knows nothing of his new fortune, and he doesn't enlighten her. Pornick, whom Kipps had met earlier, is aware of Kipps' financial windfall, but he says nothing of it to Ann because he is now a socialist and despises Kipps. Ann is a natural woman, and Kipps yearns for her simplicity and the life he could have with her. Later, when she is a servant in a house where he is a guest, Kipps throws caution to the wind and proposes to her. Having just learned of his wealth, Ann cautiously accepts.

Because of idleness, their married life falls into the doldrums. Ann feels inferior and longs for a simple life, but Kipps feels that his wealth dictates that they live "well." Ann and Kipps continually argue about the architecture and size of the house Kipps proposes to build for them.

Change occurs when Helen Walsingham informs Kipps that her brother lost Kipps' money in bad investments and fled the country. With the money Kipps still has, he and Ann open a bookshop and live the simple life for which they have both longed. Then Chitterlow's play becomes a great success, and investor Kipps is again wealthy. But Ann has presented him with a son, and he is no longer interested in wealth. In fact he already considers himself the happiest man alive!

The Dickensian flavor of *Kipps* is obvious. The novel is also somewhat autobiographical. Of the book, Wells wrote that "*Kipps* is designed to present a typical member of the English lower-class in all its pitiful limitation and feebleness, and beneath a treatment deliberately kind and general provides a fairly sustained criticism of the ideals and ways of the great mass of middle-class English people." Of course, Wells was in a position to comment on both classes.

THE FILMS

Kipps (1921) Stoll, Great Britain

CREDITS: Directed by Harold Shaw; Screenplay by Frank Miller.

CAST: George K. Arthur (Kipps), Edna Flugarth (Ann), Christine Rayner (Helen), Teddy Arundel (Chitterlow), Norman Thorpe (Mr. Coote), Arthur Helmore, John M. East.

Synopsis and Adapation

The 1922 version of *Kipps* is apparently lost. Surviving stills, however, suggest that the film followed the novel fairly closely.

Production and Marketing

George K. Arthur (1899–1985) proved a popular English actor in such films as *Kipps* and *A Dear Fool*. He went to America and found popularity in such films as *Madness of Youth* (1923), *Lights of Old*

Broadway (1925), *The Boyfriend* (1926), *Rookies* (1927, the first in a series of comedies with Karl Dane), *The Last of Mrs. Chenyey* (1929), and *Oliver Twist* (1933). He later became a distributor and financier of art shorts.

Strengths, Weaknesses, and Rating

Since the film does not exist for viewing, we can only speculate about its strengths and weaknesses. In his book *H.G. Wells in the Cinema*, Alan Wykes judges from existing stills that, probably due to the popularity of music halls, the comic scenes were played more broadly for laughs than in the 1941 version. After all, the film itself was an adaptation of a stage version of *Kipps*.

No rating is possible

The Remarkable Mr. Kipps (1941) aka *Kipps* Twentieth Century, Great Britain / Running Time: 108 minutes / Release Date: May, 1942 (in United States)

CREDITS: Directed by Carol Reed; Produced by Filippo del Giudice; Executive Producer—Edward Black; Screenplay by Frank Launder and Sidney Gilliat, based on the novel by H.G. Wells; Cinematography by Arthur Crabtree; Art Direction by Vetchinsky; Edited by Alfred Roone.

CAST: Michael Redgrave (Arthur Kipps), Philip Frost (Kipps as a Boy), Phyllis Calvert (Ann Pornick), Diana Calderwood (Ann as a Girl), Diana Wynyard (Helen Walsingham), Michael Wilding (Ronnie Walsingham), Mackenzie Ward (Pearce), Arthur Riscoe (Chitterlow), Max Adrian (Chester Coote), Helen Haye (Mrs. Walshingham), Lloyd Pearson (Shalford), Edward Rigbby (Buggins), Mackenzie Ward (Pearce), Hermione Baddeley (Miss Mergle), Betty Ann Davies (Flo Bates), Arthur Denton (Carshot), Betty Jardine (Doris), Frank Pettingell (Old Kipps), Beatrice Varley (Mrs. Kipps), George Carney (Old Pornick), Irene Browne (Mrs. Bindon-Botting), Peter Garves (Sidney Revel), Viscouint Castlerosse (Man in Bath Chair).

Film Synopsis

Fourteen-year-old Arthur Kipps wants Ann Pornick to be his girl, and she agrees. When he has to commence a seven year drapery apprenticeship, he gives Ann a love token in the form of half a sixpence, keeping the other half for himself. While slaving away in obsequious fashion as a drapery clerk, nineteen-year-old Arthur Kipps signs up for a self-improvement class offered by the Cultural Institute. He immediately becomes enamored of Miss Walsingham, an upper-crust woodcutting instructor. She, however, views Kipps as beneath her and acts accordingly. All the while, Kipps keeps the half of a sixpence he split with Ann.

A bicycling mishap leads to his acquaintance with Chitterlow, a playwright who is completing a play that makes fun of the upper class. Kipps is sacked for being late for work but soon learns from Chitterlow that he has inherited 26,000 pounds from a grandfather he never heard of. Freed at last from dull labor, Kipps visits his aunt and uncle and meets Ann after so many years. She reminds Kipps of the sixpence but is saddened because she is no longer in his social class.

Kipps invests in Chitterlow's play and quickly forgets his gesture of kindness. Soon he learns that Miss Walsingham is now interested in him and visits her at the home of a friend. Kipps is awkward during their conversation, but after a brief courtship, she talks him into proposing to her. She immediately tries to change his name to Cuyps, suggests changes in his pronunciation of words, and alters his dress. She also disapproves of his old friends and gets him to allow her wicked brother to manage his finances.

At the ocean, Kipps again meets

Ann, who is now a maid at a nearby house. At a social function at the house, Ann learns that Kipps is engaged and angrily returns his half of the sixpence. Kipps realizes the error of his ways, proposes to Ann and the two flee the house together.

Kipps soon discovers that Miss Walsingham's brother has embezzled most of his fortune. Now seemingly a poor man once again, he marries Ann and reunites the two halves of the sixpence at last. Together, they open a modest bookshop and are happy. Though neither are interested in being wealthy, they learn that Chitterlow's play is a success and Kipps and Ann will be comfortable for the rest of their lives as a result of the royalties.

Adaptation

The Remarkable Mr. Kipps is remarkably faithful to Wells' novel. No important character is cut, and the film's 108 minute running time allows screenwriter Gilliat to cross all the t's and dot the i's.

Production and Marketing

Director Sir Carol Reed (1906–1976) is one of England's most important filmmakers. Among his most notable accomplishments are *Bank Holiday* (1938), *The Stars Look Down* (1939), *Night Train to Munich* (1941), *The Way Ahead* (1944), *Odd Man Out* (1946), *The Fallen Idol* (1948, for which he earned an Academy Award nomination), *The Third Man* (1949, for which he earned an Academy Award nomination), and *An Outcast of the Islands* (1951). Though he continued making films into the fifties and sixties, the quality of his direction waned, the high point of his later years being *Oliver!* (1968, for which he won an Academy Award).

Distinguished British actor Sir Michael Redgrave (1908–1985) began as a schoolmaster but turned to acting of a different sort, graduating to stage and screen. Among his most memorable screen achievements are *The Stars Look Down* (1939), *Jeannie* (1941), *Thunder Rock* (1942), *Dead of Night* (1945), *Fame Is the Spur* (1947), *The Browning Version* (1950, my favorite of all his performances), *The Importance of Being Earnest* (1952), *The Dam Busters* (1955), *Nineteen Eighty-Four* (1956), *The Quiet American* (1958), *The Innocents* (1961), *The Loneliness of the Long Distance Runner* (1963) and *The Go-Between* (1971).

Distinguished British stage actress Diana Wynard (1906–1964) began her film career at MGM. She was the wife of director Carol Reed. Her best screen outings include *Rasputin and the Empress* (1932), *Cavalcade* (1933, for which she earned an Academy Award nomination), and *Gaslight* (1940).

British leading lady Phyllis Calvert (1915–) broke into show business as a child actress. Among her best films are *The Man in Grey* (1943), *Fanny by Gaslight* (1944), *Madonna of the Seven Moons* (1944), and *My Own True Love* (1948).

Irish stage actor Max Adrian (1903–1973) is probably best remembered today by theater goers for his impersonation of George Bernard Shaw. Among his best films are *The Young Mr. Pitt* (1942), *Henry V* (1945), *Dr. Terror's House of Horrors* (1965), *The Deadly Affair* (1966) and three films directed by Ken Russell: *The Music Lovers* (1970), *The Devils* (1971), and *The Boyfriend* (1971).

British stage actress Helen Haye (1874–1957) contributed to such films as *The Spy in Black* (1939), *Dear Octopus* (1943), *Anna Karenina* (1948), and *Richard III* (1956). She often appeared in films as a kindly dowager, as she does in *The Remarkable Mr. Kipps*.

British leading man Michael Wilding (1912–1979) might be best known today for having married four wives, including

Elizabeth Taylor and Margaret Leighton. Still, he appeared in many a good film, including *Sailors Three* (1940), *In Which We Serve* (1942), *Dear Octopus* (1943), *English Without Tears* (1944), *Picadilly Incident* (1946), *Spring in Park Lane* (1948), *Under Capricorn* (1950), *Stage Fright* (1950), *Waterloo* (1969), and *Lady Caroline Lamb* (1972). He also appeared in the top-notch television film *Frankenstein: The True Story* (1973).

British stage actress Betty Ann Davies (1910–1955) appeared in *Chick* (1934) before being tapped for *The Remarkable Mr. Kipps*. She would later appear in the Wells vehicle *The History of Mr. Polly* (1949), as well as *Trio* (1950) and *The Belles of St. Trinians*.

British screenwriter Sidney Gilliat (1908–1994) usually collaborated with Frank Launder. Together, they produced most of their films after 1940. Among his most notable screenplays are *Rome Express* (1933), *Friday the Thirteenth* (1933), *A Yank at Oxford* (1938), *The Lady Vanishes* 1938), *Ask a Policeman* (1939), *Night Train to Munich* (1935), *The Young Mr. Pitt* (1942). He both wrote and directed *Waterloo Road* (1942), *The Rake's Progress* (1945), *Green for Danger* (1946), *State Secret* (1950), and *Only Two Can Play* (1962).

Strengths

Carol Reed's sure-handed direction of such a whimsical film at the time England was entering World War II is admirable. The sturdy British cast of stage veterans are all up to the task. Especially noteworthy are Michael Redgrave as simple, good-hearted Kipps, Max Adrian as the mincing Mr. Coote, Lloyd Pearson as the hard driving and precise Shalford, Diana Wynyard as the cool Helen Walsingham, Arthur Riscoe as the haphazard Chitterlow, and Phyllis Calvert as the tender servant girl Ann. Also on the plus side of the ledger are Gilliat's meticulous screenplay, the film's old fashioned charm,

that will still make most viewers smile, and Reed's successful turning of the story's upper class snobs into stuffy, pompous, and pretentious charicatures.

Sir Carol Reed turns a three-star novel into a three-star film, treating us to fine acting and character development in the context of a slow plot. On the whole, the film is still worth watching, though it is no classic.

Weaknesses

Wells' novel is not particularly dramatic, a problem that transfers to the screen; therefore, Gilliat's meticulous screenplay is a double-edged sword, true to the novel but rather thin. At least one critic complained that many of the characters are so smug that we have difficulty caring about them. Viewers turned off by things British might beware.

Rating: 3

Half a Sixpence (1967)   Paramount, Great Britain / Running Time: 148 minutes / Release Date:

CREDITS: Directed by George Sidney; Produced by Charles H. Schneer and George Sidney; Screenplay by Beverley Cross; Based on the musical *Half a Sixpence*; Adapted by Dorothy Kingsley from the novel *Kipps* by H.G. Wells; Originally produced for the stage by Harold Fielding; Cinematography by Geoffrey Unsworth; Music and lyrics by David Heneker; Music supervised, arranged, and conducted by Irwin Kostal; Color by Technicolor; Production design by Ted Haworth; Art direction by Peter Morton; Executive producer— John Dark; Edited by Bill Lewthwaite and Frank Santillo; Choreography by Gillian Lynne; Unit manager—David Price; Location manager—Leslie Korda; Makeup by George Frost.

CAST: Tommy Steele (Arthur Kipps), Julia Foster (Ann), Cyril Ritchard (Chitterlow), Penelope Horner (Helen), Grover Dale (Pearce), Elaine Taylor (Victoria), Hilton Edwards (Shalford), Julia Sutton (Flo), Leslie Meadows (Boggins), Sheila Falconer (Date),

Christopher Sadford (Sid), Pamela Brown (Mrs. Walsingham), James Villiers (Hubert), Jean Anderson (Lady Botting), Allan Cuthbertson (Wilkins), Aleta Morrison (Laura), Gerald Campion (Fat Boy), Bartlett Mullins (Carsbott), Harry Locke (Weight Guesser), Julian Orchard (Photographer), James Bolam (Mr. Jones), Carole Walker (Edith), Humphrey Kent (The Butler), Norman Mitchell (Master of Ceremonies), Bridget Armstrong (The Maid); Jeffrey Chandler (Young Kipps), Deborah Permentor (Young Ann).

Film Synopsis

Young Arthur Kipps is sent to town to work as a draper's apprentice at Shalford's Emporium. Before leaving, he and his girlfriend Ann find a sixpence, which Arthur keeps as a memento of their friendship. Once in town, Arthur and his co-workers find themselves exploited by the rigid Shalford, whose motto is "Efficiency, System, and Economy." Arthur grows into a young man and receives a letter from Ann asking to meet him when she visits the city. They meet on the promenade and reaffirm their love for one another. As a token of their love, they split the sixpence they found as children and each keep half as a reminder of their commitment.

One of Shalford's best upper class customers, Mrs. Walsingham, offers self-improvement classes for the working class. Shalford bullies Arthur into signing up for a woodcarving class taught by Mrs. Walsingham's daughter Helen. Arthur is immediately infatuated with her, but she is out of his social class and pays him little attention.

A bicycle mishap introduces Arthur to Harry Chitterlow, an actor and playwright, who in turn introduces Arthur to life in the theater. Because of a misunderstanding, Arthur and Ann quarrel and become estranged. Chitterlow suddenly reappears with news that Arthur has inherited a massive fortune from a great grandfather he knew nothing about. On a whim, the exuberant Arthur invests in a play being composed by Chitterlow, quits Shalford's Emporium, and, as best he can, takes on the life of an independently wealthy English gentleman. With all his world travel and social niceties, Arthur nevertheless finds his life empty. When he runs into Mrs. Walsingham, Helen, and her brother Hubert at an outdoor ballet, he finds Helen, once out of his class, now interested in him. As Arthur begins socializing with the Walsinghams, he agrees to let Hubert manage his finances.

Arthur soon discovers that Ann works as a maid in the Walsingham household. At a rowing event at the lake, Arthur runs into Ann on the promenade. Ann still has her half a sixpence, but Arthur says he left his in another suit. Ann thinks that Arthur is still her man, but before he can explain otherwise, Mrs. Walsingham announces to all assembled that Arthur and Helen are engaged. A devastated Ann throws down her half a sixpence and runs away in tears. Arthur sadly retrieves the token and wonders if he is really going to find happiness with Helen and upper class living. Of course, the Walsingham's try to turn Arthur into a snobbish gentleman (e.g. "a gentleman never perspires!"), but he is still a commoner at heart.

At a palatial dinner party, Arthur's simple approach to things leads to social disaster. Mrs. Walsingham insults Ann, who is working as a maid, and Arthur leaps to her defense. Declaring his engagement off, Arthur proposes marriage to Ann and the two make preparations for their life together. Ann, however, is not happy with Arthur's insistence that they build an eleven bedroom house for entertaining guests. She wants only a simple life. Arthur soon learns that the simple life is in store for him too since Hubert has lost Arthur's inheritance through bad investments and has left the country, leaving him poor once again.

As the future looks bleak, Chitterlow

arrives and informs Arthur that the play he invested in is a great success and that Arthur is wealthy once again. This time, their sixpence now a whole, Arthur and Ann decide to live the lives they feel comfortable living, regardless of their wealth. A small house is just the thing.

Adaptation

Half a Sixpence is a musical, and while Wells' novel is tune-free, the film adapts the novel faithfully. Though Pornick and Coote are cut and Ann does not provide Arthur with a child, etc., the film doesn't notably digress from the novel. As with The Remarkable Mr. Kipps, the longer than usual running time allows for adequate development. Though one might argue that the additional time is taken up by songs and dances, the music develops the characters rather than place them in the background.

Production and Marketing

Wells' novel Kipps was adapted for the stage before it was for the screen. It resurfaced in London and New York as a very successful play in the 1960s. The star of the show on stage and film was Tommy Steele (1936–), an energetic cockney performer and popular singer. Previous to Half a Sixpence he had appeared on screen in such outings as Kill Me Tomorrow (1953), The Tommy Steele Story (1957), Tommy the Toreador (1960), and The Happiest Millionaire (1967, the last Disney film overseen by Walt himself). After Half a Sixpence, Steele appeared in the popular Finian's Rainbow (1968) and Where's Jack? (1969).

British leading lady Julia Foster's (1941–) most notable film before Half a Sixpence was Alfie (1966). She later appeared in the U.S. television production F. Scott Fitzgerald in Hollywood (1976).

British dancer and light comedian

Cyril Ritchard (1896–1977) spent most of his impressive career on stage where he played Captain Hook to Mary Martin's Peter Pan in Peter Pan. He did, however, appear on screen in Alfred Hitchcock's Blackmail (1929).

Irish producer and impresario Hilton Edwards (1903–1982) was long associated with the Abbey Theatre. His screen work includes the forgotten Return to Glennascaul (1953) and the groundbreaking film with homosexual themes Victim (1961). He also appeared in Orson Welles' television production of Filming Othello .

British stage actress Pamela Brown (1917–1975) appeared in such well-received films as I Know Where I'm Going (1945), Tales of Hoffman (1951), Richard III (1956), and Becket (1964). After 1967 she went on to appear in such fare as Wuthering Heights (1970), On a Clear Day You Can See Forever (1970), Lady Caroline Lamb (1972) and the television production of Dracula (1973).

American director George Sidney (1911–) began his career as a musician and a short subject director at MGM. Prior to 1967 he directed such notable films as Thousands Cheer (1943), Bathing Beauty (1944), Anchors Aweigh (1945), The Harvey Girls (1946), The Three Musketeers (1948), Showboat (1951), Kiss Me Kate (1953), Jeanne Eagles (1957), Bye Bye Birdie (1962), and Viva Las Vegas (1963, starring Elvis Presley). It was his obvious flare for musicals that placed him at the helm for Half a Sixpence.

British cinematographer Geoffrey Unsworth (1914–1978) racked up a number of impressive credits during his career with the camera, some prominent examples being A Night to Remember (1958), Becket (1964, for which he won a British Film Academy Award), 2001: A Space Odyssey (1968), Cabaret (1972, for which he won an Academy Award), Murder on the Orient Express (1974), and Tess (1979, for which he won both an Academy Award and a British Film Academy Award).

In 1967, due to the popularity of the Beatles and James Bond, American studios were financing anything British that carried hope for box office success. In its advertising, Paramount relied on the film's Edwardian appeal to draw audiences.

Strengths

The multi-talented Tommy Steele heads up a strong cast as all the thespians, particularly Julia Foster, Cyril Ritchard, and Hilton Edwards give fine performances. Veteran director Sidney and accomplished cinematographer Unsworth are sure-footed throughout. For example, they take us through a work day at Shalford's Emporium by quick cutting from one still photo to another, perfectly capturing the workday madness. A nice touch is achieved as the young workers discuss Marxism in the cellar of the Emporium, their room appropriately decorated with portraits of the grimacing Shalford and Karl Marx. Since the film is an energetic musical comedy, the camera suggests movement by shooting from a variety of angles. Also notable is an effective use of close-ups, one being of a bubbling Kipps as we look up at him from the bottom a horse trough as Shalford forces his head under water. In scenes depicting Kipps' growing infatuation with Helen, Unsworth employs a vaseline lens to suggest the dream-like quality of Kipps' experience. During the rowing contest we see Ann running breathlessly along the bank cheering on Kipps as Helen rides with regal serenity in a boat following the rowers. The camera holds a shot of Helen as the bridge and Ann recede in the distance, suggesting their relative social positions and the fact that Ann is receding as an important part of Kipps' life.

Dance scenes are colorfully choreographed and most of the tunes are both catchy and well dubbed, particularly "Half a Sixpence," "Flash, Bang, Wallop!" and "All in the Cause of Economy." Early in the film the camera invites us to feast visually on the beautiful English countryside. The comedy works too. Giving an over-the-top performance, Cyril Ritchard sprinkles his speech with phrases from Shakespeare. When Ritchard as Chitterlow introduces Kipps to a bottle-tipping, seductively dressed chorus girl, Kipps gasps, "She's a bit hot!" to which Chitterlow replies, "Only on the surface. Below breathes the soul of a milkmaid."

Near the end of the film, the camera tracks Kipps as he walks the perimeter of a gazebo and stares sadly at a motionless carousel, all suggesting the circularity of Kipps' journey from poverty to riches to poverty.

Half a Sixpence is fun. There are some memorable musical numbers and one will probably remember certain favorite scenes long after the final curtain. Still, the film is finally a well-done sixties popcorn movie: an underrated musical still worth seeing for its many strengths. In addition, I think it probably would have given H.G. Wells a chuckle.

Weaknesses

Audiences will either like the ever-smiling Tommy Steele or they won't. Some may find him tedious. A matter of taste, possibly. Now, audiences finding Tommy Steele tedious will be unlikely to enjoy the film, which accounts for its lukewarm reviews. There is also a fantasy sequence near the end during which Kipps imagines all the faces from his upper class past laughing at him. Unfortunately, the sequence does not work well. The film's greatest weakness is its lack of "gravitas." But what do you expect from a musical comedy, anyway!

Rating: 3

13

"The Door in the Wall" (1906)

THE SHORT STORY

Wells published his short story "The Door in the Wall" in the *Daily Chronicle*, July 14, 1906 and collected it in *The Door in the Wall and Other Stories* in 1911. In 1906, Wells also published *In the Days of the Comet*, an elaboration on his short story "The Star" (1897). A prominent message of the novel is one of free and group sex. Wells' reputation as a philanderer had been established as a result of his affairs with Fabians Amber Reeves and Rosemund Bland, as well as with several Fabian's wives. His libertine free-thinking roused the ire of conservatives and the praise of liberals, as did his political and economic positions in *Socialism and the Family* (1906). Because of the close publication of the two books, Wells found himself defending against the charge that the ultimate aim of his socialism was free love. Perhaps the turmoil in Wells' life led him to revisit in "The Door in the Wall" a theme he had explored in "Mr. Skelmersdale in Fairyland" and *The Sea Lady*—that of escape to a paradisal alternative world.

Short Story Scenario and Commentary

The story concerns Lionel Wallace, a man haunted by a childhood memory who is also a prominent politician awaiting a cabinet appointment. As a boy, he went through a green door in a white wall and discovered a world there that made the rest of his life pale by comparison. Years later he reveals to his friend Redmond the effect that this experience had on him. He entered a beautiful garden, he says, peopled by a lovely woman who showed him a living picture book and by children who taught him wonderful games that he could not remember upon leaving the garden. As years pass, Wallace sees the door six more times, but he is always too busy advancing his life to stop and re-enter that wonderful world. Finally, he realizes that the door symbolizes for him an escape from the cares and concerns crowding all the joy from his life. When Wallace is killed after falling through a door into an excavation site near East Kensington, Redmond concludes that Wallace "had, in truth, an abnormal gift, and a sense, something—I know not what—that in the guise of wall and door offered him an outlet, a secret and peculiar passage of escape into another and altogether more beautiful world."

After publishing "The Door in the Wall," Wells wrote few short stories over the last forty years of his life. Of his virtual abandonment of the short story he wrote in his autobiography:

> I was once an industrious writer of short stories, and that I am no longer anything of the kind.... I find it a little difficult to disentangle the causes that have restricted the flow of these inventions. It has happened, I remark, to others as well as to myself, and in spite of the kindliest encouragement to continue from editors and readers. There was a time when life bubbled with short stories: they were always coming to the surface of my mind, and it is no deliberate change of will that has thus restricted my production. It is rather, I think, a diversion of attention to more substantial and more exacting forms [Hammond, p. 75].

Today, "The Door in the Wall" is considered one of Wells' most disturbing and evocative short stories.

THE FILMS

The Door in the Wall (1953 or 1956)
The British Film Institute, Great Britain

CREDITS: Directed by Glenn H. Alvey, Jr.

CAST: Stephen Murray (Sir Frank), Kit Terrington (Frank as a Boy), Leonard Sachs (The Father), Ann Blake (The Aunt), and Ian Hunter.

Film Synopsis and Adaptation

Since this film never received a public showing and is unavailable today on video, I Neither a synopsis nor comment on the adaptation is provided.

Production and Marketing

In his book *H.G. Wells in the Cinema*, Alan Wykes gives 1956 as the film's date. J.R. Hammond's *The H.G. Wells Companion* recommends Wykes' book but gives the film's date as 1953. Other sources give 1956 as the date; therefore, 1956 is more likely. Regardless, we know that the British Film Institute sponsored the production with the aid of Associated British and Pathé. It was an experimental film designed to test the Matte Process, Glenn H. Alvey, Jr.'s new technique which prevented exposure on one part of the film in order to create a special effect during later exposure. This allowed audiences to see two bits of action simultaneously on different parts of the screen.

The film was never publicly shown, but stills indicate that a boy goes through a door in a wall and encounters wonders on the other side. The fact that the main character is portrayed as both a child and later as an adult indicates that Wells' plot was at least broadly followed. In one still, however, we see the schoolboy lounging against the scaly leg of a dinosaur called Yoicks, suggesting that time itself might have been altered behind the wall as it is not in the short story.

British character actor of stage and screen Stephen Murray (1912–1983) appeared in such films as *Pygmalion* (1938), *The Prime Minister* (1941), *Next of Kin* (1942), *Master of Bankdam* (1946), *London Belongs to Me* (1948), *Four-Sided Triangle* (1953), *A Tale of Two Cities* (1958), and *The Nun's Story* (1959).

British character actor of stage and screen Ian Hunter (1900–1975) appeared in many films in both Great Britain and the United States. Included in his work is *The Sign of Four* (1932, as Dr. Watson), *A*

Midsummer Night's Dream (1935), *52nd Street* (1938), *The Adventures of Robin Hood* (1938, as King Richard), *Tower of London* (1939), *Dr. Jekyll and Mr. Hyde* (1941, as Lanyon), and *Edward My Son* (1949).

Strengths, Weakness, and Rating

I can provide no comments as I have not seen the film.

14

The War in the Air (1908)

THE NOVEL

In 1907, Wells broke with the Fabians over the type of socialism each supported. Meanwhile, he continued to defend his 1906 publications *In the Days of the Comet* and *Socialism and the Family* against detractors. The attacks on his books brought Wells great notoriety and probably added to sales and an eagerness for his next writings. Public anticipation was satisfied in 1908 when Wells published *New Worlds for Old* and *First and Last Things*, originally subtitled *A Confession of Faith and Rule of Life*. Though revised in 1917, it remains the most comprehensive presentation of the author's social and political thought. In the book, Wells defends a collectivist philosophy of nature, arguing that all living things, with the exception of human beings, have as their goal the good of the species as a whole. Human beings, however possess a more selfish nature which must be altered through education. Such education is unfortunately opposed by the church, the state, and sometimes the family. In Book III, Section 3 Wells writes that:

> Socialism for me is a common step we are all taking in the great synthesis of human purpose. It is the organization, in regard to a great mass of common and fundamental interests that have hitherto been despersedly served, of a collective purpose.... We look towards the day, the day of the organized civilized world state.... Socialism is to me no more and no less than the awakening of a collective consciousness in humanity, a collective will and a collective mind out of which finer individualities may arise forever in a perpetual series of fresh endeavors and fresh achievements for the race.

Wells goes on to decry class warfare and champion women's rights.

He was then an optimist and remained so until his latter years. In 1908, the world he hoped to change had not yet turned his utopian dream into a nightmare. Also in 1908, Wells published *The War in the Air*, a science fiction adventure warning of the consequences of aerial warfare.

Novel Scenario and Commentary

Bert Smallway is part owner of a run-down Bun Hill (Bromley) bicycle shop. He is "a vulgar creature, the sort of pert, limited soul that the old civilisation of the early twentieth century produced by the million in every country of the world. He had lived all his life in narrow streets, and between mean houses he could not look over, and in a narrow circle of ideas from which there was no escape." When Bert's bicycle shop goes broke, he and his partner walk the beaches performing a song and dance act.

As Bert's inconsequential life grinds on, larger events are happening in England and the world. All the world powers, led by Germany and a united China and Japan, have their own fleets of dirigibles. Aerial flight in a heavier-than-air machine is imminent, and already an inventor named Mr. Butteridge has flown a demonstration flight around England. In exchange for a peerage for his disgraced mistress, Butteridge offers the British government his invention, but they refuse.

After a beach performance, Bert tries to aid the occupant of a malfunctioning air balloon. The occupant jumps free, but the balloon accidentally whisks Bert away. The occupant is Mr. Butteridge, who has left in the balloon the plans for his invention. The balloon carries Bert to Germany where it lands at a Zeppelin park just as Germany is sending an air fleet to attack the United States. When Bert is mistaken for Butteridge, the kindly bumbler assumes the role and travels in the flagship Zeppelin. Bert soon gives himself away, however, and the German super dirigibles, each containing several primitive one-man flying machines, launch an attack on New York under the command of the German warlord, Prince Karl Albert. New York officials surrender, but New York residents refuse to cooperate and quickly become victims of German saturation bombing. A battle then ensues between Germany and the United States, during which time the flagship Zeppelin is disabled. A storm blows the dirigible (and Bert) to Labrador, where the now-isolated Germans construct a wireless and contact the main fleet posted at Niagara Falls.

Over the wireless, the Germans learn that war has broken out all over the world. The superior air fleet of united China and Japan are conquering London, Paris, Berlin, and Rome. Other Oriental fleets have attacked India and the United States. Soon, an Oriental fleet conquers the Germans at Niagara Falls.

During the battle over Niagara Falls, Bert seeks refuge on Goat Island where he later encounters Prince Albert and his assistant. Bert is forced to shoot the monomaniacal prince and afterwards pilots a downed Oriental flyer to the United States where he turns over Butteridge's plans to the crippled government. But help has come too late. Civilization has fallen:

> The great nations and empires have become but names in the mouths of men. Everywhere there are ruins and unburied dead, and shrunken, yellow-faced survivors in a mortal apathy. Here there are robbers, here vigilance committees, and here guerilla bands ruling patches of exhausted territory, strange federations and brotherhoods form and dissolve, and religious fanaticisms begotten of despair gleam in famine-bright eyes. It is universal dissolution.

Meanwhile, India rebels against the Chinese-Japanese and small air battles commence between any countries that can get fighting fleets into the air.

After several years of wandering, Bert returns to England a mature, capable, and somewhat ruthless man. With civilization gone, with no political or economic institutions intact, he provides help for his family and neighbors.

The full title of the book was *The War in the Air and Particularly How Mr. Bert Smallways Fared While it Lasted*. It was written in 1907, serialized in the *Pall Mall Magazine* beginning in January, 1908, and published as a book that same year. It is a very uneven book. Bert Smallways is a character much like Arthur Kipps, and in the opening chapters of the book, Wells showcases the same sense of detail for rural life and human behavior that he did in *Kipps.* The last part of the book is a pessimistic picture of world disaster. The problem is that the light adventure of the first part does not fit well with the nightmarish vision of the second.

In the book, Wells warns of militarism. He also suggests that air power is incapable of conquering an area because, while it can kill earth-bound civilians, it cannot occupy the area. Also, it cannot necessarily overcome opposing air forces. Wells' novel is indeed prophetic. When he wrote the book in 1907, Bleriot had not yet crossed the English channel by air, and his prediction of the way airships would change the art of war was directly on the mark. Wells was right to call the novel a "fantasia of possibility."

THE FILMS

The Airship Destroyer (1909) aka *The Battle in the Clouds,* aka *The Aerial Torpedo*
Urban, Great Britain / Running Time: 11 minutes

CREDITS: Directed by Walter R. Booth; Screenplay by Walter R. Booth; Produced by Charles Urban.

Film Synopsis

Walter R. Booth breaks his film into three parts: preparation, attack, and defense. In the first part, supplies are landed at an aerocamp and an enemy airship flies off to conquer England. In England, an inventor proposes marriage to his girlfriend, but is rebuffed by her father. The announcement comes that England is under attack, and the young inventor rises to the occasion, partly in order to impress his girl and her father.

In the second part, as an enemy aircraft drops bombs on the English countryside, an armoured car pursues the vehicle with guns blazing. The car proves no match for the plane, however, and is quickly dispatched by a bomb. The aircraft then bombs the railway line, derailing a plane and killing a signal operator. British planes attack in self defense, but the invader shoots them down and continues its barrage of death. The inventor rescues his girlfriend when her house is hit by a bomb.

In the third part, the inventor and his girlfriend deploy his aerial torpedo, which is controlled by wireless electricity. The torpedo hits the aircraft and sends it down in flames, after which the inventor marries his girlfriend with the full approval of her father.

Adaptation

Though *The Airship Destroyer* is suggested in part by Wells' *The War in the Air,* it is no straight adaptation. The film borrows the concept of air warfare from Wells, and there is a hero of sorts in both novel and film. In the novel, however, the hero is too late to save civilization while in the film the hero manages to save the day.

Production and Marketing

The Airship Destroyer was England's first science fiction film. Writer and director Walter R. Booth had worked previously on the comic *Professor Puddenhead's Patents* film series. Ads for the film in trade papers proclaimed: "War in the Air! Possibilities of the Future! An actual motion picture prediction of the ideas of Rudyard Kipling, H.G. Wells, Jules Verne, and other powerful writers of imaginative fiction." The promotion said that the film would show what could happen if aeroplanes are perfected as engines of war, and it reminded theater owners of a recent air meet held and filmed in Doncaster and Blackpool.

The film's main literary sources are Rudyard Kipling's "With the Night Mail: A Story of 2000 A.D.," H.G. Wells' *The War in the Air* and Jules Verne's *Robur the Conqueror* and *Master of the World*. Other sources probably included Fenton Ash's *A Son of the Stars* and *A Trip to Mars*.

The film was re-released as *The Aerial Torpedo* in 1915 during the Zeppelin attacks of World War I.

Strengths, Weaknesses, and Rating

The Airship Destroyer is a lost film. It was apparently good enough to have been re-released, but, as it has not been viewed it cannot be critiqued.

15

The History of Mr. Polly (1910)

THE NOVEL

In December of 1909, Amber Reeves, after marrying G.R. Blanco-White, gave birth to Wells' illegitimate daughter. The Wellses then moved to Church Row, Hampstead. That same year, Wells published two of his most critically acclaimed novels, *Tono-Bungay* and *Ann Veronica*, the latter being a thinly disguised account of his affair with Amber Reeves. In 1910, Wells published what today some critics consider his greatest novel, *The History of Mr. Polly*.

Novel Scenario and Commentary

Mr. Polly is a frustrated thirty-five year old man. He hates everyone, particularly his wife and his co-workers. His life begins happily enough when, as a baby, he is coddled by his adoring parents. At the age of seven, however, his mother dies. After some ineffectual schooling he is apprenticed by his father as a draper's assistant. After completing his apprenticeship in a job he loathed, he goes unsuccessfully from one draper's shop to another. Mr. Polly is unsuited for shop work because he is a dreamer. He spends most of his money on books, which at intervals allows him to escape his humdrum existence. What Mr. Polly really lacks is companions.

When Polly's father dies, he inherits three hundred ninety-five pounds. Turning down advice that he open a shop, he decides to go on a holiday. At his father's funeral, the newly wealthy Mr. Polly finds himself romantically pursued by his three female cousins. He ends up marrying his cousin Miriam and opening a drapery shop. Polly spends an unhappy fifteen years as a respectable shopkeeper only to find himself in debt. Unable to predict the response of his slovenly wife to this news, Polly decides to set fire to his shop, cut his throat before being devoured by the flames, and leave Miriam with the insurance money. He waits till Sunday when most everyone is at church and sets the shop afire. When the flames lick his trouser legs, however, he runs from the shop, after which the fire burns out half the business district. In rescuing a deaf old lady Polly becomes an unlikely hero. Suddenly he looks upon himself through different eyes. Taking only twenty-one pounds for himself, he leaves the rest for Miriam and simply disappears. Wandering freely through the country, he discovers nature, makes acquaintances, and finds joy for the first time.

After a month, Mr. Polly stops at a wayside inn and makes the acquaintance of its owner, a plump cheerful woman. Mr. Polly, who is fond of the woman, takes a job as a handyman at the inn. The woman, however is periodically assaulted by her brutish nephew, Uncle Jim, who takes her money and stays away until he is again low on funds. When Uncle Jim shows up, Polly confronts the situation in heroic fashion and thrashes the woman's tormentor, who takes Polly's clothes and disappears.

After five years at the inn, Mr. Polly begins to feel sorry for Miriam and her loss of a husband and returns to the village to find that she and her sisters have opened a tea room. They considered Polly dead because a man wearing his clothes was earlier fished from the river. Miriam who has collected insurance money on her husband's assumed death, is terrified that his return lead to her paying back the amount. Polly assures her that she need not worry, asks her to be silent about his return, and leaves her with the money.

Mr. Polly returns to the inn and settles into a mellow life of peace with the plump woman. Obviously, Uncle Jim will never return.

THE FILMS

The History of Mr. Polly (1949)

Rank-Two Cities, Great Britain / Release Date: 1949 in Great Britain, October 1951 in United States / Running Time: 94 Minutes

CREDITS: Produced by John Mills; Written and Directed by Anthony Pelissier, based on the novel by H.G. Wells; Cinematography by Desmond Dickinson and Raymond Sturgess; Music by William Alwyn; Edited by John Seabourne; Art Direction by Duncan Sutherland; Production Manager—Andrew Allen.

CAST: John Mills (Alfred Polly), Sally Ann Howes (Cristabel), Megs Jenkins (Plump Woman), Finlay Currie (Uncle Jim), Diana Churchill (Annie), Betty Ann Davies (Miriam), Edward Chapman (Mr. Johnson), Shelagh Fraser (Minnie), Moore Marriott (Uncle Pentistemon), Gladys Henson (Mrs. Larkins), Wylie Watson (Mr. Rusper), Miles Malleson (Old Gentleman), Doris Hare (May Punt), Dandy Nichols (Mrs. Johnson), Irene Handl (Lady on Left), Lawrence Baskomb (Mr. Rumbold), Edie Martin (Lady on Roof), Ernest Jay (Mr. Hinks), Cyril Smith (Mr. Voules), Dennis Arundel (Clergyman), Juliet Mills (Little Polly), David Horne (Mr. Garvace), Wally Patch (Customer), Victor Platt, Michael Ripper, Muriel Russell).

Film Synopsis

Mr. Alfred Polly is often late for work at the drapery because he forgets himself reading romance adventures, a habit that leads to his firing. He searches for work but finds none. He is a "social misfit." When his father dies, Polly is repulsed by the behavior of those who arrive for the funeral. His three female cousins and others stuff their faces with food and promote gaiety. Then, they assume an heir of solemnity at the funeral itself. When it becomes known that he has inherited five hundred pounds, he turns down advice to open a shop, buys a bicycle and sets out for adventures. On one of his outings, he visits his three female cousins and enjoys their attention. He seems oblivious to the fact that they all hunger for his money. While on a bicycle journey to find a shop to purchase, he meets a girl sitting on a wall. Her name is Christabel. Polly and the girl enter into a fantasy in which he is her knight errant. He wants to marry her, but when her meetings with Polly are discovered by the school she is attending, all bets are off, and Polly is crushed.

Polly then blunders into marriage

with his cousin Miriam before he realizes what he has done.

Fifteen years later, though Polly still dreams of knighthood, he finds himself a miserable, henpecked shopkeeper. When he discovers that he and Miriam are sixty pounds in debt, and after being bullied by a local merchant, he decides to burn down the shop, commit suicide in the process, and leave Miriam with the insurance money. Sunday would be a good time because Miriam will be at church. His plan goes afoul, however, when the shop catches fire prematurely and he is frightened into the streets before he can cut his throat. The fire, which destroys the shop district, allows Polly to play knight and rescue an elderly deaf woman. Inspired by his own heroism, he realizes that "If you don't like your life you can change it," and

leaves the village in search of a more interesting existence.

Polly stops at an inn where he meets the plump woman who runs the place. They become immediate friends, and she hires Polly as a handyman. The woman's niece, however, warns Polly about Uncle Jim, a relative who occasionally shows up at the inn to terrorize the plump woman and take her money. That night, Uncle Jim threatens Polly with great bodily harm if he stands in his way. Polly undergoes an inner conflict between whether or not this is his battle to fight. At last, he becomes the knight he wants to be and battles the drunken Uncle Jim. Drunk as he is, Jim loses but returns for revenge when Polly is asleep. This time, Jim must be content only with stealing Polly's clothes. Jim pursues Polly but accidentally falls

Betty Ann Davies and John Mills eye one another with disgust in this scene from *The History of Mr. Polly* (1949).

into the stream that runs swiftly beside the inn.

After three years, Polly feels guilty about leaving Miriam. He returns to the village to find that she and her sister have opened a tea room with insurance money and from the mistaken conclusion that Polly is dead, found drowned in the stream. Satisfied that all is well with Miriam, Polly returns to the inn and to the plump woman—and to a simple life of fishing, sunsets, and sweet companionship.

Adaptation

The film *The History of Mr. Polly* is a remarkably faithful adaptation of Wells' novel. The main characters are all in place and the plot runs an exact course with the novel. Though as in most cases, the book is fuller and ultimately more satisfying than the film, the celluloid version is probably as good an adaptation as one could reasonably expect.

Production and Marketing

British leading actor Sir John Mills (1908–2000) had a long, productive career in films. Overcoming a short stature, he became a major leading performer in the 1940s and went on to become a versatile character actor thereafter. Before producing and starring in *The History of Mr. Polly*, Mills had appeared in such fare as *Those Were the Days* (1934), *Goodbye Mr. Chipps* (1939), *Cottage to Let* (1941), *In Which We Serve* (1942), *Waterloo Road* (1944), *The Way to the Stars* (1945), *The October Man* (1947), and *Scott of the Antarctic* (1948). Afterwards, he graced such films as *The Rocking Horse Winner* (1950), *Hobson's Choice* (1954), *Town on Trial* (1957), *Tiger Bay* (1959), *The Swiss Family Robinson* (1961), *The Wrong Box* (1966), *Ryan's Daughter* (1971, for which he won an Academy Award), and *Gandhi* (1982). He was the

father of actresses Hayley and Juliet Mills, the latter of whom appears in *The History of Mr. Polly*.

For discussion of actress Betty Ann Davies, see Production and Marketing for *Kipps* (1941), and for discussion of actress Sally Ann Howes, see Production and Marketing for *Dead of Night* (1945). For a discussion of actor Edward Chapman, see Production and Marketing for *The Man Who Could Work Miracles* (1937).

Plump British actress Megs Jenkins (1917–1998) appeared in *Green for Danger* (1946), *The Monkey's Paw* (1948), *Ivanhoe* (1952), *The Innocents* (1961, probably her most memorable outing), and *Oliver* (1969).

Veteran Scottish actor Finlay Currie (1878–1968) turned in memorable performances in such films as *Great Expectations* (1946, as Magwitch), *Treasure Island* (1950), *The Mudlark* (1951, as John Brown), *Quo Vadis* (1951), *People Will Talk* (1952), *Ivanhoe* (1952), *Rob Roy* (1953), *Around the World in 80 Days* (1956), *Ben Hur* (1959), *The Adventures of Huckleberry Finn* (1960), and *Corridors of Blood* (1963).

British leading lady Diana Churchill (1913–1994) appeared mainly on stage until multiple sclerosis ended her career. Her films include *House of the Arrow* (1940), *Eagle Squadron* (1944), and *Scott of the Antarctic* (1948).

While *The History of Mr. Polly* played in British mainstream theaters, in America it played mainly in art houses. Make of that whatever you will.

Strengths

As is the case with many top-rung British productions, the film's main strength is its cast. Producer and star John Mills is perfect as Mr. Polly, projecting himself as a Don Quixote on bicycle, the quintessential common man who dreams of being something more. The entire cast is up to demand, and the result is delicious.

Director and screenwriter Anthony Pelissier adapts a very good novel to the screen as faithfully as possible. Any cinematic version requires artful pruning, and here the pruning is expert.

The film delivers humor in abundance. Polly's monologues and dialogues are often humorous, as when he evaluates his shop as "pretty arsonical," and when he contrasts himself with Uncle Joe as "nothing much bicepterically." In addition, the deaf old woman Polly rescues from the fire is comically uncooperative. Underlying all this, however, is a warm and charming assessment of the common man that will please many a viewer, especially as Polly is contrasted with those following plastic convention.

The film is also technically solid. The cinematographer makes good use of close-ups and keeps visual perspectives interesting. The film is ultimately hopeful for those extraordinary ordinary people longing for a more meaningful life.

Weaknesses

It may be typical of British films and other foreign films that matters unfold more slowly than in American films. The slower pace of *Mr. Polly* may bore today's viewers who demand swift action and plot development. This, however, may be a criticism of some viewers more than a criticism of the film. Overall, this is a fine fantasy that captures the flavor of its time and carries a universal message of hope.

Rating: 3

16

Marriage (1912)

THE NOVEL

H.G. Wells wrote *Marriage* at Pont-de-l'Arche in 1911 and published it in 1912. Having had his recent novels castigated as attacks on contemporary moral codes, Wells proclaimed in a letter to Sir Frederick Macmillan that: "The next book I'm planning won't cause any of this trouble— I'm passing out of a necessary phase in handling my medium. Sex must be handled, and few writers escape the gawky phrase."

Perhaps to see that sex was indeed handled correctly in *Marriage*, Jane Wells closely monitored the book from its British publication through its American serialization. As passing months brought slow sales, Wells became concerned that the book's new tone may be hurting its popularity. In response, he pestered Macmillan to publicize the book more vigorously. Wells was in a bind. On one hand, he needed money to pay off mounting financial responsibilities, but on the other, he feared that his attacks on conventional morality had hurt both his reputation and his sales.

Novel Scenario and Commentary

Richard Andrew Godwin Trafford is a physics professor devoted to scientific research. As time passes, Trafford becomes upset with science's increasing tendency to sell out secretly to the financial and commercial world. He abandons his scientific goals when he falls in love with and marries Marjorie Pope, who had been engaged to another man. Marjorie is a beautiful woman with "an abundance of copper-red hair, which flowed back very prettily from her broad, low forehead and over her delicate ears, and she had that warm-tinted clear skin that goes so well with reddish hair."

Trafford soon finds that the stifling conventionality of married life in Edwardian London prevents him from fully satisfying his sexual needs. Both Trafford and Marjorie become increasingly aware of each other's shortcomings and temperamental differences, with Trafford experiencing "a vast hinterland of thoughts and feelings, an accumulation of unspoken and largely of unformulated things in which his life had no share. And it was in that hinterland that his essential self had its abiding place." When prostitution becomes a part of his sexual life as it had threatened to become in his scientific life, he petitions Marjorie to travel with him to Labrador where they can both rethink their fundamental attitudes about life and marriage. Trafford is successful in his request because "A great desire came upon Marjorie to go away with Trafford for a time, out of their everyday life into strange and cool and spacious surroundings.... It was the first invasion of their lives by this conception, a conception that was never afterwards to leave them altogether, of retreat and reconstruction." By pondering the question "What is life to be?," they finally solve their problems in exotic Labrador.

Though they didn't seem to help book sales, positive reviews greeted the publication of *Marriage*. The book returned to a theme dear to Wells: the need to change environments as a precursor to personal growth. Wells had in previous years moved a number of times as if a change of environment would lead to a change in his enjoyment of life. This theme informs his fiction as well, as evidenced by such stories as "The Door in the Wall" and "Mr. Skelsmerdale in Fairyland." Remember, too, that Mr. Polly flees his stifling environment with the intent of taking control of his life. Another recurrent theme is that of the intellectual who gives up his work for love, as was the case in *Love and Mr. Lewisham*. We also see echoes of Wells' science fiction novels in which dedicated scientists become disenchanted with the scientific establishment. In the science fiction novels, the disgruntled scientists pursue science beyond the establishment, whereas in *Marriage* our hero abandons science for love.

Marriage is one of those novels that, while featuring some highly effective writing and provocative social insight, tends to be preachy. Though Wells even uses third person narration in an effort to avoid preaching, he doesn't quite succeed. In some ways the novel is now dated, and it will probably not be among Wells' works known to future generations.

THE FILMS

Marriage (1927)   Fox, United States

CREDITS: Directed by Roy William Neill.

CAST: ?

Film Synopsis

No details are known of this film.

Production and Marketing

Irish-born director Roy William Neill (1890–1946) entered life with the name Roland de Gostrie. Before *Marriage* he directed *Love Letters* (1917), *Good References* (1921), and an adaptation of Victor Hugo's *Toilers of the Sea*, but it was after *Marriage* that he directed the films for which he is today remembered. In 1934, for instance, he directed Boris Karloff in *The Black Room*, which is today regarded as one of the actor's best. He also skillfully helmed such low budget thrillers as *Dr. Syn* (1937), *Eyes of the Underworld* (1941, with Lon Chaney, Jr.), and *Frankenstein Meets the Wolf Man* (1943, starring Lon Chaney, Jr. and Bela Lugosi). Perhaps he is best remembered today for having directed most of Universal Pictures' *Sherlock Holmes* series (1942–1946, starring Basil Rathbone and Nigel Bruce).

Adaptation, Strengths, Weaknesses, and Rating

Not only is *Marriage* a lost film, but little, if anything, remains today from which to readily reconstruct the plot or speculate about the degree to which the film was true to the book. Therefore, any evaluation of this film is impossible.

17

The Passionate Friends (1913)

THE NOVEL

The Passionate Friends is another in a series of books Wells devoted to sexual and marital problems. Much of the novel is autobiographical, and Wells claimed to have written it for his son to read after growing up.

Novel Scenario and Commentary

Stephen Stratton is the only son of the rector of Burnmore. Stratton spends much of his childhood at Burnmore Park, where he meets and falls in love with Lady Mary Christian. He participates in the Boar War in South Africa and returns to find Mary married to Justin, a wealthy financier. Undeterred, Stratton becomes Mary's lover, until Justin discovers the affair and has him banished from England for three years.

Stratton eventually marries Rachel More, a young woman who has been in love with him since the age of seventeen. They have three children: Stephen, Rachel, and Margaret. Meanwhile, Stephen and his friend Gidding establish the firm of Alphabet and Mollentrave, a giant enterprise aimed at bringing the world's greatest books to the public at affordable prices.

The spread of knowledge, they believe, will lead to the establishment of a peaceful world order.

Though he is married with a family, Stratton cannot forget Lady Mary Justin. The two develop a correspondence and later meet accidentally. Justin learns of the accidental meeting and threatens Lady Mary with divorce. Fearful that news of the divorce will ruin Stratton's career, she commits suicide.

Wells poses the following question in *The Passionate Friends*: "Is friendship possible between men and women?" As in the other "marital problem" novels, Wells concludes here that conventional morality holds no solutions to problems of love and marriage. As men and women spend increasing amounts of time together and engage in intellectual intimacy, physical intimacy must soon follow. As Wells writes: "On the basis of the accepted code the jealous people are right, and the liberal-minded ones are playing with fire. If people are not to love, then they must be kept apart. If they are not to be kept apart, then we must prepare for an unprecedented toleration of lovers." The novel pleads that people who choose to live outside of conventional morality not be ostracized.

It is important to note that the pessimism evident in a number of Wells' scientific romances becomes more pronounced in *The Passionate Friends*. Near the end of the book, the narrator speaks for Wells: "We idealists are not jolly people, not honest simple people ... a sense of life as of an abysmal flood, full of cruelty, densely futile, blackly aimless, penetrates my defenses." Perhaps that is why the novel lacks the humor present in many of his previous works. Could some worldwide rebirth of education save humankind? Wells had his doubts. And World War I, which broke out the following year, only added to his pessimism.

THE FILMS

The Passionate Friends (1922)   Stoll, Great Britain / Release Date: ? / Running Time: ?

CREDITS: Directed by Maurice Elvey; Screenplay by Leslie H. Gordon.

CAST: Milton Rosmer (Steven Stratton), Mlle Valia (Lady Mary), Ralph Forster (Philip Eversham), Frederick Raynham (Harrison Justin), Madge Stuart, Teddy Arundel.

Film Synopsis

The 1922 version of *The Passionate Friends* appears to be a lost film. Some stills survive, however, and their captions allow us to speculate on the film's plot:

1. "Youth and age—love and rest."
2. "Shall we tell him?"
3. "Spurned by Society."
4. "Between us we killed her."
5. "The eternal triangle."
6. "Father and Son."

From these captions, it seems that the film at least follows Wells' novel to a rec-

ognizable degree. Apparently the film juxtaposes the lovers' passion and the older banker's desire for rest. It is also clear that Mary commits suicide as she does in the novel, but would not do in the 1949 version. Perhaps Steven's children, or at least a son, even plays a role in the film.

Production and Marketing

Maurice Elvey (1887–1967) directed over three hundred films, perhaps more than anyone else in the British cinema. Though most of his work is forgotten today, he did turn out a few memorable titles: *The Hound of the Baskervilles* (1921), *The School for Scandal* (1930), *The Lodger* (1932), *The Wandering Jew* (1933), *The Clairvoyant* (1934), *The Tunnel* (1934), and *Beware of Pity* (1946). In spite of, or perhaps because of his pomposity, Elvey was regarded with affection by his acquaintances. He liked to tell anyone who would listen that his first job was that of a pageboy at the Savoy Hotel, where a talent scout persuaded him to join the company of the Theatre Royal, Nottingham. He claimed that others saw his talent as well and soon assigned him to direct his first film in 1914 at the age of twenty-seven. Because he felt revered by producers who offered him work, he rarely turned down an opportunity to direct, a situation which led to his making a great many bad films. Interestingly, he claimed that Wells would not accept producer Stoll's offer of one thousand pounds for *The Passionate Friends* unless he, Elvey, were hired to direct. To date, there is no evidence to back up Elvey's claim.

British stage actor Milton Rosmer (1881–1971) appeared in many films from 1913. Among his most notable are *Goodbye Mr. Chips* (1939), *Fame Is the Spur* (1947), and *The Monkey's Paw* (1948). He also directed such films as *Dreyfus* (1931), *Channel Crossing* (1932), and *The Challenge* (1937).

Strengths, Weaknesses, and Rating

Since this is apparently a lost film, we can only guess at its strengths and weaknesses on the basis of its 1923 reception. In the United States, critics were tough on *The Passionate Friends*. The *New York Times*, for example, called it "sedulously dull." In addition, director Elvey reputedly experienced difficulties making the picture, which sometimes bodes ill for a film's quality. In this case, though, we just don't know.

Since this is a lost film, judgment cannot be made.

The Passionate Friends (1949) aka *One Woman's Story* Pinewood/Cineguild, Great Britain / Release Date: January 20, 1949 / Running Time: 91 minutes

CREDITS: Produced by Ronald Neame; Directed by David Lean; Screenplay by Eric Ambler, based on the novel by H.G. Wells; Cinematography by Guy Green; Camera operated by Oswald Morris; Sets designed by John Bryan; Edited by Geoffrey Foot; Costumes designed by Margaret Furse; Music by Richard Addinsell; Music played by the London Philharmonic Orchestra, conducted by Muir Matheson; Assistant Director—George Pollock; Associate Producer—Norman Spencer; Sound by Stanley Lambourne and Gordon K. McCallum; Dubbing edited by Winston Ryder; Continuity by Margaret Sibley; Hair Dresser—Biddy Chrystal.

CAST: Ann Todd (Mary Justin), Claude Rains (Howard Justin), Trevor Howard (Steven Stratton), Isabel Dean (Pat), Betty Ann Davies (Miss Layton), Arthur Howard (Servant), Guido Lorraine (Hotel Manager), Marcel Poncin (Hall Porter), Wilfrid Hyde-White (Solicitor), Natasha Sokolova (Chambermaid), Helen Burls (Flower-woman), Francis Waring (Charwoman), Wanda Rogerson (Bridge Guest), Jean Serrett (Emigration Official).

Film Synopsis

Though she has always loved Steven Stratton, a university biology teacher, Mary marries international banker Howard Justin. Mary goes on a holiday in Switzerland, all the while remembering the week-long idyll that she and Steven had there nine years ago, during which they agreed that Mary would divorce Howard. Howard's money and power prevailed, however, and Steven was banished from the country while Mary remained Mrs. Justin.

While having breakfast, Mary is pleasantly surprised to find that, unknown to her, Steven is occupying the room adjoining hers. Steven is married and has two small children, and both he and Mary admit they are happier now than they have ever been. Steven and Mary cruise the lake in a speedboat and then lunch on the mountaintop, each affirming that life has been good. When they return to the hotel, Howard has arrived there early from a business trip. Howard watches the friends kiss and learns that they have adjoining rooms. Convinced that his wife is having an affair, Howard sues for divorce. Mary tries frantically to locate Steven to inform him of Howard's action, but refrains when Steven and his wife are reunited at Victoria Station. To Mary's horror, a solicitor serves Steven with the divorce papers, which name him as a correspondent. Steven's wife breaks into hysterics as he unsuccessfully tries to comfort her.

Mary and Steven finally meet and say goodbye. When Mary returns to Howard, he flies into a rage, and she heads for the underground station to commit suicide. Howard pursues her, restrains her, and lovingly invites her back home with him. The passionate friends have gone their separate ways, and there will be no divorce.

Adaptation

The film *The Passionate Friends* takes the skeleton of Wells' novel and leaves the meat behind. First, the film never seriously

Claude Rains, Ann Todd, and Trevor Howard in a scene from *The Passoniate Friends* (1949).

explores the novel's problems of love and passion versus marriage and conventional morality. Also left unexplored is Wells' political philosophy. What is left is a none-too-engrossing celluloid romance. They may be small matters that Stephen's name is now spelled "Steven" and that somewhere between the novel and the film he loses one of his three children, but it is surely not a minor departure from the book that Mary returns to Howard rather than commit suicide. It was the late forties, however, and audiences expected their happy ending.

The character of Steven's wife Rachel is undeveloped, and the important Mr. Gidding is written out entirely.

Production and Marketing

British director David Lean (1908–1991) broke into the film business as an editor and went on to earn the title of "Sir" as a result of his work as a director. Among his best efforts are *Blithe Spirit* (1945), *Brief Encounter* (1946, for which he won an Academy Award nomination), *Great Expectations* (for which he won an Academy Award nomination), *Oliver Twist* (1948), *The Sound Barrier* (1951, which he also produced), *Hobson's Choice* (1954, which he also produced), *Summer Madness* (1955, aka *Summertime*, for which he won an Academy Award nomination), *The Bridge on the River Kwai* (1957, for which he won an Academy Award), *Lawrence of Arabia* (1962, for which he won an Academy Award), *Dr. Zhivago* (for which he won an Academy Award nomination), *Ryan's Daughter* (1970), and *A Passage to India* (for which he won an Academy Award nomination for best director, an Academy Award nomination for best screenwriter, and an Academy Award nomination for best editor).

For background on top-billed Claude Rains, see Production and Marketing under *The Invisible Man.*

British actress Ann Todd (1909–
1993) so impressed director David Lean
in *The Passionate Friends* that he divorced
his wife and married her. Todd had distinguished herself in H.G. Wells' *Things
To Come* (1936), *South Riding* (1938), *The
Seventh Veil* (1945), and *The Paradine Case*
(1948, directed by Alfred Hitchcock) before
starring in Lean's *The Passionate Friends*.
She continued to appear in movies through
1979 and also produced and directed short
travel films.

Before tackling *The Passionate Friends*,
British leading man Trevor Howard (1916–
1988) had appeared in such well-received
films as *Brief Encounter* (1946), *Green for
Danger* (1946), and *They Made Me a Fugitive* (1947). Later, he contributed his talents to such successes as *The Third Man*
(1949), *The Heart of the Matter* (1953), *The
Key* (1958, as British Film Award winner),
Sons and Lovers (1960, for which he earned
an Academy Award nomination), *Mutiny
on the Bounty* (1962, as Captain Bligh), *The
Charge of the Light Brigade* (1968), *Ryan's
Daughter* (1970), *The Night Visitor* (1971),
Gandhi (1982).

British actress Isabel Dean (1918–1997)
made a career of assaying upper-class roles
on stage, but she also appeared in a number of films after *The Passionate Friends*,
among them *The Story of Gilbert and Sullivan* (1953), *The Light in the Piazza*
(1962), and *A High Wind in Jamaica* (1965).

For information on British actress
Betty Ann Davies, see Production and
Marketing under *Kipps* (1941).

British character actor Arthur
Howard (1910–1995) was the brother of
Leslie Howard. Appearing often as a
schoolmaster, clerk, or servant, his films
include *Passport to Pimlico* (1948), *The
Happiest Day of Your Life* (1949), *The Shoes
of the Fisherman* (1968), *The Missionary*
(1982), and *Curse of the Pink Panther* (1983).

British character actor Wilfrid Hyde-
White (1903–1991) appeared often in
comedy roles. A few of the most important
entries on his vita are *The Third Man*
(1949), *North-West Frontier* (1959), *My
Fair Lady* (1964), and *Ten Little Indians*
(1965). He also appeared in the popular
American soap opera *Peyton Place* in 1967.

Though the film boasted a good cast,
production problems beset *The Passionate
Friends* from the beginning. First, David
Lean, who was originally scheduled to
produce, had to switch places with Ronald
Neame, who was originally scheduled to
direct. Second, sets were budgeted and built
only to be destroyed before use. Third,
those in charge had difficulty agreeing on
suitable locations.

When the plagued film went out to
theaters, advertising posters and ads featured the prominent head of Claude Rains
above drawings of the passionate friends
and their speedboat excursion against a
background of mountains. The film was
re-titled *One Woman's Story* for American
release, presumably because the original
title was considered a bit too risqué.

Strengths

The strongest aspect of *The Passionate Friends* is its cast, particularly second-
billed Claude Rains. His angry outbursts
against Todd and Howard are among the
film's best moments. In one scene, Todd's
very mention of Stratton's name elicits the
following response:

> I didn't expect love from you, or even
> great affection. I'd have been well satisfied
> with kindness and loyalty. You gave me
> love, kindness, loyalty.... But it was the
> love you'd give a dog, and the kindness
> you'd give a beggar, and the loyalty of a
> bad servant!... You were my wife and you
> made me hate and despise myself, and I
> don't want you anymore. Now get out!

Top-billed Ann Todd delivers a fine
understated performance. Less strong, but
certainly adequate is Trevor Howard.

Weaknesses

Both the novel and film versions of *The Passionate Friends* share a common weakness: most of the characters are too priggish and reserved to be believed. Wells' Mary Justin is livelier than the character portrayed by Ann Todd, but both versions of Stratton are uninteresting. Another problem with the film is its confusing flashbacks within flashbacks which, thankfully, occur only early in the film. In addition, the whole affair is quite talky and devoid of the passion promised by the title. *The Passionate Friends* is now dated, its only importance lying in its director and a few cast members.

Rating: 2

18

Three Short Subjects: Bluebottles, The Tonic, and Daydreams (1928)

Bluebottles **(1928)** Anglo, Great Britain / Running Time: 20 minutes. / Release Date: ?

CREDITS: Directed by Ivor Montagu; Art Direction and Screenplay by Frank Wells, based on a sketch by H.G. Wells.

CAST: Joe Beckett, Dorice Fordred, Marie Wright, Charles Laughton, Elsa Lanchester, Norman Haire.

The Tonic (1928) Anglo, Great Britain / Release Date: ? / Running Time: 20 minutes

CREDITS: Directed by Ivor Montagu; Art Direction and Screenplay by Frank Wells, based on a sketch by H.G. Wells.

CAST: Renee de Vaux, Elsa Lanchester.

Daydreams **(1928)** Release Date: ? / Running Time: 20 minutes

CREDITS: Directed by Ivor Montagu; Art Direction and Screenplay by Frank Wells, based on a sketch by H.G. Wells.

CAST: Harold Warrender, Charles Laughton, Dorice Fordred, Marie Wright.

Film Scenarios

These three shorts sketched by H.G. Wells are presumed lost, and little information about them survives.

Adaptations

Since Wells' sketches were scripted by his son, we can assume that the younger fairly adhered to the elder, but we cannot be sure.

Production and Marketing

In 1928, music, color, and even sound were becoming a part of filmmaking, and Wells understood the cinema's potential as both a message bearer and a money maker. In 1927, apparently as the result of a conversation in a Paris bistro, Wells sketched three twenty minute one-reel shorts for filmmaker Ivor Montegu. According to legend, Wells wrote the sketches on the table cloth. Wells' son Frank wrote screenplays from his father's sketches, and the results were *Bluebottles*, *The Tonic*, and *Daydreams*, all produced in 1928.

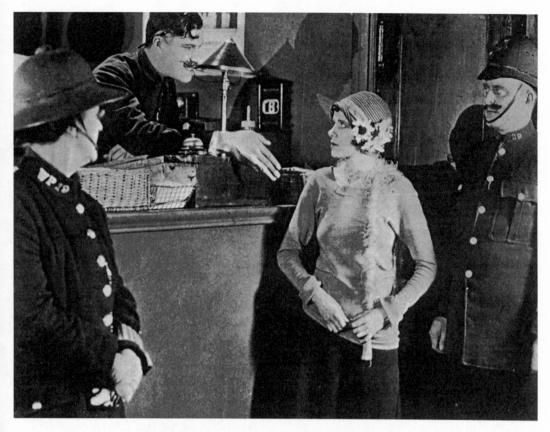

Elsa Lanchester in a scene from *Bluebottles* (1928).

Though the three shorts proved financially unsuccessful and were eventually lost, they should be remembered for at least one thing: they represent the second film appearance of Charles Laughton (1899–1962) and the first of his wife Elsa Lanchester (1902–1986). Both Laughton and Lanchester were respected stage thespians at the time. Lanchester talked Laughton into the job by convincing him that it would be fun.

Lanchester would contribute her talents to such projects as *The Private Life of Henry VIII* (1932), *David Copperfield* (1935), *The Bride of Frankenstein* (1935), *Rembrandt* (1937), *The Spiral Staircase* (1935), *Come to the Stable* (1949, for which she earned an Academy Award nomination), *Witness for the Prosecution* (1957, for which she earned an Academy Award

nomination), *Mary Poppins* (1964), and *Murder by Death* (1976).

For an account of Charles Laughton's career, see Production and Marketing under *The Island of Lost Souls* (1932)

British actor of stage and screen Harold Warrender (1903–1953) went on to star in such films as *Friday the Thirteenth* (1933), *Scott of the Antarctic* (1949), and *Pandora and the Flying Dutchman* (1951).

Strengths, Weaknesses, and Rating

Since these are lost films, a critique is impossible. The films were not financially successful, but that may or may not give us a clue to their artistry since the British were not at the time kind to short story adaptations.

19

The Shape of Things to Come (1933)

THE NOVEL

Wells began the year 1914 by visiting Russia in January. By the time Rebecca West gave birth to his son Anthony in August, the world was plunged into war, a turn of events that convinced Wells more than ever of the need for world unification.

When H.G. Wells wrote *The Shape of Things to Come*, his reputation as a novelist was in decline. He had, however, earned a large alternative readership with his historical, sociological, and scientific works, especially *An Outline of History* (1920), *The Science of Life* (1930), and *The Work, Wealth, and Happiness of Mankind* (1932).

Also, Wells' journalistic pronouncements on the issues of his day often received wide syndication.

After World War I, Wells renewed the hope expressed in his earlier scientific romances: that humankind could only be saved if a devoted group of planners could establish and impose a new pattern of living on the masses. Wells had long been influenced by such utopian architects as Plato, More, Campanella, and Bacon, and he had dabbled a bit in utopian fiction in *The Modern Utopia* (1905). In 1932, he

began his most important optimistic work about humankind's future: *The Shape of Things to Come*. Wells considered democracy inadequate because the masses have no collective will and power passes to the most clever electioneer. The future must be controlled by an elite as described by Plato and Saint-Simon.

Novel Scenario and Commentary

In 1930, Dr. Raven is dead, but he has left behind a chronicle of the years 1930–2105 which he calls a "short history of the future."

In 1933, humankind has reached a crossroads. World War I has left a frustrated, stagnant world in its wake. Modern weapons have intensified the horrors of war, the League of Nations has proven unsuccessful in deterring military aggressors, problems with world economic systems, and the harsh peace settlement imposed on Germany at Versailles all conspired to threaten civilization.

A mid–1933 meeting of the World Economic and Monetary Council ends in failure. Japan rises as a world power and Hitler attacks Poland, igniting "The Last War Cyclone" which ends in 1949, leaving

Europe racked by widespread poverty and disease.

From 1965 to 1978, the writings of Gustave De Windt give rise to the "Modern State." Led by a group of "technical revolutionaries," aviators link all parts of the world via flight, and a "Police of the Air and Sea Ways" keep order. Nationalism is replaced by a "Modern State Society" which argues for a unified world and an end to warfare and private ownership. Though these ideas spread quickly, they are opposed by intellectuals and writers who desire a return to private ownership and national sovereignty. In 1978 the second Basra conference creates a Council for World Affairs, a world government that puts down a series of armed uprising.

From 1978 to 2059, resistance to the Council of World Affairs continues. In maintaining control, the Council grows increasingly dictatorial. The spokesperson for the resistance is Ariston Theotocopulos, a talented painter and designer who argues for complete freedom in all artistic matters. A conference at Megeve, France, in 2059 declares the establishment of a World State and the end of "The Martyrdom of Man."

From 2059 to 2106 the world continues to unite under the leadership of the World State. Religious and racial bigotry dies out. Basra remains the headquarters of world government, with New York its base in the western hemisphere. The population of the earth is now 2500 million people, and Basic English is the world language. Life expectancy is rising and human beings lead better lives than ever before.

But has Dr. Raven left behind a mere dream book or a true vision of the shape of things to come?

Wells began writing his book under the title *An Outline of the Future* but later changed the title to *The Shape of Thing to Come.* As Leon Stover points out in his book *The Prophetic Soul,* along with incor-

porating the ideas of Plato and Saint-Simon, Wells also adds the Hindu Trinity to his vision. The Hindu Trinity consists of Brahma the Creator, Siva the Destroyer, and Vishnu the Possessor. For Wells, these deities correspond with Plato's three social castes. In other words, there is a creator class of intellectuals characterized by wisdom and reason, there is an administrative class characterized by force and will to enforce the plans of the creators, and there are the dull and base masses characterized by desire and passion. Like Plato, Wells recommends that the creative wisdom and destructive force of the upper two classes combine to repress the greed and self-interest of the ruled. Self-interested partisanship must be forced to conform for the good of the whole. In *The Shape of Things to Come,* The World Council unites Brahma the Creator and Siva the Destroyer to control Vishnu the Possessor. This is Wells' "Religion of Progress." The priests and warriors must join together to control the peasants for the good of civilization as a whole. When Wells finished the book he had Marjorie tell Watt that it was in the form of a student's history of 2106 and that it was in no way a fantasia or extravaganza. He insisted that the book be published in a cheap edition so that serious young men and women, laborers, schoolmasters, journalists, and others of low income could partake of his ideas. In compliance with the publisher's request, Wells modified his descriptions of two characters thought to be caricatures of arms manufacturer Sir Basil Zaharoff and the Bank of England's Montague Norman. The author took out libel insurance with Lloyds of London, but no suits proved forthcoming.

The film *Things to Come* also credits Wells' book *The Work, Wealth, and Happiness of Mankind,* wherein the author calls for a planned economy in which the State acts as "the universal buyer and seller."

Buying and selling are abolished as regulated cooperation replaces the free market. As in Plato's *Republic*, all people serve the State in roles nature intended for the good of all concerned.

Wells himself was not altogether comfortable with every aspect of his future socialist vision. Though he obviously envisioned himself among the "priestly" class, he understood the ire that artists would feel as the State cracked down on them for the good of the whole. Therefore, for any definitive classification and definition of Wells' world view, we must read all of his writings devoted to social, political and economic theory.

THE FILMS

***Things to Come* (1936)** London Films, Great Britain / Release Date: February 22, 1936 (Great Britain) and April 17, 1936 (United States). / Running Time: 130 minutes (later cut to 113 minutes and to 96 minutes)

CREDITS: Produced by Alexander Korda; Directed by William Cameron Menzies; Screenplay by H.G. Wells, based on his *The Shape of Things to Come* and *The Work, Wealth and Happiness of Mankind*; Cinematography by Georges Perinel; Special effects by Ned Mann (and Harry Zech, uncredited); Art Direction by William Cameron Menzies; Design by Vincent Korda; Music by Arthur Bliss; Costumes by Rene Hubert and John Armstrong; Consultant: Frank Wells;

CAST: Raymond Massey (John Cabal and Oswald Cabal), Ralph Richardson (The Boss), Maurice Braddell (Doctor Harding), Edward Chapman (Pippa Passworthy), Sophie Stewart (Mrs. Cabal), Derrick de Marney (Richard Gordon), Margaretta Scott (Roxana Black), Alan Jeayes (Grandfather Cabal), Pickles Liningstone (Horrie Passworthy), Anthony Holles (Simon Burton), Pearl Argyle (Catherine Cabal), Patricia Hilli Janet Gordon), Cedric Hardwicke (Theotocopulos).

Film Scenario

On Christmas Eve, 1940, aviation engineer John Cabal sits quietly in his study reading newspaper headlines that warn of impending war. At midnight, enemies launch a surprise attack that nearly demolishes the city.

War continues until 1966, at which time enemies spread a deadly disease called "the walking sickness." Those who contract the disease are shot. Rubble abounds, and civilization as previously known is nearly wiped out.

The Boss, an aggressive thug, takes the reins of what government still exists and assigns young Richard Gordon to repair a worn collection of salvaged airplanes.

By 1970 "the walking death" has ceased due to the killing of the afflicted. Cars share roads with horses. Due to lack of tools and technology, Gordon is unsuccessful at repairing the salvaged planes. At that point, John Cabal arrives in the city by air. He has settled in another part of the world and organized a group known as Wings over the World, whose aim is to restore law, order and civilization.

Recognizing Cabal's aviation skills, the Boss places him under arrest and orders him to help Gordon. Roxanna, the Boss' mistress, is attracted to Cabal and tries unsuccessfully to have him freed.

Cabal and Gordon finally perfect one of the planes. Gordon escapes to the headquarters of Wings over America and leads a fleet of planes to rescue Cabal. Using an anesthetizing gas, the fleet takes over the city and progress begins again.

By 2036, wonderful progress is taking place. Subterranean cities are being built and technology is increasing rapidly.

Oswald Cabal, John Cabal's grandson, has succeeded to his grandfather's position of leadership. The new society has invented a space gun capable of shooting manned rockets around the moon and back to earth. It is now time to substitute human beings for animals in the space experiments. Many young people volunteer, but it is Oswald's daughter Catherine and her boyfriend who get the nod.

Meanwhile, Theotocopulos, an artist of the old regime, rouses the people to rebel against this experiment and leads a mission to destroy the space gun. Before the angry masses can carry out Theotocopulos' plan, the space gun launches its cylinder, and a new age of space travel begins.

Adaptation

Wells adds characters to the broad structure of his *The Shape of Things to Come* and infuses the story with some of the philosophy from his *The Work, Wealth and Happiness of Mankind*. To that extent, Wells adapts his own speculative novel in the form of an original screenplay. In doing so, he uses characters as mouthpieces to express the ideas in his novel. The storyline follows that of the book very closely. Of course, most of the detail is missing, e.g. the 1933 economic summit and hundreds of other specifics. Such familiar names as Hitler, Mussolini, Wilson, Hoover, and Rockefeller receive mention in the book but not in the film. The book's "Last War Cyclone" is included in the film as an attack by Germany (presumably) against Great Britain, an act that leads to world war. Missing also is the name of Gustave De Windt, whose "vision" comprises the history of the Wells novel. The film's John and Oswald Cabal represent the novel's World Council, and Wells adds a minor love interest to the film with the son and daughter of major characters. The only specific character making the transition from novel to film is Theotocopulos, the leader of the resistance.

In essence, Wells strips the novel to its bare essentials for mass cinema consumption. The primary bare essential in both novel and screenplay is that a benevolent fascist state is necessary for human progress, and though fascism presents its own problems, it should be and must be the way of the future.

Production and Marketing

Things to Come is one of two screenplays H.G. Wells provided producer Alexander Korda, the other being *The Man Who Could Work Miracles*. For information on Korda, see Production and Marketing under that title.

American director and art director William Cameron Menzies (1896–1957) established himself as a great art director with such memorable films as *The Thief of Baghdad* (1924), *The Dove* (1928, for which he won an Academy Award), *Alice in Wonderland* (1933), *The Adventures of Tom Sawyer* (1938), *Gone with the Wind* (1939), *Our Town* (1940), *Foreign Correspondent* (1940), *King's Row* (1941), *For Whom the Bell Tolls* (1943), *Arch of Triumph* (1948), and *Around the World in Eighty Days* (1956). Besides *Things to Come*, Menzies is best remembered as a director for *Chandu the Magician* (1932, starring Bela Lugosi), *The Maze* (1953), and the science fiction classic *Invaders from Mars* (1953, the first outer space invasion film shot in color).

Things to Come began scripting in March, 1934, as *Whither Mankind* and wrapped in January, 1935, as England's first million dollar motion picture. Korda chose what in 1936 was, except perhaps for Cedric Hardwick, a no-name cast. For information on Hardwick, see Production and Marketing under *The Invisible Man Returns*. For information on actor Ralph Richardson, see Production and Marketing under *The Man Who Could Work Miracles*. For information on actor Edward Chapman, see Production and Marketing under *The Man Who Could Work Miracles*.

Canadian-born actor Raymond Massey (1896–1983) worked in Great Britain from 1922 and made many films in the United States. He gave excellent performances in such films as *The Old Dark House* (1932), *The Scarlet Pimpernell* (1934), *The Prisoner of Zenda* (1937), *Abe Lincoln in Illinois* (1940, for which he earned an Academy Award nomination), *Arsenic and Old Lace* (1944), *The Fountainhead* (1948), and *East of Eden* (1955). He also co-starred with Richard Chamberlain in the popular television series *Dr. Kildare* (1961–1966).

British actor, dancer, playwright, screenwriter and producer Maurice Braddell played Doctor Harding (1901–1990). Born in Singapore and schooled at Charterhouse and Oxford, Braddell studied at RADA and toured America with Mrs. Partick Campbell's acting troupe, but failed to get work in Hollywood. Returning to London, he worked as assistant producer on *The Battles of Coronel and Falkland Islands* (1927). He branched out into acting, screenwriting, etc. before retiring after World War II. He then lived in New York as a picture restorer and returned to the screen in the sixties in several films directed by Andy Warhol.

British stage actress Sophie Stewart (1909–1977) took time for such screen production *As You Like It* (1936), *The Return of the Scarlet Pimpernell* (1938) and *Uncle Silas* (1947).

British actor and producer Derrick de Marney (1906–1978) scored in *Young and Innocent* (1937) and went on to appear in such films as *Victoria the Great* (1937, as Disreali), *Uncle Silas* (1947), and *The Projected Man* (1966).

British actress Margaretta Scott (1912–) began work on the stage from 1929 and worked in films from 1934. Among her films are *Where's Charley?* (1952), *Town on Trial* (1956), and *Crescendo* (1969).

British stage and film actor Alan Jeayes (1885–1963) appeared in such screen successes as *The Scarlet Pimpernel* (1934), *Rembrandt* (1937) and *The Thief of Bagdad* (1940).

British actor Anthony Holles (1901–1950) lent his talents to such film fare as *The Lodger* (1932), *Brewster's Millions* (1937), *Bonnie Prince Charlie* (1949), and *The Rocking-Horse Winner* (1950).

Special effects director Ned Mann, film artist and originator of the split-screen effect Harry Zech, and art director Vincent Korda (1896–1979) created the magnificent visuals of *Things to Come*. The earlier science fiction masterpiece *Metropolis* (1926) was flawed by its inability to successfully place live actors in its outstanding miniatures. Mann, Zech, and Korda solved the problem by constructing life-size lower storys of buildings and then inserting miniature upper storys with matte work. Buildings were often painted on glass. Clear glass remained in portions of the paintings so the camera could film actors and fragments of sets on the other side. The technicians then fastened the glass to a camera so as to film the pane and background action simultaneously. A continuous full-sized exposure resulted. Other special effects included biplane warfare, a huge space gun, ruined cities, large airplane hangars, and a giant digging machine. For information on Ned Mann, see Production and Marketing under *The Man Who Could Work Miracles*.

British composer Sir Arthur Bliss (1891–1975) sometimes scored films, *Things to Come* being his first. His score was widely heralded and became the first film score recorded as an album.

When Wells turned in the first draft of his treatment to Alexander Korda, the director was awed by its scope and content but put off by its great length. Korda gave the treatment to scenarist Lajos Biro, who, with the aid of Korda's staff, made it

Edward Chapman and Raymond Massey contemplate the fate of their offspring in this original lobby card scene from *Things to Come* (1936).

approachable. Wells then wrote a second version which became the working script for the film. A satisfied Korda then tried to hire Lewis Milestone to direct, but Milestone turned down the opportunity in order to direct MGM's *Mutiny on the Bounty* (1935).

According to Raymond Massey, Wells, agreed to cut out some of the film's emphasis on socialism to quicken the pace. As a writer, however, Wells maintained unprecedented control over the production. Whatever Wells wanted, Korda gave him. While the film was being produced, the BBC ran a six-month survey program called *Taking Stock*. As a result of the world-wide economic slump, Wells was asked to speak on "Whither Britain?". He asked that several others, such as P.M.S.

Blackett and R.A. Gregory, join him. Wells did the broadcast from Bournmouth, where he was helping make the film. In his talk, he predicted that poverty, starvation, lack of education and general degeneration of the masses would soon lead to war. Though he said he was patriotic, he urged that British citizenship become world citizenship in order to divert imminent catastrophe. The BBC received voluminous protests over Wells' talk, and when it attempted to alter (or censor) some of Wells' later talks, friction between the author and the broadcasting system resulted.

Studio publicity for the film emphasized the famous author: "H.G. Wells' Amazing! Wonderful! Unbelievable! Mystery-Miracle Spectacle!" Other catch phrases in ads include:

"It took 3 years to make! It takes 2 hours to see! It would take a century to live! It will take an eternity to forget."

"WOMAN OF TOMORROW. Will she be SADIST, BEAST, BARBARIAN, BEAUTY? Will her KISSES KILL?"

SEE—The Birth of Superman! SEE— The Glass Cities! SEE—1,000 Passenger Air Lines! SEE—Rocket Ship to the Moon!"

As to the question of what the woman of tomorrow will be like, the film indicates that she will be pretty much as she has always been. What ballyhoo!

Both Wells and Raymond Massey attended the film's London premiere on February 22, 1936. The film did well in England but not as well in the United States. Wells was satisfied enough to participate actively in Alexander Korda's adaptation of "The Man Who Could Work Miracles." Still, Wells was not altogether satisfied with *Things to Come*, claiming later that it failed to meet his expectations.

The film was enthusiastically praised in both Great Britain and America. Though famous editor, literary agent, and film historian Forrest J Ackerman still considers *Things to Come* the best horror/science fiction film of the Thirties, and though the film made many early lists of the greatest films of all time, its reputation has suffered over the years.

Strengths

After over fifty years, the stunning futuristic cityscapes of *Things to Come* are still awesome, and its panoramic scope still magnificent. So convincing is the bombing of the cities and the resulting ruin that it could pass for newsreel footage from World War II (which was still several years away). Arthur Bliss' powerful musical score appropriately accompanies the grand sets against which brave adventurers struggle against human frailty to construct a better world. Also impressive are the cinematography and editing skills shown as the camera produces close-ups of frightened faces during air-raid warnings and later gazes up worshipfully at the towering, determined figure of John Cabal.

The costumes created by Armstrong and Hubert artfully suggest the passage of time. Clothing worn in 1940 is only slightly advanced over that worn in 1936. Over time, these clothes become shredded rags as war devastates civilization. Of course, the more time passes, the more elaborate the costumes become.

Two acting performances stand out, the more impressive being that of Raymond Massey. As the visionary John and Oswald Cabal, Massey exudes determination and self-confidence as he measures his plans for humanity's improvement even as the masses and petty tyrants resist. The film's final scene is also probably its greatest as Passworthy expresses to Cabal his concerns for their children, who have just been launched into space:

> Passworthy: I feel that what we've done is monstrous!
> Cabal: What we've done is magnificent.
> Passworthy: If they don't come back— my son and your daughter—what of that, Cabal?
> Cabal: Then, presently, others will go.
> Passworthy: Oh, God, is there ever to be any age of happiness? Is there never to be any rest?
> Cabal: Rest enough for the individual man—too much, and too soon—and we call it death. But for Man [kind], no rest and no ending. He must go on conquest beyond conquest. First this little planet with its winds and ways, and then all the laws of mind and matter that restrain him. Then the planets about him, and at last out across immensity to the stars. And when he has conquered all the deeps of space and all the mysteries of time, still he will be beginning.

Passworthy: But ... we're such little creatures. Poor humanity's so fragile, so weak. Little ... little animals.

Cabal: Little animals. If we're no more than animals, we must snatch each little scrap of happiness and live and suffer and pass, mattering no more than all the other animals do or have done. Is it this—(pointing to the spaceship now visible on the space mirror): all the universe or nothing. Which shall it be, Passworthy? Which shall it be?

The other standout performance is that of Ralph Richardson as the power-hungry Boss, his thuggish, Hitlerian manner presenting a stark contrast to the other-directed activities of John and Oswald Cabal.

Things to Come is the greatest science film of the thirties and forties. It would rank today as one of the greatest films of all time but for its aloofness and tendency to spout ideology. It is still a stunning film, however, and should be applauded for taking chances. Since much of what Wells predicts actually has come to pass, perhaps we should watch carefully for those things which may yet come.

Weaknesses

Wells claimed at the time that the characters in his *Things to Come* screenplay were symbols representing his various philosophical concerns. Unfortunately, symbols of ideas do not involve audiences in the way that real people with real problems do. Consequently, the humanity depicted in the film is too sterile. Characters do not speak; they preach—and not so much to each other as to the viewing audience. Key scenes seem to end with assaulting punctuation marks. Couple this with the film's ultimate support for a benevolent fascism much like the one condemned early in the film, and it becomes easy to see why the patriotic, na-

tionalistic working classes of America were put off.

The pacing of the film is also a problem. Decisions to cut its running time twice improved the situation, but not completely. The first third of the film is strongest, and the last third, though weakened by its pontificating, holds our attention with its grandeur and speculation. The middle third, however, is slow and sometimes tedious.

Rating: 3½

The Shape of Things to Come (1979)

Film Ventures International, Canada / Release Date: December 13, 1979 / Running Time: 95 minutes

CREDITS: Executive Producer: Harry Alan Towers. Produced by William Davidson; Directed by George McCowan; Screenplay by Martin Lager; Special Effects Directed by Wally Gentleman; Scientific Consultant: Frank Wells; Cinematography by Reginald Morris; Edited by Stan Cole; Production Manager: Marilyn Stonehouse; Art Direction by Gerry Holmes; Special Effects by Don Weed; Miniature Construction by Brick Price.

CAST: Jack Palance (Omus), Barry Morse (Dr. John Caball), Carol Lynley (Niki), John Ireland (Senator Smedley), Nicholas Campbell (Jason Caball), Eddie Benton (Kim Smedley), Sparks (himself).

Film Scenario

Two generations after Oswald Cabal launched a rocket to the moon, Earth has been destroyed by nuclear robot warfare, but civilization and science continue to exist in a domed lunar colony called New Washington. On the colony, some who survived the Earth rely on regular doses of a miracle drug that combats radiation. Omar, a renegade scientist and emperor of the planet Delta III, blackmails the colony by threatening to withhold production of the drug unless it accepts him as dictator. When his threats fail, he attacks the pacifist lunar colony. During one of those attacks, the defenders capture one of Omus' robot army and afterward convert it into Sparks, a companion robot who recites poetry and fights on the side of New Washington.

Dr. John Caball, the grandson of Oswald Caball, and his son Jason prepare a defensive counter-attack in a spacecraft called the Starstreak. Technician Kim Smedley, who converted Sparks, is upset when her ultra-pacifist father, Senator Smedley, puts a stop to the counter-attack. In response, the Caballs, Kim, and Sparks steal the Starstreak and set off for Delta III to fight Omus and rescue Niki, a captured moon colonist, and other prisoners.

Skirmish follows skirmish until a ceiling caves in on Omus and New Washington is safe from aggression—at least for awhile.

Adaptation

Though it carries the original full title (*The Shape of Things to Come* as opposed to just *Things to Come*), this film is based neither on H.G. Wells' novel nor on his screenplay. This film is a sequel. The only remaining vestige of the 1936 classic is the name Cabal, but the spelling has, for no apparent reason, been changed to Caball. The film explores none of Wells' ideas, its main theme being that pacifism does not work.

Production and Marketing

The brain behind *The Shape of Things to Come* is British producer Harry Alan Towers (1920–), a prolific maker of low-budget horror/science fiction films. Among the authors whose works have influenced his films are: Sax Rohmer—*The*

Face of Fu Manchu (1965), *The Brides of Fu Manchu* (1966), *The Vengeance of Fu Manchu* (1967), *The Million Eyes of Sumuru* (1967), *Castle of Fu Manchu* (1968), *Blood of Fu Manchu*, (1968), and *Die sieben Manner der Sumuru* (1970); Oscar Wilde—*Dorian Gray* (1970); Bram Stoker—*El Conde Drácula* (1970); Gaston Leroux—*The Phantom of the Opera* (1989); Edgar A. Poe—*The House of Usher* (1988), *Masque of the Red Death* (1990), and *Buried Alive* (1990); and Stephen King—*The Mangler* (1995). He also hit on the works of the Marquis de Sade, Robert Louis Stevenson, and Arthur Conan Doyle.

Towers decided to do a science fiction film in the wake of the popular *Star Wars* (1977). He said he optioned *Things to Come* as a multi-million dollar widescreen extravaganza and as a possible television series. Towers' history, however, would indicate that he had no realistic hope for a multi-million dollar science fiction extravaganza on the scale of *Star Wars*.

According to Towers, he planned to do the film in England, but when that plan fell apart he let go Sylvia Anderson, the technical consultant for television's *Space 1999*. Towers claimed that the next problem was with H.G. Wells' son Frank, who had been the consultant on his father's classic *Things to Come*. Frank Wells was apparently concerned about Towers' storyline, but Towers explained that he had little choice but to use the original book and screenplay as a springboard. According to Towers:

> The Korda film couldn't be redone because, frankly, it would be out of date. The whole point of the 1936 film was that Armageddon was coming quickly. The movie was written between World Wars and it really starts at the beginning of World War II. It assumes that World War II really spreads into an all-out holocaust and that people get carved up more than they actually did [Future #10].

Considering Wells' present our past, Towers concluded that only a space opera on a grand scale could hold contemporary audiences: "We took the premise contained in the original, that a world of engineers would ultimately arise and create conflict between those citizens who want to keep the world the way it is and those who want to advance it. We've merely translated that conflict onward into a futuristic era." Soon, however, what was planned as a joint Canadian/English co-production moved entirely to Canada, necessitating the release of Sylvia Anderson and other British technicians from the project. Wally Gentleman, who was hired as director of special effects, sported such notable credits on his resume as *2001: A Space Odyssey* (1968) and the television series *Project UFO* (1978). He also served as special effects director for the Canadian Film Board on such award-winning productions as *Universe* and *The Drylanders*.

Popular science fiction author Harlan Ellison was originally to have penned episodes for the envisioned television series, but he soon removed himself from the project. Producer William Davidson and screenwriter Martin Lager, who had collaborated on the Canadian science fiction series *The Starlost*, assumed the writing chores.

American leading man Jack Palance (1920–) made a career in films playing villains. Among his best remembered films are *Panic in the Streets* (1950), *Sudden Fear* (1952, for which he won an Academy Award nomination), *Shane* (for which he won an Academy Award nomination), *Man in the Attic* (1954, as Jack the Ripper) *The Big Knife* (1955), *Torture Garden* (1967), *Dracula* (1973, as Dracula), *The Strange Case of Dr. Jekyll and Mr. Hyde* (1974, made for television), *Batman* (1989), and *City Slickers* (1991, for which he won an Academy Award). Television viewers will best re-

member him as the master of ceremonies on *Believe It Or Not* (1982–1986).

British leading man Barry Morse (1919–) moved to Canada where he became a star of stage and television. Some may remember his feature film roles in *Justine* (1969), *Asylum* (1972), and *The Changeling* (1980). Television viewers will remember him for *The Fugitive* (1963–1966, as Lt. Gerard) and for *Space 1999* (1975–1976).

American leading lady Carol Lynley (1942–) appeared in theatrical features such as *Blue Denim* (1959), *Return to Peyton Place* (1961), *Bunny Lake Is Missing* (1965), and *The Poseidon Adventure* (1972) before playing mainly in made-for-television movies. Canadian leading man John Ireland (1914–1992) carved out an impressive career in such films as *I Shot Jesse James* (1940), *All the King's Men* (1949, for which he earned an Academy Award nomination), *The Good Die Young* (1954), *Queen Bee* (1955), *Gunfight at the OK Corral* (1957), and *Spartacus* (1960). His career took a downturn, however, as he later turned up in such pictures as *Arizona Bushwhackers* (1968), *The House of the Seven Corpses* (1973), *Love and the Midnight Auto Supply* (1977), *Madam Kitty* (1977), *Guyana* (1980), and *The Incubus* (1982).

Responding to the fact that *The Shape of Things to Come* has little or nothing in common with H.G. Wells, executive producer Towers said, "We have admittedly taken certain liberties with the original concept, but out of necessity. I don't think anyone will be disappointed." Someone must have been disappointed, however, since the film was never released in theaters but went straight to Canadian television without generating a series. Originally to be released by Allied Artists, the film fell into the hands of Film Ventures International when AA filed for Chapter XI bankruptcy.

Strengths

The Shape of Things to Come boasts a capable cast. Jack Palance, as usual, makes a good villain. The miniatures are mostly well executed, and in a scene in which the colonists revisit earth, some wandering, homeless children supply some pathos. Well, that's about it for the strengths.

Weaknesses

Made in the wake of *Star Wars* (1977), *Close Encounters of the Third Kind* (1977), *Superman* (1978), *Alien* (1979), *Star Trek* (1979), and *The Black Hole* (1979), the film relies primarily on special effects. Unfortunately, except for some of the miniatures, they are often bad ones. Not only do they fall far short of those in other seventies space operas, but they are also dwarfed by those of the original *Things to Come* (1936). The low budget, of course, doesn't help as we watch a styrofoam roof bounce off Jack Palance's head in his big death scene.

The capable cast is defeated by the talky, muddled script. Competing against the inspiring and grandiose language of the 1936 film, the best we get here is "Man's future is limited only by his imagination."

As is often the case with films produced by Harry Alan Towers, the weaknesses considerably outweigh the strengths. *The Shape of Things to Come* is a shameless exploitation film, full of sound and fury, signifying almost nothing. Beaming with pride, Towers told an interviewer, "I think Wells would have appreciated our *The Shape of Things to Come*. When watching our spaceships zoom across the screen, you really have to think about what H.G. Wells would have written if he was alive today." One thing he surely would have written is a bad review for Towers' film. *Variety* got it right: Towers "Should have left Wells enough alone."

Rating: 1½

Afterword

World War II proved deadly to Wells' optimism regarding the future of humanity. In 1940, he finished the novel *Babes in a Darkling Wood* in which his two otherworldly protagonists, Stella and Gemini, fall in love but then must face the horrors of the war. Gemini breaks down and undergoes psychoanalysis, during which he concludes that only women can save the world since men cannot overcome their self-centeredness and greed. His last novel, *You Can't Be Too Careful* (1941) offers little hope for humanity because people are simply what civilization makes of them.

When Wells wrote his final book, *Mind at the End of Its Tether* (1945), he still believed that humanity must adapt or perish. Now, however, he held little hope, if any, that humanity would adapt. Some new type of animal would eventually replace human beings:

> Deliberately planned legislation, food shortages, and such-like economic processes, waves of sentiment for or against maternity, patriotic feeling, or the want of it, the natural disposition of love coupled with a desire to fix a relationship by some permanent common interest, and a pride in physically and mentally well-begotten children, may play incalculable parts in the production of a new humanity, capable of an adaptation to the whirling imperatives about us, sufficient to see out the story of life on earth to its end.

For Wells, common humanity was finished, and only a highly adaptable few could possibly survive. The elitism that Wells advocated all his life as the tool for humanity's survival had become an end in itself. Common humanity would not survive because it was not open to reason, not adaptable to change, and not willing to control egocentric impulses for the good of the whole. Could common humanity overcome itself if it wished? Yes, but history offered no evidence that humanity would. Common humanity, alas, was unsalvageable due to self-imposed ignorance. The scientific elite could teach all it wanted, but common humanity was not prepared to listen.

It is interesting that in the last year of his life, Wells claimed to have begun "The Way the World is Going," a film scenario and sequel to *The Shape of Things to Come*. Disappointed by the cinema throughout his life just as he had been by humanity itself, he returned to it as his mind and body deteriorated. He approached the project not so much out of optimism as from a

183

sense of duty. The atomic bomb had been exploded, and people should understand the kind of world that it had produced. But Wells never completed his film scenario. He died on August 13, 1946.

Writers should not be judged on the basis of films adapted from their works, and H.G. Wells is no exception. Indeed, the cinema has probably betrayed Wells more than it has any other important author. He was an elitist who valued progress over sentiment, yet most film adaptations seem to approve of common humanity over Nietzschean supermen. For example, high-minded scientists such as Griffin and Moreau are turned by the cinema into mad scientists who must be stopped by the common folk. Social satires such as *The Food of the Gods* are turned into teenage exploitation flicks and "big bug" shockers designed to reassure and preserve the status quo. Wells' godless universe becomes a haven of God's providence in George Pal's *The War of the Worlds*. Though Wells was not optimistic about common humanity, he still held some fondness and sympathy for it. After all, he rose from it. The cinema has captured that side of Wells in film adaptations of *Kipps*, *The History of Mr. Polly*, and "The Man Who Could Work Miracles." The cinema treats Wells' socialism approvingly only in films based on Wells' own screenplays, and the film that most expresses Wells' world view, *Things to Come*, was a financial disappointment. Films based on Wells' liberal views of love and marriage were toned down considerably for theater audiences.

As a writer, Wells will be remembered for the following:

(1) Novels: *The Time Machine, The Island of Dr. Moreau, The Invisible Man, The War of the Worlds, The First Men in the Moon, Kipps, Tono-Bungay,* and *The History of Mr. Polly.*

(2) Short Stories: "The Country of the Blind," "Aepyornis Island," "Pollock and the Porroh Man," "The Diamond Maker," "In the Abyss," "Under the Knife," "The Sea Raiders," "The Purple Pelius," "A Catastrophe," "The Man Who Could Work Miracles," "The Star," "The Crystal Egg," "The Door in the Wall," "The Empire of the Ants," and "Valley of the Spiders." Note that the cinema has adapted only three of these stories.

(3) Non-fiction: *The Outline of History*

As one whose writings were adapted to film, Wells will be remembered for *Le Voyage dans la Lune* (1902), *The Island of Lost Souls* (1932), *The Invisible Man* (1933), *The Man Who Could Work Miracles* (1935), *Things to Come* (1936), *Kipps* (1941), *The History of Mr. Polly* (1949), *The War of the Worlds* (1953), and *The Time Machine* (1960). The other films, some good and some bad, will eventually fade from video stores and from memory.

Whether or not my prognostications are the shape of things to come, one thing is certain: H.G. Wells was one of the most influential thinkers of his time, and anyone hoping to understand that time must understand H.G. Wells. Depending on one's politics, morality, and economics, Wells was either a spokesperson for moral degeneracy masquerading as progress or a pioneer in humankind's quest for improvement. If one approves of socialism and collectivism (forced or otherwise), Wells was an angel. If one opposes the same, then Wells was a devil. I would love to see a debate between Wells and Ayn Rand! If one approves of feminism, free love, abortion, and the abolition of marriage, Wells was an angel. If one opposes the same, Wells was a devil. I would love to see a debate between Wells and Dr. Alan Keyes or Dr. James Dobson! If one

Malcolm McDowell (as H.G. Wells) and the time machine that will take him into the future in search of Jack the Ripper in *Time After Time* (1979).

approves of progressive education, Wells was an angel. If one opposes the same, Wells was a devil. I would love to see a debate between Wells and Dr. William Bennett! I would love to see a discussion between Wells and Friedrich Nietzsche on the subject of the Overman or Superman. I would love to see Wells debate or discuss history's meaning with philosophers of history and with anthropologists. Then again, Wells did not fare well in public debate, as his humiliating feud with Hillaire

Belloc demonstrates. For more on that, consult a Wells biography.

My own take is that Wells was a great man of his time who enriched the world with his fiction, distinguished himself with some of his ideas, disgraced himself with others, and who, for most of his life, overestimated humanity as a species. Films based on his writings were produced for the "mindless masses" that he tried to awaken. Unfortunately for him, those film adaptations usually catered to the climate of opinion adopted by the same "mindless masses." In the end, the cinema must be viewed as an entity opposed to Wells' ideas. He tried to harness it, but the powers of conformity were too great. Perhaps in the end, that is good. Again, it depends on where one stands politically, morally, and economically.

There may be one other Wells legacy associated with the movies: Wells himself as a movie character. This occurs in Nicholas Meyer's *Time After Time* (1979), wherein a young H.G. Wells invents a time machine in 1893 London and pursues Jack the Ripper into 1979 San Francisco. In the film, Wells (played by Malcolm McDowell) encounters a museum exhibit lionizing him as a "man before his time." He also goes to McDonald's and humorously encounters such modern American icons as television. Wells finally concludes that "Every age is the same. It's only love that makes any of them bearable." As we will recall, this was certainly not Wells' view in 1893, if ever. Speaking of television, in the 1990s Wells became a character in an episode of television's *Time Cop*, which also involved Jack the Ripper, proving that Wells still intrigues mass audiences today, though undoubtedly not always as he had hoped.

Annotated Bibliography

Books by Wells

Wells, H.G. *A Critical Edition of The War of the Worlds* (with introduction and notes by David Y. Hughes and Harry M. Geduld). Bloomington: Indiana University Press, 1996.

    Includes annotations, appendices, a glossary, works consulted, and an index.

Wells, H.G. *Experiment in Autobiography*. New York: Macmillan, 1934.

    Though Wells subtitles his autobiography *Discoveries and Conclusions of a Very Ordinary Brain (Since 1866)*, the author exhibits an extraordinary brain throughout. Contains an index, photographs, and drawings.

Wells, H.G. *H.G. Wells: Early Writings in Science and Science Fiction*. Edited with critical commentary and notes by Robert M. Philmus and David Y. Hughes. Berkeley: University of California Press, 1975.

    Contains pre–1900 writings by Wells, some of which evolved into *The Time Machine*, and shed light on *The Island of Doctor Moreau*. Includes an appendix and an index.

Wells, H.G. *The Collector's Book of Science Fiction by H.G. Wells*. Secaucus, N.J.: Castle Books, 1978.

    Selected by Alan K. Russell, this anthology features the original magazine illustrations, along with the following stories later adapted to the screen: *The War of the Worlds*, *The First Men in the Moon*, "The Story of the Inexperienced Ghost," "The Empire of the Ants," and "The Man Who Could Work Miracles." The 1898 serialization presented here differs in important ways from the book published in 1901.

Wells, H.G. *The First Men in the Moon: A Critical Text of the 1901 London First Edition, with an Introduction and Appendices*. Edited by Leon Stover. Jefferson, N.C.: McFarland, 1998.

    Top Wells scholar Leon Stover provides indispensable annotations in this and the following three volumes of McFarland's annotated H.G. Wells series, all of which include appendices, a bibliography, and an index.

Wells, H.G. *The Invisible Man: A Grotesque Romance. A Critical Text of the 1897 New York First Edition, with an Introduction and Appendices*. Edited by Leon Stover. Jefferson, N.C.: McFarland, 1998.

Wells, H.G. *The Island of Doctor Moreau: A Critical Text of the 1896 London First Edition, with an Introduction and Appendices*. Edited by Leon Stover. Jefferson, N.C.: McFarland, 1996.

Wells, H.G. *The Time Machine: An Invention. A Critical Text of the 1895 London First Edition, with an Introduction and Appendices*. Edited by Leon Stover. Jefferson, N.C.: McFarland, 1996.

Wells, H.G. *The Short Stories of H.G. Wells*.

Garden City, N.Y.: Doubleday, Doran, 1895.

Includes the following stories adapted to film: "The Time Machine," "The Empire of the Ants," "The Door in the Wall," The Man Who Could Work Miracles," and "The Inexperienced Ghost."

Wells, H.G. *The Works of H.G. Wells*: 28 volumes. London: Atlantic, 1924–27.

This 28 volume set includes all of Wells' important writings through 1924. Wells provides brief introductions to each. I consulted this set for novels that are generally unavailable or out of print.

BOOKS ABOUT WELLS AND/OR HIS WORKS

Bergonzi, Bernard. *The Early H.G. Wells: A Study of the Scientific Romances*. Manchester, England: Manchester University Press, 1961.

Explores key themes in Wells' *fin de siecle* scientific romances, and argues that Wells was a symbolic and mythopoetic writer whose quality deteriorated after 1901. Leaves you interested to note how many of Wells' major themes were actually adapted in the films.

Bloom, Harold (ed.). *Classic Science Fiction Writers*. New York: Chelsea House, 1995.

Contains a brief biographical sketch of Wells, critical extracts related to his writings, and a Wells bibliography.

Clareson, Thomas D. (ed.). *Voices for the Future: Essays on Major Science Fiction Writers*. Bowling Green, Ohio: Bowling Green University Popular Press, 1976.

Contains the essay "Jack Williamson: The Comedy of Cosmic Evolution," in which author Alfred D. Stewart compares and contrasts the science fiction visions of Wells and Williamson.

Coren, Michael. *The Invisible Man: The Life and Liberties of H.G. Wells*. New York: Atheneum, 1993.

Argues that Wells was on the wrong side in the major political and literary debates of his age and suggests that he was an anti–Semite who advocated concentration camps, racial eugenics and the incarceration or execution of misfits. Contains a list of sources and an index.

Foot, Michael. *H.G.: The History of Mr. Wells*. Washington, D.C.: Counterpoint, 1995.

A biography traces Wells' involvement in social movements and argues that the author's open defiance of Victorian prudery helped push England into the twentieth century. Contains a chronology and an index.

Haining, Peter (ed.) *The H.G. Wells Scrapbook*. New York: Clarkson N. Potter, 1978.

Contains articles, essays, letters, anecdotes, illustrations, photographs and memorabilia about H.G. Wells. Of special interest is "The Man Who Did Work Miracles—in the Movies," by Denis Gifford.

Hammond, J.R. *An H.G. Wells Companion*. London: Macmillan, 1979.

An indispensable companion to the works of H.G. Wells. Contains two dictionaries: an alphabetically arranged key to the characters and locations in the fiction, and a dictionary of the titles of novels, romances, stories, and essays. Also contains a select bibliography, a dated and incomplete filmography, and index.

Philmus, Robert M. *Into the Unknown: The Evolution of Science Fiction from Francis Godwin to H.G. Wells*. Berkeley: University of California Press, 1970.

Illustrates "some of the continuities of theme and myth subsisting among works that belong to the history of science fiction," and goes on to consider the myths of science fantasy. The concluding chapter focuses on Wells' *The First Men in the Moon*. Includes a selective bibliography and index.

Smith, David C. *H.G. Wells: Desperately Mortal*. New Haven, Conn.: Yale University Press, 1986.

This is probably the definitive biography of H.G. Wells to date. Even-handed and complete.

Stover, Leon. *The Prophetic Soul: A Reading of H.G. Wells's Things to Come*. Jefferson, N.C.: McFarland, 1987.

Leon Stover, one of the world's most knowledgeable H.G. Wells scholars, provides an in-depth critique of the film *Things to Come*. Includes the film treatment by Wells and the release script along with photographs, references, a bibliography, and an index.

BOOKS ABOUT THE SCIENCE FICTION/HORROR GENRES AND WELLS CINEMA

Berenstein, Rhona J. *Attack of the Leading Ladies.* New York: Columbia University Press, 1996.

Focuses on gender, sexuality, and spectatorship in the classic horror cinema, including a well-foundationed discussion of homosexuality in *The Island of Lost Souls.* Includes a filmography, bibliography, and index.

Baxter, John. *Science Fiction in the Cinema.* New York: Paperback Library, 1970.

Comments perceptively on most pre–1970 Wellsian science fiction films. Illustrated. Contains a bibliography and select filmography. No index.

Brosnan, John. *Future Tense: The Cinema of Science Fiction.* New York: St. Martin's Press, 1987.

Good critical history of science fiction films. Devotes ample space to Wells-based pictures. Illustrated. Contains an appendix and index.

Brosnan, John. *The Primal Scream: A History of Science Fiction Film.* Boston: Little, Brown, 1991.

An informative history of the genre with ample attention paid to films inspired by Wells. Illustrated. Contains an index.

Brunas, Michael, Brunas John, and Weaver, Tom. *Universal Horrors.* Jefferson, N.C.: McFarland, 1990.

Contains excellent critical overviews of fine Universal films based on or inspired by Wells' *The Invisible Man.* Illustrated. Contains an appendix and an index.

Butler, Ivan. *Horror in the Cinema.* New York: Paperback Library, 1971.

This is still a valuable overview for understanding the pre-seventies horror cinema. Butler addresses horror elements in several early Wellsian pictures. Illustrated. Contains a bibliography and index of principle references.

Hardy, Phil (ed.). *The Overlook Film Encyclopedia: Horror.* Woodstock, N.Y.: Overlook Press, 1995.

This and its companion volume *The Overlook Film Encyclopedia: Science Fiction* are well-researched, insightful tools for anyone doing research in the horror/science fiction film genres. Pays more attention than other such books to non–Euro American productions. Contains entries on most Wells-inspired genre films. Illustrated. Contains an index and appendices.

Jensen, Paul M. *The Men Who Made the Monsters.* New York: Twayne, 1996.

This is probably the best book ever written about horror/science fiction genre directors and special effects men. Delivers Insightful, informative critiques of Wells films made by director James Whale and special effects wizard Ray Harryhausen. Illustrated. Contains a filmography, a selected bibliography, and an index.

Johnson, William (ed.). *Focus on the Science Fiction Film.* Englewood Cliffs, N.J., 1972.

This anthology of critical writings in the science fiction film genre contains an excerpt from "Paul and 'The Time Machine'" by Terry Ramsaye, an excerpt from the *Things to Come* film script by H.G. Wells, "Things to Come" by Anonymous, "Things to Come: A Critical Appreciation" by Elizabeth Bowen, "A Brief, Tragical History of the Science Fiction Film" by Richard Hodgens, and "Filming *The Time Machine*" by Darrin Scot, all of which pay valuable attention to Wells' contribution to science fiction film genre. Illustrated. Contains a filmography, a bibliography, and an index.

Pohl, Frederik, and Pohl, Frederik IV. *Science Fiction Studies in Film.* New York: Ace Books, 1881.

Offers useful critiques of the major Wells-inspired productions. Illustrated. No index.

Rey, Lester del. *The World of Science Fiction: The History of a Subculture.* New York: Ballantine, 1979.

This excellent introductory history of science fiction literature covers Wells under "Background: Before 1926." In the recommended reading list, Rey singles out Wells' *The Time Machine* and *The War of the Worlds* for special attention.

Rovin, Jeff. *A Pictorial History of Science Fiction Films*. Secaucus, N.J.: Citadel, 1975.

Profusely illustrated general history of the science fiction film genre. Devotes thumbnail attention to most significant science fiction films, including several inspired by Wells. Comes with an annotated "Best and the Worst" list and a filmography of the films and their studios. No index.

Saleh, Dennis. *Science Fiction Gold*. New York: Comma, 1979.

Examines fourteen science fiction classics of the fifties, one of which is *The War of the Worlds* (1953). Illustrated. Contains a filmography. No index.

Schneider, Kirk J. *Horror and the Holy*. Chicago: Open Court, 1993.

Psychologist Schneider explores how cinematic and literary horror can lead to spiritual understanding. He identifies three types of horrors: hyperconstrictive, hyperexpansive, and bipolar. The film *The Invisible Man* (1933) is an example of hyperconstriction. Though the author proclaims his book aimed at both academic and lay audiences, the former will profit from it more than the latter. Contains a bibliography, filmography, and index.

Scholes, Robert, and Rabkin, Eric S. *Science Fiction: History—Science—Vision*. Oxford: Oxford University Press, 1977.

A readable, accurate, and comprehensive history of science fiction literature. Places Wells in context and explains his undeniable importance to the genre.

Senn, Bryan. *Golden Horrors: An Illustrated Critical Filmography, 1931–1939*. Jefferson, N.C.: McFarland, 1996.

The best, most comprehensive examination of thirties horror films available. Contains excellent chapters on *Island of Lost Souls* and *The Invisible Man*. An appendix addresses "borderline horrors," including *The Man Who Could Work Miracles* and *Things to Come*. Includes a second appendix, a bibliography, and an index.

Sevastakis, Michael. *Songs of Love and Death*. Westport, Conn.: Greenwood Press, 1993.

This interesting and informed critique of classic American horror films of the 1930s includes a chapter on *The Island of Lost Souls*, which the author compares to James Whale's Frankenstein films. Contains a bibliography and index.

Skal, David J. *The Monster Show: A Cultural History of Horror*. New York: W.W. Norton, 1993.

Probably the best book of its kind, this cultural study of the horror film devotes some informative space to *The Island of Lost Souls* and mentions *The Invisible Man*. Illustrated. Contains notes and an index.

Skal, David J. *Screams of Reason: Mad Science and Modern Culture*. New York: W. W. Norton, 1998.

Treats Wells' themes in fifties' cinema along with much else relevant to that era's science fiction films.

Warren, Bill. *Keep Watching the Skies!* Two vols. Jefferson, N.C.: McFarland, 1982 and 1986.

Contains intelligent, personal critiques of Wells adaptations *The War of the Worlds*, *Terror Is a Man*, and *The Time Machine*. Warren doesn't cover Mexico's *The New Invisible Man*. Nevertheless, these volumes represent the best work done on the science fiction cinema, 1950–1962. Sparsely illustrated. Contains complete filmographies, a selected bibliography, appendices, and index.

Weaver, Tom. *Attack of the Monster Movie Makers*. Jefferson, N.C.: McFarland, 1994.

In an interview with Ann Robinson, Weaver (as usual) goes more deeply than other interviewers have gone in getting the actress to discuss her experiences filming *The War of the Worlds*.

Willis, Donald (ed.) *Variety's Complete Science Fiction Reviews*. New York: Garland, 1985.

This book is just what it says it is. Reviews a number of Wells-inspired films.

Wykes, Allan. *The Films of H.G. Wells*. London: Jupiter Books, 1977.

Supplies scant but important information on some lost Wells films. Otherwise, except for being the first book on the Wells cinema, it is useless. Illustrated.

ARTICLES

Asherman, Allan. "*Things to Come*." *Space Wars* Vol. 2, No. 3 (1978).

The author argues that *Things to*

Come (1936) is a better film than its reputation would indicate.

Asherman, Allan. *"First Men in the Moon." Star Warp* Vol. 1, No. 3 (1978).

The author provides a detailed plot summary of the film and then focuses on the screenwriters and on Ray Harryhausen's special effects.

Ashton, Eric. *"The Food of the Gods." Famous Monsters of Filmland* 128 (1976).

A plot summary, followed by a brief interview with Special Effects Coordinator Jody Richardson.

Bernewitz, Fred von. "The Genius of George Pal." *Castle of Frankenstein* 25 (1975).

In an interview, director Pal discusses his work on *The War of the Worlds* and *The Time Machine.*

"Blood Creature." *Famous Monsters of Filmland* 37 (1966).

A filmbook for *Terror Is a Man* (1959), an adaptation of Wells' *The Island of Dr. Moreau.* Concludes with some minor production information.

Delson, James. "'Move That Monster, Mister': An in-depth Interview with Ray Harryhausen." *Fantastic Films* Vol. 1, No. 4 (1978).

Special effects wizard Ray Harryhausen answers two questions related to his work on *The First Men in the Moon.*

Fleisher, Martin. "An Interview with Ann Robinson." *Science Fantasy Film Classics* 2 (1978).

Robinson discusses her work in *The War of the Worlds.* She doesn't reveal much more here than she did with me during our lunch interview.

Holliss, Richard. *"The Time Machine." Starburst* Vol. 8, No. 7 (1986).

A short but informative account of George Pal's 1960 classic.

Houston, David. "Nicholas Meyer: Putting Finishing Touches on *Time After Time." Starlog* 27 (1979).

Director Meyer discusses his work on *Time After Time.*

Hutchinson, David and Everitt, David. "Special Effects Extra." *Starlog* 56 (1982).

An informative piece discussing in capsule fashion the special effects in *The Time Machine, The War of the Worlds, The Invisible Man,* and *Things to Come.*

"The Island of Dr. Moreau." *Famous Monsters of Filmland* 138 (1977).

A filmbook for *The Island of Dr. Moreau* (1977). Concludes with some minor production information.

Kay, Joseph. *"The Shape of Things to Come." Future Life* 10 (1979).

A preview of Harry Alan Towers' *The Shape of Things to Come.* It appears with Barbara Lewis' "The Return of the Time Traveller" as part of a feature titled "H.G. Wells Revival."

Kinnard, Roy. "Are We Not Men?" *Fantastic Films* 20 (1980).

A positive retrospective of *The Island of Lost Souls* (1933). Also comments briefly and negatively on *The Island of Dr. Moreau* (1977).

Lewis, Barbara. "Return of the Time Traveller." *Future Life* 10 (1979).

A preview of *Time After Time.* It appears with Joseph Kay's "The Shape of Things to Come" as part of a feature titled "H.G. Wells Revival."

Malanowski, Tony and Rizzo, Charlie. "William Tuttle: Make-up Genius." *Children of the Night* 3 (1977).

The article and accompanying interview touch on portions of Tuttle's makeup career but fail to address his creation of the Morlocks for *The Time Machine.*

Maronie, Samuel J. "Yvette Mimieux." *Starlog* 36 (1980).

The article and interview focus in part on Mimieux's work in *The Time Machine.*

Maronie, Samuel J. "George Pal 1908–1980." *Starlog* 38 (1980).

A retrospective on the career of George Pal, producer of *The War of the Worlds* and director of *The Time Machine.*

"Memories of Tomorrow." *Modern Monsters* 1 (1966).

Revisits highlights of the early science fiction cinema, including *Things to Come.*

Naha, Ed. "The Worlds of George Pal." *Starlog* 10 (1977).

Naha interviews George Pal, the director of *The Time Machine* and producer of *The War of the Worlds.* Pal discusses how he came to direct *The Time Machine* and reveals plans for the sequel he never made.

Naha, Ed. *"The Time Machine." Starlog* 13 (1978).

Naha incorporates an interview with director Pal into this retrospective on the title film.

Pal, George. "How Mars Attacked the World." *Spacemen* 2 (1961).

    This reprint and revision of producer Pal's 1953 *Astounding Science Fiction* article discusses his work on *The War of the Worlds*.

Roegger, Berthe. "The Shape of Things to Come." *Starlog* 22 (1979).

    A preview of Harry Alan Towers' *The Shape of Things to Come* (1979).

Rogers, Tom. "*The War of the Worlds*." *Starlog* 2 (1976).

    Rogers discusses Wells' novel, Garrett P. Serviss' sequel, Orson Welles' "Mercury Theatre of the Air" broadcast, and the 1953 film adaptation.

Swanson, Glen E. "The War That Never Was." *Starlog* 137 (1988).

    Swanson gives a complete account of Orson Wells' radio production of *The War of the Worlds*, and much else.

Swires, Steve. "Rod Taylor: Time-Travelling Hero." *Starlog* 108 (1986).

    The article and interview focus on Taylor's work in *The Time Machine*.

Tryforos, Laurel Anderson. "The Martian Kind." *Science Fantasy Film Classics* 2 (1978).

    Analyses the attitude toward aliens projected in the film *The War of the Worlds*.

Villard, Robert. "*War of the Worlds* Revival." *Cinefantastique* Vol. 6, No. 3 (1977).

    Director George Pal and cast members gather for the film's 25th anniversary.

Wolfe, Michael. "How Earth Won the War of the Worlds." *Starlog* 117 (1987).

    Points out possible lapses, inconsistencies, errors and anomalies in the *War of the Worlds* screenplay.

NOVELIZATIONS OF SCREENPLAYS AND TIE-INS

Silva, Joseph. *The Island of Dr. Moreau*. New York; Ace Books, 1977.

    A novelization of the screenplay based on Wells' book. Contains shots from the 1977 film on front and back covers.

Wells, H.G. *Kipps*. Montreal: Fontana Books, 1967.

    Wells' novel published to tie in with *Half a Sixpence*, "Paramount's musical film of H.G. Wells' hilarious masterpiece *Kipps*."

Wells, H.G. *The Invisible Man*. New York: Grosset and Dunlap, 1933.

    Wells' novel published to tie in with *The Invisible Man* (1933). Contains stills from the film.

Wells, H.G. *The Island of Dr. Moreau*. New York: New American Library, 1977.

    "The famed horror classic, now a sensational new film starring Burt Lancaster, Michael York."

Wells, H.G. *The Island of Dr. Moreau*. New York: Tom Doherty Associates, 1996.

    Paperback tie-in of Wells' novel issued to coincide with the release of the 1996 film. "Basis for a major motion picture ... A brilliant doctor's mad obsession: To create a powerful new breed of animal—half man and half beast. Is it a miracle of science? Or a crime against nature." Contains a new foreword pointing out the continuing relevance of the novel.

Wells, H.G. *The Island of Dr. Moreau*. New York: Modern Library, 1996.

    Hardback tie-in issued to coincide with the 1996 film. Contains a new introduction by Peter Straub and film credits on the dust jacket.

Wells, H.G. *The Time Machine*. New York: Berkley Medallion Books, 1960.

    Wells' novel published to tie in with *The Time Machine* (1960), the "spellbinding story of a man who invents a Time Machine and travels into the future to the world of 802,701 A.D."

Wells, H.G. *The War of the Worlds*. New York: Pocket Books, 1953.

    Wells' novel published to tie in with *The War of the Worlds* (1953). Features cover art from the film of a Martian war machine creating havoc.

COMIC BOOKS

First Men in the Moon. Gold Key, number 10132-503, 1964.

The Island of Dr. Moreau. Marvel, 1977.

The Time Machine. Dell Movie Classics, number 1085, 1960.

Index